M000310322

What readers are saying about
Enterprise Recipes with Ruby and Rails

Enterprise Recipes with Ruby and Rails covers most of the tasks you need to accomplish in the enterprise, including integration with other systems, databases, and security measures. I wish I'd had this book three years ago.

▶ **Ola Bini**
  JRuby Core Developer, ThoughtWorks Studios

This book is full of practical, *relevant* advice instead of theoretical background or "Hello, World" samples. Once you move beyond the basic skills of using Ruby and Rails, this is exactly what you need— real-world recipes that you can put to use immediately. It's like getting condensed experience on paper, giving you a two-year head start on those who have to acquire this knowledge by making their own mistakes.

▶ **Stefan Tilkov**
  CEO and Principal Consultant, innoQ

If you're responsible for developing enterprise software, after reading this book you'll want to review all your projects to see where you can save time and money with Ruby and Rails. Maik Schmidt shows us once again that enterprise software doesn't have to be "enterprisey."

▶ **Steve Vinoski**
  IEEE Internet Computing Columnist and Member of Technical Staff, Verivue, Inc.

On exactly the right level, this book explains many interesting libraries and tools invaluable for enterprise developers. Even experienced Ruby and Rails developers will find new information.

▶ **Thomas Baustert**
  Rails Book Author, b-simple.de

Enterprise Recipes with Ruby and Rails

Enterprise Recipes with Ruby and Rails

Maik Schmidt

The Pragmatic Bookshelf
Raleigh, North Carolina   Dallas, Texas

Many of the designations used by manufacturers and sellers to distinguish their products are claimed as trademarks. Where those designations appear in this book, and The Pragmatic Programmers, LLC was aware of a trademark claim, the designations have been printed in initial capital letters or in all capitals. The Pragmatic Starter Kit, The Pragmatic Programmer, Pragmatic Programming, Pragmatic Bookshelf and the linking *g* device are trademarks of The Pragmatic Programmers, LLC.

Every precaution was taken in the preparation of this book. However, the publisher assumes no responsibility for errors or omissions, or for damages that may result from the use of information (including program listings) contained herein.

Our Pragmatic courses, workshops, and other products can help you and your team create better software and have more fun. For more information, as well as the latest Pragmatic titles, please visit us at

http://www.pragprog.com

Copyright © 2008 Maik Schmidt.

All rights reserved.

No part of this publication may be reproduced, stored in a retrieval system, or transmitted, in any form, or by any means, electronic, mechanical, photocopying, recording, or otherwise, without the prior consent of the publisher.

Printed in the United States of America.

ISBN-10: 1-934356-23-9
ISBN-13: 978-1-934356-23-4
Printed on acid-free paper.
P1.0 printing, November 2008
Version: 2008-10-29

For my girls:
Mia, Henriette, and Caro.

Contents

Foreword

I'm glad someone finally wrote this book.

Let me explain. I've been bullish on Ruby in the enterprise for a long time now, both with and without Rails. And, the company for which I work, ThoughtWorks, has also been a strong advocate for enterprise Rails. It happened for me shortly after I fully understood what sets Rails apart from other web frameworks. At the time, the last thing I wanted to see was another web framework, recently having completed a book comparing the dizzying array of web frameworks in the Java space (the now very outdated *Art of Java Web Development* [For03]). Once you've spent that much time looking at frameworks, a new one is not high on your list of priorities. But when Rails came along, I could tell that it was completely different and that it had lots of compelling, obvious-in-hindsight ideas embedded inside it. I remember thinking "Wow, this is going to be a really cool thing when all the libraries catch up." For something to be "enterprise ready," you have to have tons of libraries to support all the interactions with the outside world and repositories of reusable code, so I estimated at the time that it would take five or six years for Ruby to even sit at the table in the enterprise world.

But I was wrong in two ways. First, I greatly underestimated the passion and fire in the Ruby community to roll up their sleeves and create all the libraries needed to let Rails play in any space it wants. The second way I was wrong reflects the first: it's just plain easier to write stuff in Ruby. I was carrying all the prejudices from my experience with other languages, where it takes a lot of work to write reusable libraries of code. And the reason for that comes from what I call the "Lockdown Experiment."

Back in the mid-90s, an experiment started as a way to make average developers more effective, because the demand continued (as it does today) to outstrip the supply of good developers. If the software industry can figure out a way to make mediocre developers productive, software development can expand to enterprise scales. Thus, we saw the rise of languages like Visual Basic and Java and later C#. These languages were specifically made less powerful than alternatives (like Smalltalk). The goal of the Lockdown Experiment: make tools to keep average developers out of trouble while still being able to write code. But then a couple of interesting things happened. First, creating restrictive tools and languages didn't really keep average developers out of trouble, because average developers sometimes apply great ingenuity to coming up with ridiculously complex solutions to problems. But while this didn't really make the average developers better, it put a serious governor on the best developers. The whole industry seemed to be optimizing for the wrong thing: safety at the expense of power, with the stated goal of creating software faster. Yet, we didn't produce software faster; we just annoyed the best developers. The second effect was this new wave of languages was so restrictive that they immediately had to start supplementing them to get real work done. For example, in the Java world, the second version added a bunch of new features (like anonymous inner classes), and eventually some limited metaprogramming was added to Java via aspect-oriented programming.

The real underlying problem with lots of "enterprise languages" is one that Stuart Halloway of Relevance software summed up brilliantly: ceremony vs. essence. Languages that require you to jump through hoops to achieve results are highly ceremonious, whereas languages that make it easy to do sophisticated things are more essential. At the end of the day, you have to solve problems. You want languages and frameworks that lessen the distance from intent to result. Ceremonious languages sometimes make that distance quite far, requiring lots of work that doesn't really move your solution forward. More essential languages get out of your way, making the distance from intent to result shorter.

That comes back to the second reason I was wrong about the appearance of libraries in Ruby: it's just plain easier to write stuff in Ruby because it's a more essential language. And that's where this book really shines. It brilliantly illustrates both of my points. It shows how mature the libraries are in Ruby for doing "enterprisey" stuff like security, networking, reporting, and interoperability. And it does a great job of showing how concise solutions to typical problems leverage the combination of Ruby and Rails. If this book were written for a more ceremonious language, it would be twice as thick! This book covers the gamut of ways that Ruby and Rails fits into and complements enterprises, including how to interact with existing infrastructure like message queues, handle monitoring and administration via Ruby libraries, and even bridge to existing Java and .NET code.

Ultimately, this book shows that Ruby is indeed a first-class citizen in the enterprise and will continue to grow in stature. The characteristics that make Rails compelling also make other solutions in Ruby compelling. Every time someone in an enterprise setting rejects Ruby as a solution to a problem because it isn't "enterprise ready," just toss a copy of this book on their desk. With readable code, concise examples, and compelling examples, this book will help accelerate Ruby's rise as a serious player in the enterprise. That is why I'm so happy this book was written.

Neal Ford
Software Architect/Meme Wrangler
ThoughtWorks, Inc.

Acknowledgments

If you want to experience the loneliness of the long-distance runner, you have to run a marathon or write a book. Most of the time writing is a lonely, exhausting business, and the finish line does not seem to ever get nearer. In these moments, you need someone who cheers you up, and I thank my editor Susannah Davidson Pfalzer for her patience, for her professional advice, for her cheerful emails, and for always motivating me to take the next step.

A hearty "Thank you very much!" goes to the whole crew of the Pragmatic Bookshelf. This book has been another great experience, and I still cannot imagine writing for any other publisher.

I am deeply grateful to my reviewers for their invaluable comments and suggestions: Holger Arendt, Matthew Bass, Thomas Baustert, Ola Bini, Jeff Cohen, Jens-Christian Fischer, Ralf Graf, Kaan Karaca, Bill Karwin, Matthias Klame, Beate Paland, Uwe Simon, Stefan Tilkov, and Steve Vinoski. This book wouldn't be half as good without your help!

Beta books are in my opinion the best thing since the invention of sliced bread. I highly appreciate the comments and suggestions sent by Joseph Grace, Eric Kramer, Robert McGuire, Tim Sullivan, and Andrew Timberlake.

I'd like to thank my family and friends for their patience and support: Mom, Dad, Yvonne, André, Christian, Agnieszka, AleX, Roland, and Greta.

Last but not least, I'd like to thank Mia for ignoring all my quirks, for being infinitely patient, and for constantly reminding me that there's more to life than this "computer stuff."

Preface

It's a fact: Ruby and Rails are ready for the enterprise. Whether you're going to implement only a small service or build a full-blown distributed application, Ruby will be a strong ally.

That is especially true for web applications, because Ruby on Rails makes creating even the fanciest web applications a breeze. It has never been easier to implement not only prototypes but also industrial-strength applications and services in record time.

The term *enterprise* is a tricky one, with different meanings to different people. When I talk about "the enterprise," I adhere to Martin Fowler's definition in his book *Patterns of Enterprise Application Architecture* [Fow03]. In a nutshell, enterprise applications enable you to display, manipulate, and store large amounts of complex data, and they support or automate business processes with that data.

From this definition, you might think you would need special tools such as databases and message brokers to develop enterprise applications. Fortunately, Ruby's tool support has become much better over the years. Today it doesn't matter which database system you prefer, because Ruby supports all the popular commercial and open source products. Similarly, you can build asynchronous messaging systems without worrying much about the message-oriented middleware you'd like to use.

Ruby's openness and its strong support for popular network protocols make it an excellent tool for solving integration problems. You can easily integrate with HTTP/REST/SOAP/*your favorite protocol here* services, and you can create new services based on these protocols, too. The same applies for legacy code written in C/C++, Java, or C#; that is, you can reuse your existing code base without much difficulty.

Of course, all your projects will adhere to the highest-quality standards, because testing and generating reports and documentation are a piece of cake with Ruby.

And it's getting even better every day, because some of the biggest IT companies spend a lot of money to create and enhance new Ruby platforms that better fit their needs. Both Sun and Microsoft, for example, pay developers to build JRuby and IronRuby (a Ruby interpreter implemented in C#), respectively, and the whole community benefits from their efforts. In addition, companies like Oracle have already developed applications using JRuby on Rails.[1]

There's so much you can do in the enterprise with Ruby and Rails, and this book will be your guide.

Who This Book Is For

This book is for anyone, beginner to experienced in Ruby/Rails, who wants to learn how to apply their knowledge of Ruby/Rails in their jobs (that is, "the enterprise") and now needs some orientation and quick solutions to urgent problems.

Learning the basics and keywords of a new language is comparatively easy, and the biggest task is learning all the new libraries. Enterprise programmers need to know how to parse XML files, how to execute stored procedures, and how to integrate with SOAP services. These are things—among many others—that you'll learn in this book.

What's in This Book

Enterprise software is different from software that gets shipped to customers on a CD or DVD, because it often depends on a complex infrastructure. Databases, message-oriented middleware, and daemon processes are rarely needed in desktop applications, for example, but for enterprise programmers they are a commodity.

Also, the life cycle of enterprise applications is special compared to other domains. Applications are not only created; they also have to be operated. Many special tools and techniques are needed to make software that runs 99.99999 percent of the year.

This book deals with all the specialties of typical enterprise applications and shows you how to address them with Ruby as well as the Rails framework.

---

1. http://mix.oracle.com/

Here's a short road map of all the things we will cover:

- Protecting your system from unwanted access and protecting your customers' privacy are extremely important requirements. Learn how to fulfill them in Chapter 1, *Implement Enterprise-wide Security*, on page 3.

- Outsourcing particular parts of your infrastructure often makes sense, especially if they aren't related to your core business. In Chapter 2, *Process E-commerce Payments*, on page 49, you'll learn how to integrate with popular payment gateways so you can get money from your customers without ever talking to a credit card company.

- Databases often come to mind first when thinking about enterprise software. Read further about Ruby's database support in Chapter 3, *Get the Most Out of Databases*, on page 77.

- In Chapter 4, *Tame File and Data Formats*, on page 107, you'll see how easy it can be to work with all kinds of textual and binary data formats.

- In enterprises, XML can be found everywhere, and you're better off when you know how to process XML without thinking about it. See how to do it in Chapter 5, *Process XML Documents the Ruby Way*, on page 133.

- Distributed applications became a commodity in enterprise environments long ago, and they're advantageous if you know how to integrate with all varieties of popular network protocols. See Chapter 6, *Perform Basic Networking Tasks with Ease*, on page 175 to learn about it.

- For a more formal approach to combining applications and services, see Chapter 7, *Use and Build Web Services*, on page 199.

- Communication between processes often happens synchronously, because synchronous protocols are easy to implement. But they can lead to performance problems and limit both robustness and scalability. In Chapter 8, *Talk to Message Brokers*, on page 223, you'll learn how to build and integrate with asynchronous messaging systems to overcome these problems.

- Legacy code written in arcane languages such as C/C++, Java, or C# is not a bad thing if you know how to reuse it with ease. Chapter 9, *Speak Foreign Languages*, on page 259 shows you how.

- Building enterprise software often also means operating it. Chapter 10, *Maintain and Administer Your Applications*, on page 289 shows you strategies and techniques for making the administration and monitoring of processes a breeze.

- Like every piece of software, enterprise applications have to be tested carefully and thoroughly. To reduce time and effort needed for testing, read Chapter 11, *Test the Easy Way*, on page 323.

- Software does not solely consist of code; it also needs documentation, and so does the poor guy who has to add a feature to your shiny new application in a year from now. Do everyone a favor and write some documentation (it might be you who needs it). Most of it can be generated automatically anyway, as you can see in Chapter 12, *Get Documentation Nearly for Free*, on page 355.

How You Should Read This Book

As a software developer who writes code in big companies for a living, I know how stressful a typical working day can be. I also know the pain you feel when you urgently need a solution to an important problem. That's why I've chosen the recipes format for this book.

Each recipe deals with a concrete problem and its solution. You want to know how to improve performance of your XML parsing? Take a look at Recipe 24, *High-Performance Parsing*, on page 153. You need a versioned database back end? Find a solution in Recipe 16, *Manage Data with Subversion*, on page 101. You'd like to start developing Ruby programs on the .NET platform? Recipe 43, *Mix Ruby and .NET with IronRuby*, on page 279 brings you up to speed.

All recipes start with a *Problem* section explaining the exact problem that will be solved. They continue with an *Ingredients* section listing all libraries you need, and they have a *Solution* section that shows in detail how to solve the problem with Ruby. An optional *Discussion* section follows that discusses potential shortcomings or alternative solutions, and you'll often find a *See Also* section that refers to related material. Usually, the recipes do not depend on each other, but whenever I think it's advantageous to read some of them in a certain order, I'll give you a hint in the *See Also* section.

Most of the tools and technologies described in the recipes are complex enough to devote a whole book to every single one of them. I tried to keep all recipes as brief as possible, because I wanted to give you a basic template to follow and a good starting point for getting up to speed quickly. In addition, all recipes offer plenty of information about other resources to go to for more information, so if you'd like to learn more, you can go off on your own to do so.

Code Examples and Conventions

This is a book about Ruby and Rails, so it should come as no surprise that it contains many code examples. But this is not an introductory book, and I assume you are familiar with Ruby's syntax and with Rails. For example, I won't explain Rails basics such as working with Active-Record or installing a RubyGem.

Most examples were written in Ruby, but in today's enterprise environments you'll still find much more software written in other languages. I use C/C++, Java, and C# code in some recipes to show you how to mix them with Ruby, for example. Knowing these languages is certainly helpful but not required, and the same is true for libraries such as the Spring framework[2] that is used in some recipes in Chapter 8, *Talk to Message Brokers*, on page 223.

I've tried to keep all examples platform independent, but sometimes it was not possible, because some gems are not available on the Microsoft Windows platform, for example. You'll find a note in the recipes whenever that is the case.

Also, you'll find many README files in the code distribution belonging to this book. They contain detailed information about setting up the environment I've used for the samples. I prefer that over long-winded installation instructions in a book's text.

When you find a "slippery" road icon beside a paragraph, you should slow down and read carefully, because they announce difficult or dangerous techniques.

Installing and Using RubyGems

Many recipes depend on one or more RubyGems that you have to install to run the samples on your own machine. Whenever you have to install a RubyGem by executing a command such as this:

```
$ gem install <gem-name>
```

---

2. http://springframework.org/

you might actually have to execute the command as the root user or administrator or whatever your operating system insists on:

```
$ sudo gem install <gem-name>
```

For brevity, require 'rubygems' statements have been left out in the code examples (if you're using Ruby 1.9 or a more recent version, they aren't needed anyway).

What Version Do You Need?

All the recipes were prepared with Rails 2.1.0 and the latest versions of gems and plug-ins as of this writing. In the book's examples (see the next section for more information), you'll find a detailed list of all RubyGems currently installed on my machine. Everything has been tested with Ruby 1.8.6.

Online Resources

The Pragmatic Programmers have set up a forum for *Enterprise Recipes with Ruby and Rails* readers to discuss the recipes, help each other with problems, expand on the solutions, and even write new recipes. You can find the forum at http://forums.pragprog.com/forums/80/.

The book's errata list is located at http://pragprog.com/titles/msenr/errata/. Submit errata by clicking the "Report erratum" link in the PDF version of the book or by posting them directly to the errata list.

You'll find links to the source code for almost all the book's examples at http://pragprog.com/titles/msenr/code/. If you have the PDF version of the book, you can access an example's source code by clicking the gray lozenge containing the code's filename that appears before the listing.

Let's get started!

Maik Schmidt
September 2008
contact@maik-schmidt.de

Tags and Thumb tabs

So you can better find topics in this book, I have added tabs to each recipe. To find recipes that deal with automation, for example, look for the Automation tab at the edge of this page. Then look down the side of the book: you'll find a thumb tab that lines up with the tab on this page for each appropriate recipe.

Administration

Automation

Databases

Documentation

Integration

Messaging

Monitoring

Performance

Rails

REST

Security

Testing

Web applications

Web services

XML

Part I

Security & E-commerce Recipes

Chapter 1

Implement
Enterprise-wide Security

Web applications and enterprise applications often have one thing in common: they work with sensitive data. Whenever you are working with sensitive data, it's absolutely necessary that you protect it. Data security is important for a lot of reasons:

- Customer data always has to be kept secret to protect your customers' privacy. If your customers do not trust you any longer, because someone was able to steal their data, you will quickly be out of business.

- Credit cards, passwords, and so on, have to be protected from unauthorized usage to protect you and your customers from fraud and identity theft.

- Your data might contain important trade secrets that have to be hidden from your competitors. Industrial espionage is more common than you might think.

But there's more to security than just protecting data. Often you have to prevent your systems from being accessed without permission, and you have to build strong and secure authentication systems. That is not as easy as many people think, especially if the authentication systems should be convenient to use, too.

Your biggest ally for solving all these problems is cryptography. Thanks to the efforts made by the OpenSSL community, you get some of the most advanced cryptographic technologies for free in nearly every modern programming language, and Ruby is no exception.

Whenever you have to exchange sensitive data, you have to encrypt it. Basically, there are two ways to do this: symmetrical and asymmetrical cipher algorithms. You'll learn how to use both of them in Recipe 1, *Protect Information with Symmetric Ciphers*, on the facing page and Recipe 2, *Protect Secrets with Asymmetric Ciphers*, on page 11.

When exchanging sensitive data with other companies or customers, it's important to make sure data does not get tampered with during transmission. It is also important to verify the identity of a message's sender. Learn how to do this in Recipe 3, *Verify Data Integrity with Signatures*, on page 15.

For many cryptographic algorithms, random numbers are important. The more random they are, the more secure your software will be. I explain how to create real random numbers in Recipe 4, *Generate Real Random Numbers*, on page 19.

Passwords are still the basis of nearly all authentication systems in the world. Consequently, you'll learn how to create secure passwords in Recipe 5, *Create Strong and Convenient Passwords*, on page 23, and you'll learn how to store them in a really secure way in Recipe 6, *Store Passwords Securely*, on page 29.

There are countless ways to implement an authentication system, and you'll see a few in this book. Sometimes it's most efficient to use basic technology, so you will learn how to protect your actions using HTTP basic authentication in Recipe 7, *Reanimate Good Old Basic Authentication*, on page 33. A more secure, more advanced, and more convenient technology is OpenID; you'll see how to add its power to your applications in Recipe 8, *Implement a Single Sign-on System with OpenID*, on page 37. Last but not least, I have devoted a whole recipe to LDAP (Recipe 9, *Authenticate with LDAP*, on page 45), a reliable partner in the authentication business.

Protect Information with Symmetric Ciphers

Your problem:

C4whIgO5mhRpyiv9BqKSIAcXZFZeb76hMU5GO/sX3LM=

Real geeks can see that this seemingly random sequence of characters is a byte string that has been encoded in Base64. What they cannot see is that this is really a credit card number that has been encrypted with the Advanced Encryption Standard (AES) in Cipher Block Chaining Mode (CBC)[1] using a key length of 256 bits.

In this recipe, you'll learn how to encrypt and decrypt data in Ruby with symmetric cipher algorithms.

Ingredients

- We use the *creditcard*[2] library to make things more tangible:

  ```
  $ gem install creditcard
  ```

Solution

OpenSSL[3] is one of the most advanced and most complete implementations of cryptographic algorithms that is currently available. It's fast, it's free, and you can find a binding for nearly every programming language. There's one for Ruby, too, and it's even bundled with Ruby. It can be used as follows to decrypt the previous ciphertext (if you know the secret key, that is):

`security/symmetric_cipher.rb`

```
Line 1  require 'openssl'
   -    require 'digest/sha1'
   -
   -    ciphertext = 'C4whIgO5mhRpyiv9BqKSIAcXZFZeb76hMU5GO/sX3LM='
```

---

1. http://en.wikipedia.org/wiki/Cipher_block_chaining
2. http://creditcard.rubyforge.org/
3. http://openssl.org/

```
 5   cipher = OpenSSL::Cipher::Cipher.new('aes-256-cbc')
 -   cipher.decrypt
 -   cipher.key = Digest::SHA1.hexdigest('t0p$ecret')
 -   cipher.iv = '1234567890abcdef' * 2
 -   plaintext = cipher.update(ciphertext.unpack('m*').to_s)
10   plaintext << cipher.final
 -   puts "Plaintext: #{plaintext}"
```

First we create a new Cipher object for the algorithm used to encrypt our data. We use the cipher named aes-256-cbc, because we know how the data has been encrypted. To get a list of all cipher commands that are supported on your platform, run the following command:

mschmidt> **openssl list-cipher-commands**

aes-128-cbc	cast5-ecb	des3
aes-128-ecb	cast5-ofb	desx
aes-192-cbc	des	rc2
aes-192-ecb	des-cbc	rc2-40-cbc
aes-256-cbc	des-cfb	rc2-64-cbc
aes-256-ecb	des-ecb	rc2-cbc
base64	des-ede	rc2-cfb
bf	des-ede-cbc	rc2-ecb
bf-cbc	des-ede-cfb	rc2-ofb
bf-cfb	des-ede-cfb	rc4
bf-ecb	des-ede-ofb	rc4-40
bf-ofb	des-ede3	rc5
cast	des-ede3-cbc	rc5-cbc
cast-cbc	des-ede3-cfb	rc5-cfb
cast5-cbc	des-ede3-ofb	rc5-ecb
cast5-cfb	des-ofb	rc5-ofb

In line 6, we turn the Cipher object into a decryption engine, and in the following line, we set the decryption key. Typically, keys that are used in modern encryption algorithms are a long sequence of bytes. Because humans are bad at memorizing such byte sequences, we use a little trick and create the key from an easy-to-remember password with the SHA1 hash function (this is not as secure as using a random byte sequence as a key!). This way, the key length will not be exactly 256 bits (32 bytes), but that doesn't matter as long as it is unambiguous.

Line 8 looks harmless, but it is very important, because here we set the *initialization vector* to a byte sequence that is as long as the cipher algorithm's block length. Usually, a symmetric encryption algorithm encrypts a block of input data as long as the key size and appends the encrypted block to the result. Then it encrypts the next block until all blocks have been encrypted. In CBC, every block that is going to be encrypted is XORed with its encrypted predecessor before it gets encrypted itself. (XOR, or *exclusive or*, is a binary operation whose output is 1 if its two input bits are different. Otherwise, the output is 0.) The first block has no predecessor, so it is XORed with the initialization vector.

CBC is an effective weapon against *known plaintext attacks*. If an attacker knows, for example, that you encrypt business letters, then the attacker can guess that all your plaintexts start with a phrase such as "Dear Sir or Madam," which gives him a better chance to break your encryption. With CBC, the same plaintext never results in the same ciphertext and makes such attacks much harder.

In contrast to the key, the initialization vector can be safely transferred over public networks, but it is important that it is never used twice with the same key. The best strategy is to generate a random initialization vector for each encryption, and there's even a method for this named Cipher#random_iv().

The rest of our program is simple, and in line 9, we turn the Base64 string into the original byte string and decrypt it with the update() method. We store the result in plaintext and could decrypt more data with subsequent update() calls, but we are finished and call final() instead in line 10.

That's all! When we run our program, it prints the following:

```
Plaintext: 5431111111111111
```

It certainly looks like a credit card number, but is it really one? Credit card numbers are built according to a fixed scheme. The last digit of a credit card number is a check digit that is calculated with the Luhn algorithm,[4] and the first six digits determine which organization issued it. Typically, the first two digits are sufficient to identify the credit card organization. For example, cards issued by Visa always start with 4, and cards issued by MasterCard start with 51, 52, ..., 55. The *creditcard* library hides all these ugly details:

security/symmetric_cipher.rb

```ruby
require 'creditcard'

if plaintext.creditcard?
  puts "Credit card was issued by #{plaintext.creditcard_type}."
else
  puts 'Sorry, but this is not a credit card number.'
end
```

---

4. http://en.wikipedia.org/wiki/Luhn

Key Management

Don't be misled by the simplicity of the code samples in this and in the following recipe. The biggest problem when building a cryptographic infrastructure is implementing a secure key management infrastructure, not choosing and applying the right encryption algorithm. You can use the most secure algorithms in the world, but if you scribble your keys on a sticky note and attach it to your monitor, it won't help much.

Storing and distributing cryptographic keys is a difficult business and should not be taken lightly. If you have not studied the topic yourself for several years, please leave it to the pros and get a *key server*.* A key server securely stores all the keys you need and makes sure that these keys can be accessed only by authorized applications in a secure manner.

A lot of commercial products are available, and many of them are implemented as hardware security modules (HSMs).† Those who prefer an open source software alternative should refer to StrongKey.‡ StrongKey is a pretty complex Java enterprise application, but once you've installed it, it silently runs in the background. At the moment, it has client support only for Java (commercial support for C++ is available, too), but you can integrate it with the Ruby Java Bridge or JRuby (see Recipe 41, *Mix Java and Ruby Code*, on page 269 for details).

---

*. http://en.wikipedia.org/wiki/Key_server_%28cryptographic%29
†. http://en.wikipedia.org/wiki/Hardware_Security_Module
‡. http://www.strongkey.org/

Run the previous program; it outputs the following:

```
Credit card was issued by mastercard.
```

Nice, eh? You cannot really check whether this is an existing credit card number without sending a request to a payment service provider, but you can at least verify whether the credit card number is syntactically correct, and you can even determine the credit card company that issued it.

They wouldn't call it a *symmetric cipher* if it did not work the other way around, would they?

To encrypt a credit card number, do the following:

`security/symmetric_cipher.rb`

```
Line 1   plaintext = '5431111111111111'
   -     cipher = OpenSSL::Cipher::Cipher.new('aes-256-cbc')
   -     cipher.encrypt
   -     cipher.key = Digest::SHA1.hexdigest('t0p$ecret')
   5     cipher.iv = '1234567890abcdef' * 2
   -     ciphertext = cipher.update(plaintext)
   -     ciphertext << cipher.final
   -     ciphertext = [ciphertext].pack('m*')
   -     puts "Ciphertext: #{ciphertext}"
```

That's symmetrical, isn't it? It differs from the decryption code only in a single line: line 3. Here we turn our Cipher object into an encryption machine. The rest stays the same, and the most interesting line is line 8, because there we convert our encrypted plaintext into a Base64 string. That's not a necessity, but if you work with encrypted data and store it in a database, for example, you are better off when you encode it into something readable.

Protect Secrets with Asymmetric Ciphers

Symmetric cipher algorithms have a lot of advantages: they are fast, they can be used to encrypt documents of arbitrary size, and they are easy to implement. Their biggest disadvantage is key management. If only two parties want to exchange confidential information, they have to agree on a single key over a secure channel. But if n parties want to exchange confidential information, $0.5 * (n^2 - n)$ keys have to be exchanged.

Asymmetric ciphers solve this problem by splitting a key into a public part and a private part. You can freely publish your public key, and anyone can send you a confidential message by encrypting it with the public key. Only you can decrypt the message using your private key. It's like a mailbox: everyone can throw in letters that only you can read, because only you have the key.

All asymmetric cipher algorithms are based on more or less complicated mathematical algorithms, but don't be afraid—you do not have to implement them yourself; you will learn how to use them in this recipe.

Solution

Before we get into the details of all the cryptography stuff, we first generate a public/private key pair using OpenSSL:[5]

```
mschmidt> openssl genrsa -des3 \
> -out private_key.pem 2048
Generating RSA private key, 2048 bit long modulus
.................................................+++
.................................................+++
e is 65537 (0x10001)
Enter pass phrase for private_key.pem:
Verifying - Enter pass phrase for private_key.pem:
```

---

5. http://openssl.org/

This command creates public and private key information for the RSA algorithm and stores it in a file named private_key.pem in the current directory (PEM stands for *Privacy-enhanced Electronic Mail*). The file has been encrypted using the symmetric triple DES algorithm[6] and can be used only by people who know the right passphrase (*tOp$ecret* in our case).

To communicate with other parties securely, we have to send them our public key, so let's extract it:

```
mschmidt> openssl rsa -in private_key.pem -out \
> public_key.pem -outform PEM -pubout
Enter pass phrase for private_key.pem:
writing RSA key
```

This creates another .pem file named public_key.pem that contains the public key part of our RSA key pair. .pem files are nothing special,[7] so we can safely take a look at our public key:

```
mschmidt> cat public_key.pem
-----BEGIN PUBLIC KEY-----
MIIBIjANBgkqhkiG9w0BAQEFAAOCAQ8AMIIBCgKCAQEAmCSsvH67RCuPqIRjGrEW
t2yE7O7xFel+Vze4QmEZqtEkRfHQp7oR4FLVfKcsnJdDPY7/ISYZplVTMZHX7VRO
7v7IH/WtgCS5zQT2o8DiftH2zOdu4T2lmtrx5CMKu/M9Tk56IpvRkNiOwQUdxTxK
lyABhMg96zerqErdcgkiSMNfHwcmsAJLivKR9NmRZ9V2Y9OZULHbzgYm/QXRmm8V
VX99MPnk9o9fIof2DGFw3JewLRqxB9LUOOcJlWVXfRKUDj7Vvo0QvRuq6F6g7+IB
dTDiLtvto6HR+gun74XriLNOFke9eRh4rUqjIl2cbLbcPm9FRrWI6i8n9P9Mpjj9
YQIDAQAB
-----END PUBLIC KEY-----
```

We could have created a key pair using Ruby, but you probably will not exclusively communicate with people who use Ruby, so I chose OpenSSL as a common denominator. That makes it easier to explain to your business partner's IT department how to create key files (see Recipe 3, *Verify Data Integrity with Signatures*, on page 15 if you want to learn how to create key pairs using Ruby).

Now that we have a public key, let's use it to encrypt something:

security/rsa_encrypt.rb

```
Line 1  require 'openssl'
   -
   -    plaintext = 'Hello, world!'
   -    public_key = OpenSSL::PKey::RSA.new(IO::read('public_key.pem'))
   5    ciphertext = public_key.public_encrypt(plaintext)
   -    puts "Ciphertext length is #{ciphertext.length} bytes."
   -    puts [ciphertext].pack('m*')
```

---

6. http://en.wikipedia.org/wiki/Triple_DES
7. http://en.wikipedia.org/wiki/X.509#Certificate_file_extensions

The previous program prints the following (for better readability we've converted the encrypted data into Base64):

```
Ciphertext length is 256 bytes.
Mx1GNDudFZAu/64gpQ5YEhUR7HWUCO3JyLJm4yQoWpd01jwbOiIuGxu3Jg+I
2CecmCpo1GrjgNG+ieHVDKDqstW7WvUywFY8Sc6ocF1P3HoNkUwCdg/IMnMF
snkHOwQK/YQNkJOn96nAkP32+9+9Bm5kSQ+oWkUoMnGMEfPZSwbfXNer3VC/
J3YBePI2YVwD1qOMPJqCGoA2zALsknhmGHTvjYtQfcideRgjpS169tjCbg9r
Qkoey+/Ng22qi+zeAtl+9O67eHuy7VWhCQDJPWuILlf30cBa+OW5vXOAkN2Q
AepqAk5Spwi81dbJUQbiFRyLOaJbDg1uWguPrz7VRA==
```

You have to keep another important aspect about asymmetric ciphers in mind (especially in your unit tests): their results are rarely deterministic, because they often depend on modulus operations. If we run our program again, it will probably produce a completely different result:

```
Ciphertext length is 256 bytes.
ksqr7cpL22Wn2jM3VgEriKugWtTYjQKMqkOuRz38JjfmvDHwl8faGk8KXUFZ
PMopWrmZ6Ozk9nYeCeORpCqNOvzOirt+qkI2hPMADNsn+gcSr1iEcnSOtyUE
5HExswY6Ip1CbYKtezfHsK7tzFqJIBB8DBLBwkGsq/yBFGA/baf59dmllpiq
B8ELKc7+b8EHQIj/eHfXSXJXlzm9cwA1V2RJdPEPF+mqQzUArOHYf4vGzPSa
e8cCVBaKACv5cNTIVrJe+KZiBV5Ot9mbnZxH2qWbC3+ay3/mQTHgthzCpAte
w45KIuMq9/ifdViKnMSVi/OZES9+NQBYUprLUvIYJg==
```

Although this looks completely different from the first one, it still results in the same plaintext when we decrypt it. Decryption works like this:

`security/rsa_decrypt.rb`

```
Line 1  require 'openssl'
   -
   -    ciphertext = IO.read('ciphertext.txt').unpack('m*').to_s
   -    password = 't0p$ecret'
   5    private_key_data = File.read('private_key.pem')
   -    private_key = OpenSSL::PKey::RSA.new(private_key_data, password)
   -    plaintext = private_key.private_decrypt(ciphertext)
   -    puts plaintext
```

First we read the ciphertext to be decrypted and turn it from Base64 into its original binary representations (see the sidebar on page 117 to learn how pack() and unpack() work). Then, in line 6, we read the private key we need to decrypt the data in line 7. One thing is very important: RSA should be used to encrypt small pieces of information only. The high-order 11 bytes of the RSA output are used to implement its padding scheme. Thus, for a 2048-bit key (256 bytes), you get 256 - 11 = 245 bytes for your own data (for a 1024-bit key it's 117). That's perfectly fine for a credit card number or something similar, but it's certainly not sufficient for encrypting movie files. Asymmetric ciphers are normally used to encrypt keys for symmetric ciphers that are used to encrypt the actual payload.

Verify Data Integrity with Signatures

You have to exchange sensitive data with other companies; that is, you have to send and receive encrypted messages. For any message you send, you also want to prove that it actually has been sent by you. On the other side, you want to make sure the data you get comes from the right source and has not been tampered with during transmission.

Although the problem sounds difficult, it can be solved easily using asymmetric cipher algorithms. In addition to the data you want to send, you send a cryptographic signature proving that the data has been sent by you. In this recipe, we'll discuss several strategies for creating this signature.

Interestingly, asymmetric ciphers have a symmetric facet, too; that is, if you encrypt data with your private key, it can be decrypted using your public key. That doesn't affect the security of your private key, but the ciphertext's recipient can prove that the message has been encrypted by you if the recipient has your public key. We'll use this to create a solution to our problem, but first we'll set up our environment.

We assume that Alice wants to send an extremely important message to Bob. In our test code we'll need a key pair for Bob and one for Alice. They are generated as follows:

`security/signatures/signature.rb`

```
require 'openssl'

def generate_key_pair(name)
  private_key = OpenSSL::PKey::RSA.generate(1024)
  File.open("#{name}_private.pem", 'w+') do |f|
    f.puts private_key.to_pem
  end
  File.open("#{name}_public.pem", 'w+') do |f|
    f.puts private_key.public_key.to_pem
  end
end
```

```
-    generate_key_pair('alice')
-    generate_key_pair('bob')
-
15   def key(name)
-      OpenSSL::PKey::RSA.new(File.read("#{name}.pem"))
-    end
```

Ruby's OpenSSL binding allows us to generate a 1024-bit RSA key by calling generate(), as we did in line 4. We write both the public part and the private part of the key in PEM format into two different files (PEM stands for *Privacy-enhanced Electronic Mail*). The private part gets extracted in line 9. In addition, we have defined a helper method named key() that reads an RSA key identified by its name.

After running this code, you'll find four files containing the private and public keys of Alice and Bob in the current directory: alice_private.pem, alice_public.pem, bob_private.pem, and bob_public.pem. We can use these keys now to send an encrypted message together with a signature from Alice to Bob:

`security/signatures/signature.rb`

```
Line 1   alice_private_key = key('alice_private')
-        alice_public_key = key('alice_public')
-        bob_public_key = key('bob_public')
-        plaintext = "Alice's extremely important message!"
5        ciphertext = bob_public_key.public_encrypt(plaintext)
-        signature = alice_private_key.private_encrypt(plaintext)
```

In line 5, Alice's message is encrypted using Bob's public key, and in line 6, we create a signature by encrypting the message again, but this time we use Alice's private key (please note that Alice has to know only Bob's public key and her own keys). Now Alice sends the ciphertext and the signature to Bob, and here's what he has to do to decrypt the message and make sure it has been sent by Alice:

`security/signatures/signature.rb`

```
Line 1   bob_private_key = key('bob_private')
-        plaintext = bob_private_key.private_decrypt(ciphertext)
-        if alice_public_key.public_decrypt(signature) == plaintext
-          puts "Signature matches."
5          puts "Got: #{plaintext}"
-        else
-          puts 'Signature did not match!'
-        end
```

Bob regularly decrypts Alice's message using his private key in line 2. Then, in line 3, the message's signature is decrypted using Alice's public key. Only if the result of both decryption calls is the same can Bob be sure that the message has not been tampered with and has been sent by Alice. Also, Bob has to know only Alice's public key and his own keys.

Run the program, and it will print the following:

```
mschmidt> ruby signature.rb
Signature matches.
Got: Alice's extremely important message!
```

If you change a single bit of the ciphertext or of the signature, the program will print an error message. All in all, our problem seems to be solved.

The downside of this approach is that you have to send twice as much data: the message and the signature that is as long as the message. It will also consume twice as much processing time if you encrypt your message with the recipient's public key, too.

A much better solution would be not to use the whole message as a signature but only a digest (or fingerprint). In this case, the plaintext would be encrypted only once, and the signature would be very small. To achieve this, Alice has to do the following:

security/signatures/signature.rb

```
Line 1    plaintext = "Alice's extremely important message!"
   -      ciphertext = bob_public_key.public_encrypt(plaintext)
   -      digest = OpenSSL::Digest::SHA1.new
   -      signature = alice_private_key.sign(digest, plaintext)
```

The message is encrypted with Bob's public key, and in line 4, a signature is created by calling the private key's sign() method. sign() expects two things: the digest to be used (SHA1 in our case) and the plaintext to create a signature for. If Alice sends the ciphertext and the signature to Bob, he can decrypt and verify it as follows:

security/signatures/signature.rb

```
Line 1    bob_private_key = key('bob_private')
   -      plaintext = bob_private_key.private_decrypt(ciphertext)
   -      digest = OpenSSL::Digest::SHA1.new
   -      if alice_public_key.verify(digest, signature, plaintext)
   5        puts "Signature matches."
   -        puts "Got: #{plaintext}"
   -      else
   -        puts 'Signature did not match!'
   -      end
```

Decrypting the ciphertext is business as usual, but in line 4, we use the verify() method to make sure the signature matches the plaintext and Alice's public key. Bob has to use the same digest algorithm as Alice.

That's it. With minimal overhead you can verify the integrity of all the messages you receive and send.

Discussion

The techniques demonstrated in this recipe make sense only if you can be sure that the public keys you're using actually belong to the people or companies you'd like to communicate with. In extreme cases, public keys are handed over personally, but usually it's sufficient to load public keys via a communication link secured by SSL where the server's identity is verified by a certificate (learn how to verify certificates with Ruby in Recipe 5, *Create Strong and Convenient Passwords*, on page 23).

Also See

- See Recipe 2, *Protect Secrets with Asymmetric Ciphers*, on page 11 to learn more about asymmetric ciphers and how to use them in Ruby.

Generate Real Random Numbers

For real security, good random numbers are extremely important, because if your keys and your initialization vectors are as random as possible, they are also as secure as possible. Unfortunately, on a deterministic machine, you won't find any random numbers; that is, the rand() function you can find in nearly every programming language is only a *pseudorandom number generator* (PNG).[8] It creates numbers that seem random, but actually they aren't.

Real randomness can be found only in nature, such as in atmospheric noise, during radioactive decay, or in a lava lamp. But before you deposit some uranium in your office and attach a Geiger counter to your computer's USB port, you'd better read this recipe to learn about a healthier alternative.

- Install the *realrand*[9] gem:

  ```
  $ gem install realrand
  ```

Some nice people already have attached sources of true randomness to their computers and have made the data available as web services. All service interfaces look similar (after all, they merely produce a bunch of bytes), but they differ in some details. The *realrand* library hides the details of three of the most popular services (more will be added):

- RANDOM.ORG[10] generates real random numbers from atmospheric noise.

---

8. http://en.wikipedia.org/wiki/Pseudorandom_number_generator
9. http://realrand.rubyforge.org/
10. http://www.random.org/

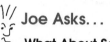

Joe Asks...

What About SecureRandom?

Since Ruby 1.8.7, SecureRandom is part of the standard library. It generates much better random numbers than the original rand() method, but it's still based on deterministic algorithms. For environments that require real security, it's still not sufficient.

- The HotBits[11] generator creates real random numbers by timing successive pairs of radioactive decays detected by a Geiger counter connected to a computer.

- EntropyPool[12] uses various sources of truly random noise including local processes, files and devices, and remote websites.

realrand offers a simple API for all these services and can be used as follows:

`security/random_bytes.rb`

```
Line 1    require 'rubygems'
          require 'random/online'
          include Random

    5     [RandomOrg, FourmiLab, EntropyPool].each do |source|
            generator = source.new
            puts "#{generator.class}:\t" + generator.randbyte(5).join(',')
          end
```

If you run the previous program on your computer, it will output something that looks similar to the following (the output on your machine will be different, because the generated numbers are truly random):

```
Random::RandomOrg:    202,222,43,186,55
Random::FourmiLab:    121,115,208,181,221
Random::EntropyPool:  46,218,53,191,254
```

In line 5, we iterate over the different services that are currently supported by *realrand*. Then, we create the appropriate generator that will actually connect to the service, and finally in line 7, we call randbyte() to generate five random bytes.

---

11. http://www.fourmilab.ch/hotbits/
12. http://random.hd.org/

Although the program is as simple as it can be, true randomness comes at a price, because you have to get the random data from an external source, which in our case is from an Internet service. This might add a noticeable performance overhead, and if performance is an issue, you should cache random bytes locally. For example, you can use the following class:

security/convenient_password.rb

```
class RandomBytesPool
  def initialize(poolsize = 1024, source = Random::RandomOrg.new)
    @poolsize = poolsize
    @random_source = source
    @position = @poolsize + 1
  end

  def next
    if @position >= @poolsize
      @pool = @random_source.randbyte(@poolsize)
      @position = 0
    end
    @position += 1
    @pool[@position - 1]
  end
end
```

RandomBytesPool caches a configurable amount of random bytes locally, and its next() method returns them byte by byte. Whenever the pool is exhausted, it gets refilled with fresh random bytes from one of the random byte sources that are supported by *realrand*. We will use this class in Recipe 5, *Create Strong and Convenient Passwords*, on page 23.

A final note: if you decide to use one of the services we have discussed in this recipe, take a look at their websites and obey their rules. Often you are allowed to generate only a certain amount of random numbers per day, but some of the services offer commercial premium accounts that allow you to generate more random numbers than with the free accounts.

Create Strong and Convenient Passwords

Whenever you create an application where users have to authenticate themselves using a password, you'd better implement a "Forgot your password?" function, too. If a user forgot his password, he can use this function to get a new one via email.

But what password do you send to the user? It does not make sense to send the same password to all users, because that would be compromised within seconds. You have to generate a new password for every user. One approach could be to randomly choose a word from a long list of words such as a dictionary, for example. But words that actually exist in the real world are never good passwords, because all crackers know these dictionaries, too, and could try to attack your system by trying all the dictionary entries.

The only alternative is to generate a random password character by character, and in this recipe you'll learn how to do this in Ruby.

Ingredients

- Install the *realrand*[13] gem:

  ```
  $ gem install realrand
  ```

- Install the *ngrams*[14] gem:

  ```
  $ gem install ngrams
  ```

Solution

We begin with a rather elegant but naive approach:

`security/naive_password.rb`

```
def create_password(length)
  chars = ('a' .. 'z').to_a + ('1' .. '9').to_a + '%$?@!'.split(//)
  Array.new(length, '').collect { chars[rand(chars.size)] }.join
end
```

---

13. http://realrand.rubyforge.org/
14. http://ngrams.rubyforge.org/

```
3.times { puts create_password(8) }
```

It's only two lines of code: we create an array named chars containing all characters that are allowed to appear in our passwords. Then we create a password by randomly choosing length characters from the array. Here's its output (yours will vary):

```
4wd%j!48
mxxhs!vn
nhve@1%!
```

That is certainly sufficient for applications that do not have to meet strong security requirements. But to create better passwords, we have to use a better random number generator, and as you can see in Recipe 4, *Generate Real Random Numbers*, on page 19, some are available on the Internet. One of them, RANDOM.ORG, even offers a password generation service that can be used like this:[15]

security/random_org_password.rb

```
Line 1  require 'net/https'
   -
   -    def create_passwords(quantity, length, options = {})
   -      parameters = {
   5        'rnd'      => 'new',
   -        'format'   => 'plain',
   -        'unique'   => options[:unique] ? 'on' : 'off',
   -        'digits'   => options[:digits] ? 'on' : 'off',
   -        'upperalpha' => options[:upperalpha] ? 'on' : 'off',
   10       'loweralpha' => options[:loweralpha] ? 'on' : 'off',
   -        'num' => quantity.to_i,
   -        'len' => length.to_i
   -      }
   -      send_request(parameters)
   15   end
   -
   -    def send_request(parameters)
   -      query = parameters.inject([]) do |l, p|
   -        l << "#{p[0]}=#{p[1]}"
   20     end.join('&')
   -      https = Net::HTTP.new(
   -        'www.random.org', Net::HTTP.https_default_port
   -      )
   -      https.use_ssl = true
   25     https.ssl_timeout = 2
   -      https.verify_mode = OpenSSL::SSL::VERIFY_PEER
   -      https.ca_file = '/usr/share/curl/curl-ca-bundle.crt'
   -      https.verify_depth = 2
```

---

15. http://random.org/clients/http/

```
     -       https.enable_post_connection_check = true
    30       https.start do |http|
     -         request  = Net::HTTP::Get.new("/strings/?#{query}")
     -         response = https.request(request)
     -         case response
     -         when Net::HTTPSuccess
    35           response.body.split(/\n/)
     -         when Net::HTTPServiceUnavailable
     -           []
     -         else
     -           response.error!
    40         end
     -       end
     -     end
```

In the create_passwords() method, we create a Hash object named parameters that contains all the query parameters we are going to submit to
the web service:

- rnd: We set this parameter to new; that is, a new randomization
  will be started for our request.

- format: This can be plain or html.

- unique: If set to on, this option makes sure we do not get back the
  same password twice.

- *digits*: If set to on, our password will contain digits.

- upperalpha: If set to on, our password will contain uppercase characters.

- loweralpha: If set to on, our password will contain lowercase characters.

- num: This is the quantity of passwords to be generated.

- len: This is the length of the passwords to be generated.

After we have prepared all parameters, we have to send them to the
RANDOM.ORG web service; we do this in send_request(). We use HTTPS,
because it would be dangerous to transmit our new passwords over
public routers without encrypting them.

We use some Ruby magic in line 18 to turn the parameters hash into a
URL query string. From line 21 to 25, we prepare the HTTPS request. In
other words, we set the request timeout to two seconds, and we verify
the certificate returned by RANDOM.ORG to make sure we are talking
to the right server. It's important to set enable_post_connection_check

to true, because otherwise Net::HTTP silently ignores warnings related to SSL errors.

To verify a server certificate, you do not have to install it locally. It's sufficient to have root certificates for the most important certificate authorities (CAs). Web browsers and similar tools such as curl need these trusted certificates, too, so chances are good that you have them already somewhere on your hard disk. On my machine I use curl's curl-ca-bundle.crt file and assign it to the ca_file member in line 27 (see Chapter 6, *Perform Basic Networking Tasks with Ease*, on page 175 if you want to learn more about HTTP clients).

In line 30, we actually start the request and check its results immediately afterward. If everything went fine, we get back the HTTP status code OK, and we turn the result document into an array of password strings by splitting the result document at every newline character.

We handle the case "service unavailable" separately, because it has a special meaning: random numbers do not grow on trees and have to be generated continuously. Usually, they are generated bit by bit depending on some natural process, and the bits are put into a pool. Whenever a client requests a new random byte, eight bits are taken out of the pool and are sent back. If there are no more bits left in the pool, you'll get back an empty result, which is represented by the HTTP status code 503 (service unavailable).

If we get back an error, we raise an exception by calling response.error!.

With only two lines of code, we can generate new passwords:

`security/random_org_password.rb`

```
Line 1  quantity, length = ARGV
     -  puts create_passwords(quantity, length, :loweralpha => true).join("\n")
```

Let's create three passwords of twelve lowercase characters each:

```
mschmidt> ruby random_org_password.rb 3 12
dklgjjfnymkw
fexuslaykjir
zrljqhzirypr
```

That looks good, and it's certainly the right way to use real random processes to create user passwords, but our current solution might not fit every possible requirement. First, you have to trust your random number provider, because all your users' passwords are created on its machines. Second, the set of password characters is limited. That is, you cannot add punctuation characters, for example, which makes your passwords less secure. According to the experts in the field (see *Perfect Passwords* [BK05]), passwords consisting of only eight characters are not secure, especially if the password consists solely of letters and digits and does not contain any punctuation characters (if all this makes you feel bad about your own passwords, you'd better create new ones with the code in this recipe!).

Finally, the passwords we have generated so far are difficult to remember, mainly because they are not pronounceable. If you want your users to keep their strong passwords and not change them back into something like *maik123* immediately, you'd better add some convenience. Even government standards deal with this topic.[16]

The trick is not to generate a password character by character but as a sequence of *n-grams*.[17] Simply put, n-grams are sequences of two or more characters, and every language has a set of rules for combining such fragments to build words; that is, some of them are valid, and some are not. For example, *zza* is a trigram that is allowed to appear at the end of a word such as *pizza*, but you won't find an English word beginning with *zza*.

Using the *ngrams* library, we can extract all bigrams and trigrams from a dictionary, and the library even has methods for building new words based on the extracted information. That makes it easy to build a password generator:

security/convenient_password.rb

```ruby
require 'ngrams'

class PasswordGenerator
  def initialize(file = Ngram::Dictionary::DEFAULT_STORE)
    @dictionary = Ngram::Dictionary.load(file)
  end

  def generate_password(length)
    @dictionary.word(length)
  end
end
```

Only one problem remains: internally, the *ngrams* library uses Ruby's rand() method to generate random numbers, and there's no official way to inject a better random number generator. But Ruby wouldn't be called a dynamic language if we couldn't change that, would it?

---

16. http://www.itl.nist.gov/fipspubs/fip181.htm
17. http://en.wikipedia.org/wiki/Ngram

> security/convenient_password.rb

```ruby
require 'ngrams'

module Ngram
  class Dictionary
    @@random_bytes_pool = RandomBytesPool.new

    def rand
      @@random_bytes_pool.next / 255.0
    end
  end
end
```

What a beautiful hack: we have reopened class Ngram::Dictionary to add the class variable random_bytes_pool (see Recipe 4, *Generate Real Random Numbers*, on page 19) and a new rand() method. Please note that this solution is not thread-safe, because access to random_bytes_pool is not synchronized!

The following sample program:

> security/convenient_password.rb

```ruby
generator = PasswordGenerator.new
3.times { puts generator.generate_password(12) }
```

produces something like this:

```
nazoanonocya
yailipticand
frutellibear
```

Although they are truly random, some of these words actually look like real words (be honest: do you know if the frutelli bear actually exists?), so you'd better check with a dictionary to see whether any existing words were created.

Store Passwords Securely

Problem

Believe me, even if you think you already know how to store passwords securely, you probably don't. There's a lot of folklore code wandering around the Internet, and most of it is wrong. In this recipe, you'll learn what the biggest threats to your passwords are and how to store them the right way.

Ingredients

• Install the *bcrypt-ruby*[18] gem (at the time of this writing, it is not available for the Windows platform):

```
$ gem install bcrypt-ruby
```

Solution

Let's say we have a User model that is represented in the database as follows:

`security/bcrypt_demo/db/migrate/20080803070736_create_users.rb`

```ruby
class CreateUsers < ActiveRecord::Migration
  def self.up
    create_table :users do |t|
      t.string :name
      t.string :hashed_password

      t.timestamps
    end
  end

  def self.down
    drop_table :users
  end
end
```

Admittedly, it's rather simplistic, but it's sufficient for demonstration purposes: our users have a name and a password. At least most people know that they should never store passwords as plaintext, so usually

---

18. http://bcrypt-ruby.rubyforge.org/

passwords are run through a mathematical one-way function such as MD5 or SHA1. These algorithms produce a hash value (also called a *fingerprint*). In other words, the same input value always results in the same output value, and you should not be able to deduce the input value from the output value. Instead of storing the password itself, you store only its hash value.

If a user tries to log in now, she sends her username and password to the application as plaintext (over a secure network connection such as HTTPS, of course). Then the server calculates the password's hash value and compares it to the hash value that has been stored in the database. If they are equal, the password is correct. Otherwise, it's not.

The biggest security threat is that someone gets a copy of all usernames and their according password hashes, because in the worst case (that is, if you did not store your passwords really securely) the attacker could derive the original passwords from the hash values. If, for example, you have hashed your passwords using MD5, this is easier than you think, because of *rainbow tables*. Simply put, these tables contain the MD5 hashes for all possible character sequences up to a certain length. Breaking a password is basically reduced to a table lookup.

To protect yourself from rainbow table attacks, you can add a little bit of random information, called *salt*, to every password before you turn it into a hash value. This way, an attacker would need a new rainbow table for every single password. But that's still insufficient, because with today's computing power, it's actually possible to perform this kind of attack. Typical hash algorithms can be computed very quickly on a modern computer, and they can be calculated even faster on special devices that have become pretty cheap in the past few years.

Most of today's password-cracking tools aren't based on tables anymore; instead, they use sophisticated algorithms based on cryptanalysis and statistics. That is, if you want to make an attacker's life more difficult, you have to drastically increase the time needed to crack your passwords. This can be achieved by hashing your passwords not only once but several times and by adding a new random bit of salt for every iteration. Several algorithms are available for doing this. One of the most popular is *bcrypt*, which is used by OpenBSD for encrypting passwords, for example.[19]

---

19. You can find an excellent article explaining all this in detail at http://www.matasano.com/log/958/.

We use a *bcrypt* library for Ruby to add a secure password scheme to our User model:

`security/bcrypt_demo/app/models/user.rb`

```
Line 1  require 'bcrypt'
  -
  -     class User < ActiveRecord::Base
  -       def password
  5         @password ||= BCrypt::Password.new(self.hashed_password)
  -       end
  -
  -       def password=(new_password)
  -         @password = BCrypt::Password.create(new_password, :cost => 10)
 10         self.hashed_password = @password
  -       end
  -
  -       def self.authenticate(name, password)
  -         if user = self.find_by_name(name)
 15           user = nil if user.password != password
  -         end
  -         user
  -       end
  -     end
```

We define a virtual password attribute. That is, we can read and write it, but it is not stored in the database. Only the hashed password gets stored. In line 5, we implement the reader. If the password has been created already, we simply return it. Otherwise, we create a new BCrypt::Password object from the hashed password and return this. The Password class hides all the cryptographic details and provides some convenience methods that we will use later.

Our writer's implementation starts in line 9. Here we create a new Password object from a plaintext password that has been input by a user. The cost attribute allows us to control the security level of the password. The higher the cost value, the longer it takes to break the password. We store the hashed password in @password and in self.hashed_password, so it gets stored in the database, too. Note that we do not have to store a salt value separately.

Finally, we need an authenticate() method that actually checks whether a certain combination of username and password is valid. First we check whether the user exists in the database, and if the user does, we compare the password entered to the password that has been stored in the database in line 15. Because the Password class overrides the ==() operator, the code looks very elegant, doesn't it? Be assured: behind the scenes a lot of cryptography is performed.

Let's use our new User class on the Rails console:

```
mschmidt> ruby script/console
Loading development environment (Rails 2.1.0)
>> user = User.create(:name => 'Maik', :password => 'tOp$ecret')
=> #<User id: 2, name: "Maik",
   hashed_password:
     "$2a$10$fveY1Zte2p37XsQOtTtsYeUGLWRgJtWPx8zXYcuFleOZ...",
   created_at: "2008-06-30 13:22:14",
   updated_at: "2008-06-30 13:22:14">
>> User.authenticate('Maik', 'wrong password')
=> nil
>> User.authenticate('Maik', 'tOp$ecret')
=> #<User id: 2, name: "Maik",
   hashed_password:
     "$2a$10$fveY1Zte2p37XsQOtTtsYeUGLWRgJtWPx8zXYcuFleOZ...",
   created_at: "2008-06-30 13:22:14",
   updated_at: "2008-06-30 13:22:14">
>>
```

We created a new user named *Maik* who has the password *tOp$ecret*. As you can see, only a hashed version of the password has been stored. Then, we tried to authenticate ourselves using a wrong password. As expected, we've got nil as a result. Finally, we used the right password and got a User object back.

Although it's easy to use the *bcrypt* library directly, there is even a Rails plug-in named *acts_as_authentable*[20] for it.

Discussion

Whenever you are writing code related to security, you should be extremely cautious and skeptical. Always try to get the latest information available about security holes in all the tools and algorithms you're going to use. That's true for *bcrypt*, too.

At the moment, *bcrypt* is sufficient for most purposes, but it uses the *Blowfish* encryption algorithm[21] internally, which has been succeeded already by *Twofish*.[22] It's a good idea to look for alternative solutions as early as possible, and stronger hashing algorithms such as SHA-256 are interesting candidates.[23]

Your software can never be totally secure, but it should be as secure as possible.

---

20. http://code.google.com/p/acts-as-authentable/
21. http://en.wikipedia.org/wiki/Blowfish_(cipher)
22. http://en.wikipedia.org/wiki/Twofish
23. http://csrc.nist.gov/groups/ST/toolkit/secure_hashing.html

Reanimate Good Old Basic Authentication

Problem

Often the simplest solutions are the best. If you have to restrict access to some part of your web application and do not want to build an elaborate access control systems, consider using good old HTTP basic authentication.[24]

Solution

Before we start, please note the following: basic authentication offers a minimum level of security, and you should use it to protect only non-critical data. The HTTP standard defines a more secure authentication method named *digest authentication*, but at the moment Rails does not support it.

However, basic authentication is well supported, and it's amazing how easy it is to protect controller actions from unwanted access with Rails 2.*x*:

`security/basic_authentication/app/controllers/authentication_controller.rb`

```
Line 1   class AuthenticationController < ApplicationController
           before_filter :authenticate, :except => [ :unprotected ]
    -
    -      def unprotected
    5        render :text => "Access granted to anyone.\n"
    -      end
    -
    -      def forbidden
    -        render :text => "Access granted exclusively to you.\n"
   10      end
    -
    -      private
    -
    -      def authenticate
   15        authenticate_or_request_with_http_basic do |user_name, password|
    -          user_name == 'maik' && password == 't0p$ecret'
    -        end
    -      end
    -    end
```

---

24. http://www.ietf.org/rfc/rfc2617.txt

Our controller implements two actions named forbidden() and unprotected() that both render a short text message. In line 2, we install a filter, so authenticate() gets called before forbidden() is invoked. authenticate() protects our forbidden() method from unauthorized access using HTTP basic authentication.

Rails 2.0 added a new method named authenticate_or_request_with_http_basic(). It expects a code block and passes it the username and password that have been transmitted on the HTTP layer. If it returns true, the request is allowed. Otherwise, it is not.

When we invoke an unprotected method, everything works as expected:

```
mschmidt> curl http://localhost:3000/authentication/unprotected
Access granted to anyone.
```

That was not too surprising, so let's see what happens if we try to access the restricted part of our application:

```
mschmidt> curl -i http://localhost:3000/authentication/forbidden
HTTP/1.1 401 Unauthorized
WWW-Authenticate: Basic realm="Application"
Status: 401 Unauthorized
Content-Type: text/html; charset=utf-8
Content-Length: 27

HTTP Basic: Access denied.
```

It works exactly as expected; we get back the HTTP status code 401 and an HTTP header named WWW-Authenticate with the value t;Basic realm='Application'. This tells us we have requested a resource in the realm "Application" that requires basic authentication. If you access the URL using an ordinary web browser, you'll get a dialog box that looks similar to the one in Figure 1.1, on the facing page.

So, let's pass a username (maik) and a password (t0p$ecret) and see what happens:

```
mschmidt> curl -i \
> maik:t0p\$ecret@localhost:3000/authentication/forbidden
HTTP/1.1 200 OK
Status: 200 OK
Content-Type: text/html; charset=utf-8
Content-Length: 35

Access granted exclusively to you.
```

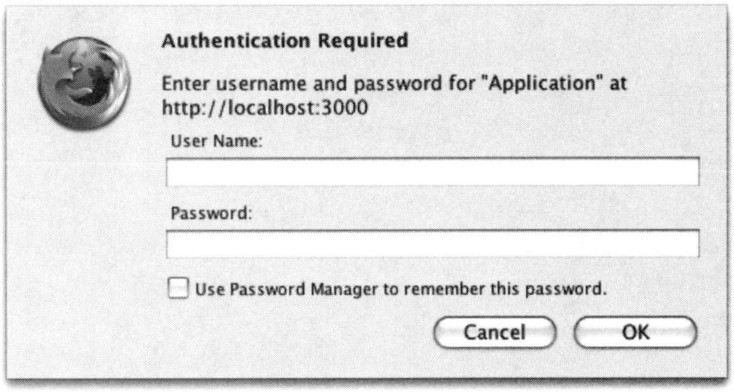

Figure 1.1: BASIC AUTHENTICATION DIALOG BOX

To use basic authentication, separate the username/password with a colon, and put it in front of the host name. Everything worked as expected; we were granted access to the forbidden() action. Behind the scenes, our username and password have been transmitted with the following HTTP header:

```
Authorization: Basic bWFpazpOMHAkZWNyZXQ=
```

It seems that our credentials have been encrypted, but they haven't. In fact, they have only been encoded with Base64, which is as secure as plaintext:

```
mschmidt> ruby -e 'puts "bWFpazpOMHAkZWNyZXQ=".unpack("m*")'
maik:t0p$ecret
```

Implement a Single Sign-on System with OpenID

Problem

With more and more new services appearing on the Web every day, it gets harder and harder to manage all your login names and passwords, doesn't it? Wouldn't it be great if you could use the same username and passwords on any website?

OpenID[25] is a framework for managing digital identities that is gaining popularity. It is based on open standards, and it is decentralized. In other words, it is not controlled by a single—potentially evil—company. In addition, it is supported by a lot of big players such as AOL and Technorati.

Perhaps you already have implemented a sophisticated authentication system for your new application but also want to support OpenID. In this recipe, you'll learn how you can support OpenID in parallel to your own authentication system so your users get the best of breeds.

Ingredients

- Install the *ruby-opendid*[26] gem:

  ```
  $ gem install ruby-openid
  ```

- Change to your Rails application's root directory, and install the *open_id_authentication* plug-in:

  ```
  mschmidt> ./script/plugin install \
  > http://svn.rubyonrails.org/rails/plugins/open_id_authentication
  ```

  The plug-in depends on the existence of a few database tables, and it comes with a rake task for creating them:

  ```
  mschmidt> rake open_id_authentication:db:create
  mschmidt> rake db:migrate
  ```

---

25. http://openid.net/
26. http://openidenabled.com/ruby-openid/

Solution

Every authentication system needs a representation of its users, and here's how our users are stored in the database:

`security/openid/demo/db/migrate/20080803114216_create_users.rb`
```ruby
class CreateUsers < ActiveRecord::Migration
  def self.up
    create_table :users do |t|
      t.string :name, :hashed_password, :identity_url
      t.timestamps
    end
    User.create(:name => 'maik', :password => 'tOp$ecret')
  end

  def self.down
    drop_table :users
  end
end
```

In a real application, we would have many more attributes, but for our purposes here, a username, a hashed password, and an identity URL (needed by OpenID) are sufficient. We need a model for our Rails application, too, and for the password authentication mechanism we use the same model as in Recipe 6, *Store Passwords Securely*, on page 29:

`security/openid/demo/app/models/user.rb`
```ruby
require 'bcrypt'

class User < ActiveRecord::Base
  def password
    @password ||= BCrypt::Password.new(self.hashed_password)
  end

  def password=(new_password)
    @password = BCrypt::Password.create(new_password)
    self.hashed_password = @password
  end

  def self.authenticate(name, password)
    if user = self.find_by_name(name)
      user = nil if user.password != password
    end
    user
  end
end
```

We already know how to authenticate users with a password, but we still have to add support for OpenID. We do not have to implement the underlying protocols ourselves but instead can use *ruby-openid*. It is

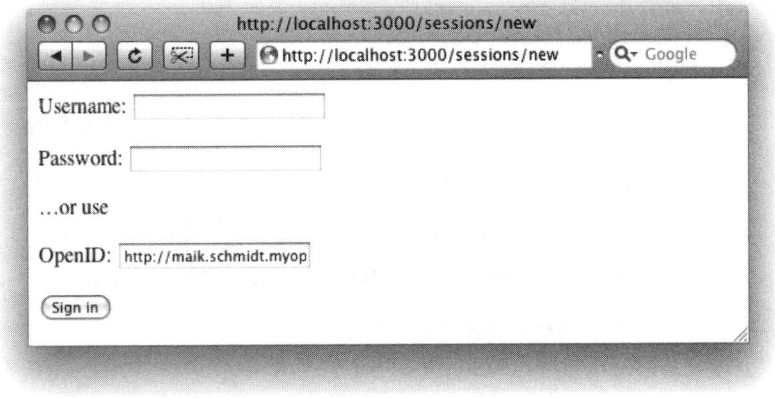

Figure 1.2: Sign in with your OpenID.

a full-blown OpenID library that allows you to create both clients and servers. Although the library is easy to use, you still have to care about a lot of details when using it directly. The Rails core team decided to build a thin wrapper around it and made it available as a plug-in named *open_id_authentication*.

After you've installed the plug-in, you can create your shiny new login page supporting both OpenID and authentication via a username and password (see Figure 1.2):

security/openid/demo/app/views/sessions/new.html.erb
```
<% if flash[:error] %>
  <div><%= flash[:error] %></div>
<% end %>

<% form_tag(session_url) do %>
  <p>
    <label for='name'>Username:</label>
    <%= text_field_tag 'name' %>
  </p>
  <p>
    <label for='password'>Password:</label>
    <%= password_field_tag %>
  </p>
  <p>
    &hellip;or use
  </p>
```

```erb
<p>
  <label for='openid_url'>OpenID:</label>
  <%= text_field_tag 'openid_url' %>
</p>
<p>
  <%= submit_tag 'Sign in', :disable_with => 'Signing in&hellip;' %>
</p>
<% end %>
```

Users can freely choose, if they'd like, to sign up with their OpenID or with their username. Here's the controller that makes all this possible:

security/openid/demo/app/controllers/sessions_controller.rb

```ruby
Line 1  class SessionsController < ApplicationController
     -    def create
     -      if using_open_id?
     -        open_id_authentication
     5      else
     -        password_authentication(params[:name], params[:password])
     -      end
     -    end
     -
     10   protected
     -
     -    def password_authentication(name, password)
     -      if @user = User.authenticate(name, password)
     -        successful_login
     15     else
     -        failed_login "User name and/or password is wrong."
     -      end
     -    end
     -
     20   def open_id_authentication
     -      authenticate_with_open_id do |result, identity_url|
     -        unless result.successful?
     -          failed_login(result.message) and return
     -        end
     25       if @user = User.find_or_create_by_identity_url(identity_url)
     -          successful_login
     -        else
     -          failed_login "Identity URL #{identity_url} is unknown."
     -        end
     30     end
     -    end
     -
     -    private
     -
     35   def successful_login
     -      session[:user_id] = @user.id
     -      redirect_to :controller => 'Main'
     -    end
```

> **Build or Buy?**
>
> Implementing an OpenID client with Ruby is not very difficult, and the same is true for an OpenID server. In principle, you could become an OpenID provider within a couple of days. But as with all things related to security, the devil is in the detail, so you'd better leave such tasks to the pros.
>
> Some OpenID providers such as myOpenID have started to offer products and services for companies that want to create an OpenID infrastructure on the client side or server side but that do not want to gain the expertise to do so themselves. Before implementing a solution yourself, check whether you can get one off the shelf.

```
40    def failed_login(message)
        flash[:error] = message
        redirect_to(new_session_url)
      end
    end
```

At first sight that's a lot of code, but it's really easy to understand, and it actually achieves a lot. In the create() method, we check whether the user wants to sign in with OpenID by calling the *open_id_authentication* plug-in's using_open_id?() method in line 3.

If the user prefers to authenticate using a password, we use a password authentication mechanism that works exactly like the one we have described in Recipe 6, *Store Passwords Securely*, on page 29, so we'll concentrate on open_id_authentication().

The core of our authentication check is the authenticate_with_open_id() method we call in line 21. It transparently handles all OpenID transactions and expects a code block that gets passed the overall result of the OpenID authentication and the identity URL that should be authenticated. First it redirects the user to the user's OpenID provider. In Figure 1.3, on the following page, you can see how this looks for myOpenID, for example.

Figure 1.3: MYOPENID LOGIN SCREEN

After a successful login at your OpenID provider, it usually asks you whether you'd like to authenticate the requesting party. Typically, you can deny this, you can allow it once, or you can allow it forever (to see how such a page looks for myOpenID, refer to Figure 1.4, on the next page).

If the identity URL can be authenticated successfully and if we can find or create the appropriate User object in the database, we call successful_login(), which redirects to the main controller of our application. Otherwise, we call failed_login() and redirect to the login page after setting an error message. This redirection mechanism works only if we adjust routes.rb accordingly:

`security/openid/demo/config/routes.rb`

```
map.open_id_complete 'session',
  :controller   => 'sessions',
  :action       => 'create',
  :requirements => { :method => :get }
map.resource :session
```

Figure 1.4: AUTHENTICATE THE TEST APPLICATION AT MYOPENID.

That's it! With a few lines of code, our application supports two convenient and secure authentication mechanisms. There's really no excuse for not offering both of them.

Authenticate with LDAP

A lot of companies use the Lightweight Directory Access Protocol (LDAP) for storing user account information, and in this recipe you'll learn how to access a LDAP repository from your Rails application to authenticate user information.

Ingredients

- Install the *ruby-net-ldap* gem:

  ```
  $ gem install ruby-net-ldap
  ```

Solution

The structure and content of our repository are defined as follows:

`security/ldap/init.ldif`

```
# Create the EnterpriseRecipes organization.
dn: dc=enterpriserecipes,dc=com
objectclass: dcObject
objectclass: organization
o: EnterpriseRecipes
dc: enterpriserecipes

# Create some users.
dn:cn=Maik Schmidt,dc=enterpriserecipes,dc=com
objectclass: top
objectclass: inetOrgPerson
cn: Maik Schmidt
sn: Schmidt
mail: Maik.Schmidt@example.com
userPassword: maik123

dn:cn=Jane Rodriguez,dc=enterpriserecipes,dc=com
objectclass: top
objectclass: inetOrgPerson
cn: Jane Rodriguez
sn: Rodriguez
mail: jane@example.com
userPassword: booze
```

Here we have an organizational unit representing the Enterprise Recipes company, and we have two users who have to authenticate using an email address and a password. Typically, you'd store more attributes in the repository, and you would not store passwords in plaintext (see Recipe 6, *Store Passwords Securely*, on page 29 for a much better approach), but for demonstration purposes we have everything we need.

Ruby has excellent support for LDAP, and you can choose between several libraries:

- A C extension library named *Ruby/LDAP*[27]

- A pure Ruby implementation named *Net::LDAP*[28]

- *Ruby/ActiveLDAP*,[29] a wrapper around Ruby/LDAP that behaves like ActiveRecord

In this recipe, we use Net::LDAP, because it's the easiest to install and because it does not depend on a local LDAP system as Ruby/LDAP does, for example. We will build a complete user authentication mechanism; it looks like this:

`security/ldap/user.rb`

```
Line 1  require 'net/ldap'

        class User
          BASE = 'dc=enterpriserecipes,dc=com'
     5    LDAP_USER = 'cn=root,dc=enterpriserecipes,dc=com'
          LDAP_PASSWORD = 't0p$ecret'

          def self.authenticate(email, password)
            email_filter = Net::LDAP::Filter.eq('mail', email)
    10      ldap_con = connect(LDAP_USER, LDAP_PASSWORD)
            dn = ''
            ldap_con.search(:base => BASE, :filter => email_filter) do |entry|
              dn = entry.dn
            end
    15      !dn.empty? and connect(dn, password).bind
          end

          private

    20    def self.connect(dn, password)
            Net::LDAP.new(
              :host => 'localhost',
              :port => 389,
```

27. http://ruby-ldap.sourceforge.net/
28. http://net-ldap.rubyforge.org/
29. http://ruby-activeldap.rubyforge.org/

```
25
30
        :auth => {
          :method   => :simple,
          :username => dn,
          :password => password
        }
      )
    end
  end
```

One class, two methods, and we are done. Let's take a look first at the connect() method beginning in line 20. We create a new Net::LDAP object using the usual parameters—the name of the host to connect to, the port of the LDAP server, a username, and a password. Note that the username is named dn, which is an abbreviation for *distinguished name*. In LDAP a distinguished name uniquely identifies an entry in the repository. We have done this because in authenticate() we can use connect() to connect to the repository itself and then to authenticate a user entry, if we have found one.

We create a Net::LDAP::Filter object in line 9 that filters all entries in the repository that have a certain email address. The eq() method returns a filter that makes sure that the mail attribute exactly matches the content of the email argument. Net::LDAP comes with more filters, and most of them even accept wildcards. For example, to get email addresses belonging to the domain example.com, you'd pass *example.com.

Then we connect to the repository using the credentials of the administrative user. In line 12, we look up the distinguished name of the entry that has a certain email address using the search() method and our filter. When we have found an entry, we try to connect to the LDAP server again using the password belonging to the entry we have just found. If this works, everything is fine, and the user can be authenticated. Here's how you'd use the authenticate() method:

security/ldap/user.rb

```ruby
if User.authenticate('Maik.Schmidt@example.com', 'maik123')
  puts 'You are logged in!'
else
  puts 'Sorry!'
end
```

With only thirty lines of client code, we have implemented a complete LDAP authentication mechanism that can be used with a single line of code. To make this authentication system as secure as possible, we should use the Secure Sockets Layer (SSL) protocol or its successor, Transport Layer Security (TLS).

In this case, we have to only slightly change the connect() method:

`security/ldap/ssl_user.rb`

```ruby
def self.connect(dn, password)
  Net::LDAP.new(
    :host => 'localhost',
    :port => 636,
    :auth => {
      :method   => :simple,
      :username => dn,
      :password => password
    },
    :encryption => :simple_tls
  )
end
```

We have changed the port number to 636 (LDAPS), and we have added the :encryption option and set it to :simple_tls. That's all, and now the authentication system works on an encrypted connection.

## Chapter 2

Process E-commerce Payments

"If you can't bill it, kill it!" is a popular mantra in the enterprise world, because companies exist to earn money. Building software is a very expensive business, and regardless of whether you offer services on the Internet or ship applications to your customers, you have to get paid for them somehow.

A common approach to obtain your customers' money is to charge their credit cards. Credit cards are widespread, reasonably secure, and easy to use. Also, they can be processed electronically and without human intervention, which makes them a good means of payment for web shops and similar applications.

The biggest problem with credit cards is that you have to process them via *payment gateways* offered by *payment service providers*. They all have their own idea of what makes up a good API, and it can be tricky to integrate with them. Fortunately, there's a Ruby solution that prevents you from the hassle of programming against a payment gateway's native API, and in Recipe 10, *Charge Credit Cards with ActiveMerchant*, on page 51, you'll learn how to use it. You should read this recipe before reading the rest of this chapter.

The focus of Recipe 11, *Integrate ActiveMerchant with Rails*, on page 57 is the integration of ActiveMerchant with your Rails applications. It's easy, but you have to pay attention to a few important details.

Sometimes charging a customer's credit card directly is not an option. In European countries, for example, credit cards aren't as widespread as they are in the United States, and many people are reluctant to enter their credit card information into a web form. For these cases, special services exist that allow users to manage their payment details centrally so they have to trust only one party. One of the most popular services is PayPal, and in Recipe 12, *Transfer Money with PayPal*, on page 65, you can learn how to add PayPal support to your Rails applications.

Charge Credit Cards with ActiveMerchant

Problem

Your company is building a new service, and customers should be able to pay by credit card. The financial department has chosen a payment service provider already, so you only have to integrate with the payment gateway's API. In this recipe, you'll learn how to do this.

Ingredients

- Install the *ActiveMerchant* gem:[1]

```
$ gem install activemerchant
```

Solution

When charging credit cards in an application, you certainly never work directly with a bank or even with one of the big credit card companies. Usually, you have to delegate credit card transaction to a *payment service provider* that itself gives you access to a *payment gateway* and the according API.

The biggest problem with these payment gateways is that there are so many to choose from. They all have their pros and cons, and they all have their own proprietary APIs. In addition, their features often differ tremendously. Some of them allow you to charge only a customer's credit card, while others offer sophisticated address verification services or support recurring payments.

Fortunately, some brave people created ActiveMerchant, a framework that abstracts a lot of payment gateways' APIs and hides them behind a nice, clean interface. Simply put, ActiveMerchant is for payment gateways what ActiveRecord or JDBC are for databases. In this recipe, you'll learn how to access a payment gateway via ActiveMerchant in principle, and in Recipe 11, *Integrate ActiveMerchant with Rails*, on page 57, you'll learn how to add payment functionality to a Rails application.

---

1. http://www.activemerchant.org/

When developers start to integrate with a payment gateway, they usually do not know a lot about the payment industry's business processes and do not see the system from a customer's perspective. Often they think that it's sufficient to have a function for charging a customer's credit card, which is pretty easy with ActiveMerchant:

`ecommerce/samples/purchase.rb`

```
require 'active_merchant'

ActiveMerchant::Billing::Base.mode = :test
gateway = ActiveMerchant::Billing::BraintreeGateway.new(
  :login => 'demo',
  :password => 'password'
)

credit_card = ActiveMerchant::Billing::CreditCard.new(
  :first_name => 'Maik',
  :last_name => 'Schmidt',
  :number => '4111111111111111',
  :month => '10',
  :year => (Time.now.year + 1).to_s,
  :verification_value => '999'
)

options = {
  :billing_address => {
    :name => 'Maik Schmidt',
    :address1 => 'Musterstraße 42',
    :city => 'Musterstadt',
    :state => 'XX',
    :country => 'US',
    :zip => 'X12345',
    :phone => '555-123-4567'
  },
  :description => 'Beer Anthology (PDF)'
}

if !credit_card.valid?
  puts 'Credit card is invalid!'
  credit_card.errors.each_full { |m| puts m }
else
  amount_in_cents = 699
  response = gateway.purchase(
    amount_in_cents, credit_card, options
  )
  if response.success?
    puts "We've got the money!"
    puts "Transaction ID: #{response.authorization}"
    if response.avs_result['code'] != 'Y'
      puts "Address is suspicious:\n#{response.avs_result['message']}"
    end
```

```
45   else
       puts "Could not purchase the product:\n#{response.message}"
     end
   end
```

First we set ActiveMerchant into test mode, because we do not actually want to perform any real credit card transactions. Nearly all payment gateways have a sandbox for testing purposes, and ActiveMerchant uses a sandbox when in test mode (for production mode replace :test with :production).

In line 4, we create a proxy object for the payment gateway we'd like to use. We use the Braintree gateway,[2] because it has great testing features that can be used without registering up front (at the moment of this writing it does not accept any applications from merchants processing less than $100,000 USD a month). To authenticate against the gateway's API, we pass a login name and a password.

Then, in line 9, we create a CreditCard instance that gets all the arguments you'd probably expect, such as the card holder's name, the card number, its expiration date, and the verification value (a number comprising three to four digits that proves you have the cards in hand and did not get its data from anywhere else). We could have specified the credit card company that issued the card with the :type attribute, but usually that's not necessary, because it's encoded in the leading digits of the credit card number anyway (the 4 indicates that this is a card issued by Visa). The credit card we are using in this example is an official test card that can be found on the Braintree website, so don't get any ideas!

In principle, the credit card information is sufficient for payment purposes, but to increase security and customer convenience, you can often provide more information when accessing a payment gateway. That's why many ActiveMerchant commands accept an options hash, and we fill ours with the customer's billing address so it can be verified by the payment gateway. In addition, we add a description text that might appear on the customer's bill.

In line 31, the real payment processing starts. First we check the credit card syntactically by calling valid?(). This makes sure the credit card number has the right checksum (the last digit is a checksum calculated with the Luhn algorithm[3]). Also, it checks whether the card holder

---

2. http://www.braintreepaymentsolutions.com/
3. http://en.wikipedia.org/wiki/Luhn

name is empty, whether the card has expired already, and so on. If the credit card is invalid, we iterate over its errors attribute (it's a kind of Hash object) and output error messages similar to those provided by ActiveRecord. We could have used each(), but the messages returned by each_full() look better.

All checks happen on the client side, and even if valid?() returns true, it doesn't mean that the credit card actually exist or wasn't stolen (this can be checked only by the payment gateway). Always perform these checks before transmitting a transaction, because it prevents unnecessary transaction fees and gives your customers faster feedback if they have mistyped something.

We actually access the payment gateway for the first time in line 36 when we invoke the purchase() method. It gets the amount we'd like to charge (to prevent rounding errors, ActiveMerchant processes all amounts as integer values in cents), the credit card to get the money from, and the options we have previously defined. It returns an Active-Merchant::Billing::Response object that tells us whether the purchase has been successful. If it was successful, we output the response' authorization attribute. This attribute is some kind of transaction ID generated by the payment gateway, and it uniquely identifies our credit card transaction. Depending on the provider, it's possible to set a transaction ID yourself. It can be set with the :order_id option. Then, we check the results of the address verification service in line 42 (usually you'd expect a negative result if the address verification has failed, but some payment gateways process the transaction anyway).

It's time for a first test run:

```
mschmidt> ruby purchase.rb
We've got the money!
Transaction ID: 768198172
Address is suspicious:
Street address and postal code do not match.
```

All in all, everything worked as expected. The money will be transferred, although the address verification failed. Now, you could get yourself a merchant account and an account at your favorite payment service provider and start to get rich. But as stated earlier, this approach works only for some business models. The purchase() command is great for charging products that get delivered immediately such as most digital products (e-books, MP3 files, screencasts, and so on). For physical goods, it's rarely appropriate, because customers would not expect their credit cards to be charged when the order has been filled.

There is another mechanism splitting the payment process into two parts: authorize() and capture(). When a customer places an order, the money gets authorized at the payment gateway. In other words, the money is only reserved and not transferred to the merchant's account. This reservation usually lasts for a week (sometimes up to a month), and during this time, the money can be actually transferred with a capture() command. This way, the merchant makes sure it will eventually get the money, and the customer can be charged after the goods have been shipped.

There's another advantage in processing payments in two steps: if the customer wants to modify or cancel the order, there's time left to change the price or to skip the order altogether. Payments can be rolled back (this action is called *credit*), but it's best to cancel a transaction before it has been settled. It prevents costs and hassle. With ActiveMerchant, the authorize/capture cycle can be implemented with ease:

`ecommerce/samples/purchase.rb`

```
Line 1  amount_in_cents = 1000
   -    response = gateway.authorize(amount_in_cents, credit_card, options)
   -    if response.success?
   -      puts "Amount has been authorized!"
   5      puts "Transaction ID: #{response.authorization}"
   -      response = gateway.capture(amount_in_cents, response.authorization)
   -      if response.success?
   -        puts "We've got the money!"
   -      else
   10        puts "Could not capture the money:\n#{response.message}"
   -      end
   -    else
   -      puts "Could not authorize transaction:\n#{response.message}"
   -    end
```

The call to authorize() in line 2 looks exactly like a purchase() call, and its response can be treated equally, too. The only difference is that no money actually gets transferred. Usually you'd store the amount to be transferred and the responses' authorization attribute in a database so you could use them after the goods have been shipped. Then, you'd pass them to capture() (as we do in line 6) to get your money. You have to pass the amount again, because it may be different from the amount that has been authorized. For example, you might be unable to deliver all the goods the customer ordered.

That's all you have to do to add support for credit card payments to your web application, because ActiveMerchant simplifies the interaction with typical payment gateways as much as possible. But it does not support all payment gateway APIs on the planet at the moment (it supports mostly gateways that are hosted in the United States). But more gateways get added frequently, and if the one you need isn't supported, consider adding an appropriate extension to ActiveMerchant instead of implementing your own proprietary solution.

Also See

- See Recipe 11, *Integrate ActiveMerchant with Rails*, on the next page if you want to learn how to integrate ActiveMerchant with your Rails applications.

Integrate ActiveMerchant with Rails

Problem

You've built a web shop with Rails, and now you want to integrate with a payment gateway so your customers can pay with their credit cards.

Ingredients

- Change to the application's root directory, and install the Active-Merchant plug-in:

```
$ ./script/plugin install \
> git://github.com/Shopify/active_merchant.git
```

  This isn't necessary if you have installed the *ActiveMerchant* gem already.

- Install the *ssl_requirement* gem:

```
$ ./script/plugin install \
git://github.com/rails/ssl_requirement.git
```

Solution

Integrating ActiveMerchant with a Rails application doesn't differ much from using it directly, but you have to take care of a few details. Let's see how all this works in a very simple Rails shop application where users can buy regular paper books and e-books.

First add the following to config/environments/development.rb:

`ecommerce/demoshop/config/environments/development.rb`

```
config.after_initialize do
  ActiveMerchant::Billing::Base.mode = :test
end
```

This makes sure ActiveMerchant runs in test mode during development, and you can add similar statements to the test and production environments.

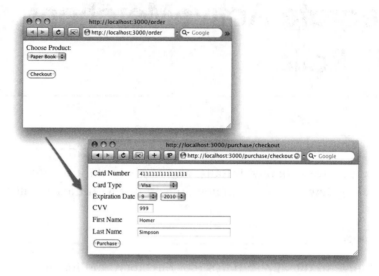

Figure 2.1: SIMPLIFIED CHECKOUT PROCESS

In a real-world application, you'd use SSL everywhere, and the *ssl_ requirement* plug-in helps you make sure that some actions can be requested only using SSL. It does not add SSL support to your application; it checks only whether certain actions are accessed using SSL! Adding SSL support right from the beginning makes testing and developing the application more complicated, so we patch *ssl_requirement* a bit in the ApplicationController:

`ecommerce/demoshop/app/controllers/application.rb`

```ruby
include SslRequirement
alias :original_ssl_required? :ssl_required?
def ssl_required?
  return false if local_request? || RAILS_ENV == 'test'
  original_ssl_required?
end
```

In addition, add the following line to the ApplicationController to prevent CreditCard objects from being written to log files:

`ecommerce/demoshop/app/controllers/application.rb`

```ruby
filter_parameter_logging :creditcard
```

Now generate the following models and controllers:

```
$ ./script/generate model Order product:string total_amount:integer
$ ./script/generate model Purchase order_id:integer amount:integer \
>  description:string xaction_id:string completed:boolean
$ ./script/generate controller Order index ship
$ ./script/generate controller Purchase checkout purchase
```

Two models and two controllers are all we need to build a simple web shop for selling books (of course, we could build a completely different business with this staff). Orders can contain only a single product—a hard-copy book that costs $30 or an e-book that costs $20. E-books can be purchased immediately, but if a customer buys a hard-copy book, her credit card will be charged after the book has been shipped.

Each order is associated with a Purchase object that contains the payment details and tracks the payment status. In Figure 2.1, on the facing page, you can see the transition from the order page to the checkout page, where the customer has to enter all credit card information needed to fulfill the payment process. Here's the Purchase model that contains the whole payment business logic:

`ecommerce/demoshop/app/models/purchase.rb`

```
Line 1   class Purchase < ActiveRecord::Base
  -        belongs_to :order
  -
  -        def purchase(order, credit_card)
  5          response = gateway.purchase(
  -            order.total_amount, credit_card,
  -            :description => self.description
  -          )
  -          return response.message if !response.success?
  10         self.xaction_id = response.authorization
  -          self.completed = true
  -          save
  -          nil
  -        end
  15
  -        def authorize(order, credit_card)
  -          response = gateway.authorize(
  -            order.total_amount, credit_card,
  -            :description => self.description
  20         )
  -          self.xaction_id = response.authorization
  -          self.completed = false
  -          save
  -          response.success? ? nil : response.message
  25       end
  -
```

```
     -    def capture(order)
     -      unless self.completed
     -        response = gateway.capture(order.total_amount, self.xaction_id)
    30        return response.message if !response.success?
     -        self.completed = true
     -        save
     -      end
     -      nil
    35    end
     -
     -    private
     -
     -    def gateway
    40      @gateway ||= ActiveMerchant::Billing::BraintreeGateway.new(
     -        :login => 'demo', :password => 'password'
     -      )
     -    end
     -  end
```

If you read Recipe 10, *Charge Credit Cards with ActiveMerchant*, on page 51, this code should look familiar, because all the model's methods delegate their work to ActiveMerchant. But there are some differences: to initialize the connection to the payment gateway only once, for example, we've put the according code into a private method named gateway(). There we check if a payment gateway reference has been assigned to the @gateway attribute already before creating a new one.

Also, the code that manipulates the completed attribute is interesting. In line 11, for example, we set it to true, because after we have successfully transmitted a purchase command to the payment gateway, the purchase is complete. That's different in the authorize() method. There we set completed to false and store the transaction ID we got from the payment gateway in line 21. That way, we can use it later in capture() to complete the purchase.

In line 28, we check whether the capture() action has been invoked for a purchase that has been completed already. If it has, we do not send a capture command again. The Purchase model is mainly used in the PurchaseController:

ecommerce/demoshop/app/controllers/purchase_controller.rb

```
Line 1  class PurchaseController < ApplicationController
     -    ssl_required :checkout, :purchase
     -
     -    def checkout
    5      session[:order] = params[:order]
     -    end
     -
```

```
     def purchase
       product = session[:order][:product]
10     credit_card = ActiveMerchant::Billing::CreditCard.new(
         params[:creditcard]
       )
       total_amount = product == 'ebook' ? 2000 : 3000
       order = Order.create(
15       :product => product,
         :total_amount => total_amount
       )
       purchase = Purchase.create(
         :amount => total_amount,
20       :description => "You bought: #{product}",
         :order => order,
         :completed => false
       )
       result = if product == 'ebook'
25       purchase.purchase(order, credit_card)
       else
         purchase.authorize(order, credit_card)
       end
       gateway_error(result) if !result.nil?
30   end

     private

     def gateway_error(message)
35     render :text => message
     end
   end
```

We start by declaring that SSL is needed to invoke any of the controller's
actions. In the checkout() action in line 5, we store the current order in
the session to make this sample application as short as possible. Usually, you'd create a shopping cart and store the order in the database
right from the beginning.

We read the order from the session at the beginning of the purchase()
method, and in line 10 we create a CreditCard object from the data that
has been transmitted using the form shown in Figure 2.1, on page 58.
Usually you'd check locally whether the credit card is syntactically correct by calling credit_card.valid?! I've skipped this check, so you can
provoke errors in the payment gateways by sending wrong credit card
information.

After we have determined the price of the product in line 13, we create
an order and a purchase object in the database, and in line 24 we
determine which payment strategy we should use: e-books are handled
by purchase(), and hard-copy books are passed to authorize().

The only action that's missing is ship(), which gets invoked after the book has been shipped:

`ecommerce/demoshop/app/controllers/order_controller.rb`

```ruby
class OrderController < ApplicationController
  def ship
    order = Order.find(params[:id])
    result = order.purchase.capture(order)
    render :text => result if !result.nil?
  end
end
```

It reads the order from the database and then invokes capture() on the according Purchase object. If something went wrong, an error message will be output. Otherwise, the regular view will be rendered:

`ecommerce/demoshop/app/views/order/ship.html.erb`

```erb
<h2>Order has been shipped and money has been captured.</h2>
```

In a final version, the ship() method would not be called by a regular customer but by a process handling shipments. But we're done, and thanks to ActiveMerchant, our web shop seamlessly handles the payment process for both physical and digital goods.

Discussion

Now that you know how easy it is to perform typical credit card transactions, you might think about much more sophisticated solutions. Perhaps you'd like to store credit card data in your database so your customers do not have to enter it every time they buy something in your shop.

It's not by accident that we did not store any credit card data in this recipe, because as soon as you store credit card information in your system, you have to get it certified according to the rules of the Payment Card Industry Data Security Standard (PCI-DSS).[4]

Its most important rules deal with the encryption of credit card information and especially with key management. Usually, you have to implement the "split key – dual control" scheme where no single person has access to a complete cryptographic key (it's like in those spy movies from the 60s where two people had to turn a key simultaneously to start

---

4. https://www.pcisecuritystandards.org/

a nuclear missile). This scheme typically has to be implemented with a key management server or a Hardware Security Module (HSM).

Of course, you have to apply all the typical security measures, too. That is, you need to have a firewall, antivirus software, an intrusion detection system, audit logs, and so on. But the certification has a lot of organizational impacts—for example, your data center will be checked, and you have to create an "incident response plan"—that makes sure somebody can be called in case of any problems.

If you have the system running, you're allowed to store encrypted credit card information in the part of your infrastructure that has been certified. You are not allowed to store credit card information outside this scope (not even encrypted!). If you have a messaging system, for example, that communicates with your credit card processing system, it is not allowed to use any message persistence mechanisms.

All in all, getting your infrastructure certified according to the rules of PCI-DSS takes a lot of work and costs a lot of money. If you absolutely have to store your customer's credit card data, delegate the task to your payment service provider! Many of them offer a secure credit card storage system where you can register your customers' credit card data once and get back a unique reference number for each card. This reference number can be stored locally (even unencrypted) and can be used in all transactions.

Alternatively, you should consider delegating payment processing to services such as PayPal, Google Checkout, or Amazon FPS. It might cost a bit more for each transaction, and it might scare away a few customers who do not use these services, but it will certainly pay off for most businesses. Implementing and maintaining an infrastructure that gets certified according to the PCI-DSS rules can be really expensive. And news about security problems in your company can take you out of business in the worst case.

No matter what you eventually do, always keep in mind that credit card fraud is some kind of identity theft, too. How would you feel if someone bought tons of porn movies using not only your money but also your name? Even worse: what if your card had been used for illegal activities? Before building a payment system yourself, do your homework. Talk to the experts, and do everything that's possible to protect your customers' privacy and money.

Also See

- In order to learn how to process your orders in the background, see Recipe 39, *Connect to Message Queues with ActiveMessaging*, on page 249.

- See Recipe 12, *Transfer Money with PayPal*, on the facing page to learn how to integrate your applications with PayPal.

- To learn ActiveMerchant's basics, see Recipe 10, *Charge Credit Cards with ActiveMerchant*, on page 51.

Transfer Money with PayPal

You'd like to give your customers the opportunity to pay using PayPal in your web shop.

- Change to the application's root directory, and install the Active-Merchant plug-in:

```
$ ./script/plugin install \
> git://github.com/Shopify/active_merchant.git
```

This isn't necessary if you have installed the *ActiveMerchant* gem already.

To demonstrate how to use the PayPal API in a more or less real-world example, we'll build a small web shop for selling screencasts. The shop will be very simplistic: you can choose between two screencasts, and you can buy only one at a time. Despite this, the checkout process will work and look like what you are used to when paying with PayPal in any other shop.

First you need to create an account for PayPal's developer sandbox.[5] After you have done this, point your browser to the sandbox, and create test accounts for a seller and a buyer. It's best to follow the "Create Manually" link and to walk through the regular registration processes (always keep in mind that you are in a sandbox, so fill out the mandatory form fields, but do not provide real-world data for bank accounts or credit cards). When you're done, your test account list should look like Figure 2.2, on the following page.

Select the seller account, and click "Enter Sandbox Test Site." Log in with the username and password you chose before, and go to the buyer account's profile page. Follow the "API Access" link, and request your

---

5. https://developer.paypal.com/

Figure 2.2: PayPal test accounts.

These materials have been reproduced with the permission of PayPal, Inc. © 2008 PAYPAL, INC. ALL RIGHTS RESERVED.

API credentials (choose the signature style, not the certificate). After the credentials have been created, log out, and go back to the developer sandbox. Click the "API Credentials" link to see your login, password, and signature.

Now create a new Rails application:

```
mschmidt> rails paypaldemo
```

and add the following lines to config/environments/development.rb (you have to insert your own credentials):

ecommerce/paypaldemo/config/environments/development.rb

```
config.after_initialize do
  ActiveMerchant::Billing::Base.gateway_mode = :test
end

PAYPAL_API_CREDENTIALS = {
  :login => 'Your PayPal API login.',
  :password => 'Your PayPal API password.',
  :signature => 'Your PayPal API signature.'
}
```

This enables ActiveMerchant's test mode and makes your sandbox API credentials available to your application. In production, you would encrypt the credentials and manage the encryption key with a key server (see Recipe 1, *Protect Information with Symmetric Ciphers*, on page 5).

The whole application is based on two models that are defined in the database as follows:

ecommerce/paypaldemo/db/migrate/20080724163157_create_orders.rb

```
create_table :orders do |t|
  t.string  :product, :state, :paypal_token
  t.decimal :amount, :precision => 10, :scale => 2
  t.timestamps
```

ecommerce/paypaldemo/db/migrate/20080724163243_create_purchases.rb

```
create_table :purchases do |t|
  t.belongs_to :order
  t.decimal    :amount, :precision => 10, :scale => 2
  t.timestamps
```

An Order object contains the name of the ordered product, the order's current state, the total amount to be paid by the customer, and a PayPal token (more on that in a few paragraphs). Every order is associated with a Purchase object containing the amount that has actually been paid by the customer (which might differ from the amount in the order).

Figure 2.3: ORDER PAGE WITH PAYPAL BUTTON.

THESE MATERIALS HAVE BEEN REPRODUCED WITH THE PERMISSION OF PAYPAL, INC. © 2008 PAYPAL, INC. ALL RIGHTS RESERVED.

To place a new order, we can use the following form:

```
ecommerce/paypaldemo/app/views/order/index.html.erb
<% form_for :order, @order, :url => {
    :controller => :purchase ,
    :action => :express_checkout } do |f| %>
  <label>Choose a Screencast:</label><br/>
  <br/>
  <%= f.select :product,
    [
      ['Rails Screencast', 'rails'], ['Erlang Screencast', 'erlang']
    ] %>
  <br/><br/>
  <input type='image'
         src="<%= image_path('btn_xpressCheckout.gif') %>">
<% end %>
```

The form contains only two hardwired products, but for our purposes, it's sufficient. You can see the order form with the PayPal checkout button in Figure 2.3. When you click the checkout button, all the work is delegated to the express_checkout() action in the PurchaseController (you have to be logged in on your PayPal sandbox while testing):

```
ecommerce/paypaldemo/app/controllers/purchase_controller.rb
Line 1  class PurchaseController < ApplicationController
          PRODUCTS = {
            'rails' => {
              :price => 4.95, :description => 'Rails Screencast'
        5   },
```

```ruby
      'erlang' => {
        :price => 5.95, :description => 'Erlang Screencast'
      },
    }

  def express_checkout
    product = params[:order][:product]
    order = Order.create(
      :state   => 'open',
      :product => product,
      :amount  => PRODUCTS[product][:price]
    )

    @response = gateway.setup_purchase(
      amount_in_cents(order.amount),
      :ip => request.remote_ip,
      :description => PRODUCTS[order.product][:description],
      :return_url => url_for(:action => :express_checkout_complete),
      :cancel_return_url => url_for(:action => :cancel_checkout)
    )

    if !@response.success?
      paypal_error(@response)
    else
      paypal_token = @response.params['token']
      order.update_attributes(
        :paypal_token => paypal_token,
        :state => 'purchase_setup'
      )
      paypal_url = gateway.redirect_url_for(paypal_token)
      redirect_to "#{paypal_url}&useraction=commit"
    end
  end

  private

  def gateway
    @gateway ||= ActiveMerchant::Billing::PaypalExpressGateway.new(
      PAYPAL_API_CREDENTIALS
    )
  end

  def paypal_error(response)
    render :text => response.message
  end

  def amount_in_cents(amount)
    (amount.round(2) * 100).to_i
  end
end
```

Admittedly, that's a whole bunch of code, but it should look familiar if you've read Recipe 11, *Integrate ActiveMerchant with Rails*, on page 57, and it's really not complicated. As mentioned before, customers can buy only one of two products that are defined in the PRODUCTS hash. Each product has a price and a description that will appear on the customer's order receipt.

express_checkout() reads the name of the product that has been ordered and creates a new order in the database in line 13. The order's state is set to :open, so we know we've received the order but did not start the payment process yet.

PayPal offers more than one API, and we use the "Express" variant that is represented by PaypalExpressGateway in ActiveMerchant. The gateway gets initialized only once in the gateway() method in line 42. In line 19, we prepare the communication with PayPal by calling setup_purchase(). setup_purchase() expects the amount the customer has to pay in cents (amount_in_cents() is defined in line 52 and does the conversion for us) and has several options:

- The customer's IP address is passed to PayPal, because it helps PayPal reduce the risk of fraud.
- PayPal gets a short :description of the product the customer has bought. It will appear on PayPal's order receipt.
- PayPal's API implements a callback interface. That is, the customer gets redirected from your web shop to the PayPal site, and with :return_url we tell PayPal where the browser should be redirected to after the customer has successfully paid for the order.
- :cancel_url contains the URL to be invoked by PayPal if the customer cancels the payment process.

If the purchase could not be set up, we print an error message by calling paypal_error(), which is defined in line 48. Otherwise, we get back a security token uniquely identifying our session with PayPal in line 30. We store this token in the database and set the order's state to purchase_setup, so we know that the order is not finished yet but has been prepared for purchase. Then, we invoke redirect_url_for() to determine the PayPal checkout URL for the token we've received and redirect the customer.

After clicking the "Checkout" button, you'll be redirected to the PayPal login page first. Log in with you buyer account, and you'll see a confirmation page that looks like Figure 2.4, on the facing page. That's what you are used to if you've ever paid something using PayPal.

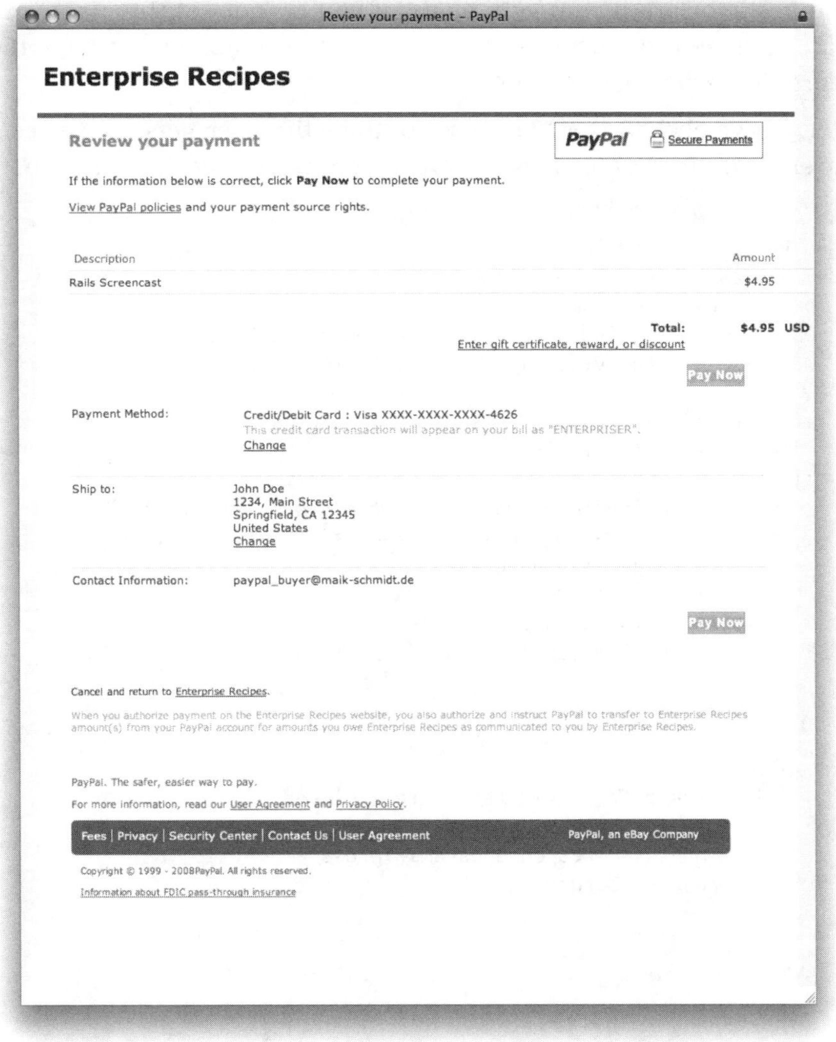

Figure 2.4: PAYPAL CONFIRMATION PAGE.

THESE MATERIALS HAVE BEEN REPRODUCED WITH THE PERMISSION OF PAYPAL, INC. © 2008 PAYPAL, INC. ALL RIGHTS RESERVED.

Please note the "Pay Now" button on the confirmation page. Usually, it'd be a "Checkout" button, but we have set the URL parameter useraction to commit in line 36. This tells PayPal there won't be a confirmation step on our site before a charge is made. If you do not set this parameter, you can present the whole order details to the customer one more time before the card is actually charged.

After you've clicked the "Pay Now" button, the user gets redirected to our site, and PayPal invokes the express_checkout_complete() action:

ecommerce/paypaldemo/app/controllers/purchase_controller.rb

```
Line 1   class PurchaseController
    -      def express_checkout_complete
    -        paypal_token = params[:token]
    -        @order = Order.find_by_paypal_token(paypal_token)
    5        @details = gateway.details_for(paypal_token)
    -
    -        if !@details.success?
    -          paypal_error(@details)
    -        else
    10           logger.info "Customer name: #{@details.params['name']}"
    -          logger.info "Customer e-mail: #{@details.params['payer']}"
    -          @response = gateway.purchase(
    -            amount_in_cents(@order.amount),
    -            :token => @details.params['token'],
    15            :payer_id => @details.params['payer_id']
    -          )
    -          if !@response.success?
    -            paypal_error(@response)
    -          else
    20             @order.update_attribute(:state, 'closed')
    -            @purchase = Purchase.create(
    -              :amount => @response.params['gross_amount'],
    -              :order => @order
    -            )
    25           end
    -        end
    -      end
    -    end
```

PayPal passes back the security token, and we use it to read the appropriate order from the database in line 4. Then we determine the details of the purchase by calling details_for(). This returns a PaypalExpressResponse object containing a lot of information about the customer, such as name, address, email address, and so on. It also contains information about the customer's verification status (both address verification and bank account verification). You could use this information to present a final confirmation page to your customers, but we only write some attributes into the application's log file and proceed with the purchase process in line 12.

purchase() gets the amount to be payed in cents, the PayPal token, and the payer's ID that we've gotten back with all the other details. If the purchase process has been completed successfully, we set the order's state to closed and create a new Purchase object in the database for this order. The Purchase object's amount attribute is set to the amount we've gotten back from PayPal in line 22.

Now the payment process is over, and you'll find an email in your developer's sandbox email inbox that looks like Figure 2.5, on the next page. For the sake of completeness, let's take a look at the cancel() method that is invoked by PayPal when the customer changes his mind anywhere in the payment process:

`ecommerce/paypaldemo/app/controllers/purchase_controller.rb`

```
class PurchaseController
  def cancel_checkout
    @order = Order.find_by_paypal_token(params[:token])
    @order.update_attribute(:state, 'cancelled')
  end
end
```

We read the order from the database and set its state to cancelled. We can use @order now to display an appropriate message:

`ecommerce/paypaldemo/app/views/purchase/cancel_checkout.html.erb`

```
<p>
  The payment process for order <%= @order.id %> has been cancelled.
</p>
```

Again, ActiveMerchant simplified our job significantly, although Pay-Pal's callback interface differs from the usual request/response cycle of many other payment gateways. Because PayPal is very popular and its integration is really easy, you should think about giving your customers the opportunity to pay with PayPal.

⌐ Also See ⌐

- In order to learn more about ActiveMerchant's basics, see Recipe 10, *Charge Credit Cards with ActiveMerchant*, on page 51.

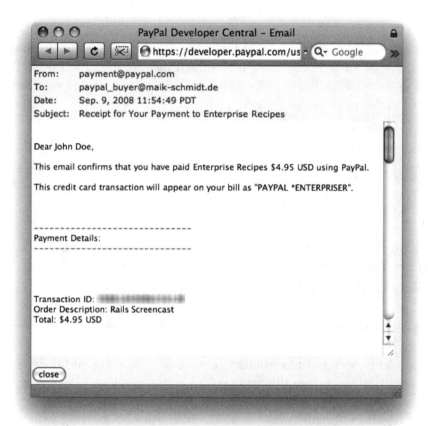

Figure 2.5: PAYPAL CONFIRMATION EMAIL.

THESE MATERIALS HAVE BEEN REPRODUCED WITH THE PERMISSION OF PAYPAL, INC. © 2008 PAYPAL, INC. ALL RIGHTS RESERVED.

Part II

Databases & XML Recipes

Chapter 3

Get the Most Out of Databases

If there's a single most important technology for enterprise software, it's certainly databases. Enterprise software is often expected to store and manipulate large and complex data sets, managed by relational database systems (RDBMSs).

Relational database systems are a mature technology, and several excellent products (both commercially and open source) are available. Their vendors usually support the SQL standard, but nearly all products come with proprietary extensions.

Some support nonstandard data types, some support nonstandard functions, and many of them even support stored procedures, which can be implemented in the vendor's own programming languages (some products allow you to write stored procedures using regular languages such as Perl, Python, or even Ruby).

Rails developers usually use the excellent ActiveRecord library to prevent themselves from having to deal with all these nitty-gritty SQL details, but by design ActiveRecord cannot cover specialties such as stored procedures. It's still possible to use them with ease, and in Recipe 13, *Execute Stored Procedures*, on page 79, you'll learn how to do it.

In Web 2.0 applications, databases get filled by excited users providing lots of content. Enterprise environments are different in this respect, because databases are typically filled by importing large data files. ActiveRecord does not have elaborate import or batch features right now, so see how to import data into your Rails applications in Recipe 14, *Feed Rails Databases from the Outside*, on page 87.

If your company uses products from different vendors, you might be happy to hear that you can actually use them simultaneously in your Rails applications. Learn more about it in Recipe 15, *Access Databases from Different Vendors Simultaneously*, on page 95, and learn how to incrementally migrate your applications from one database system to another.

For most tasks, relational database systems are a perfect fit, but in some situations other tools are more appropriate. If you have to store documents including their history of changes, for example, you'd be better off using a version control system instead of a database. Take a look at Recipe 16, *Manage Data with Subversion*, on page 101 to learn more about this useful technique.

Execute Stored Procedures

You are a big ActiveRecord fan, and one of your New Year's resolutions was to never write SQL statements yourself again. Unfortunately, ActiveRecord only maps tables to objects, and vice versa. It does not support stored procedures, which is really a pity, because you can find them in many legacy databases and there are still companies that do not allow their developers to access table data directly. Their database admins insist on using stored procedures.

In this recipe, you'll learn how to use ActiveRecord's raw connection to execute arbitrary SQL statements and how to invoke stored procedures.

Ingredients

- Install the *ruby-plsql* gem:[1]

  ```
  $ gem install ruby-plsql
  ```

- Install the *activerecord-oracle_enhanced-adapter* gem:[2]

  ```
  $ gem install activerecord-oracle_enhanced-adapter
  ```

Solution

The database we are working with is an Oracle database containing the following objects:

databases/stored_procedures/create_db.sql

```sql
CREATE TABLE customer (
  id            NUMBER(10) NOT NULL PRIMARY KEY,
  forename      VARCHAR2(60),
  surname       VARCHAR2(60),
  date_of_birth DATE
);

CREATE SEQUENCE customer_id;
```

---

1. http://ruby-plsql.rubyforge.org/
2. http://oracle-enhanced.rubyforge.org/

There is a table named customer for storing customer data and a sequence named customer_id for generating new customer IDs. Usually, creating a new customer would be easy and could be implemented with a single INSERT statement. But you have to use the following PL/SQL function instead:

databases/stored_procedures/create_db.sql

```
CREATE OR REPLACE FUNCTION add_customer(
  forename     IN VARCHAR2,
  surname      IN VARCHAR2,
  date_of_birth IN DATE
)
RETURN PLS_INTEGER
IS
  l_customer_id PLS_INTEGER;
BEGIN
  INSERT INTO customer
  VALUES (customer_id.NEXTVAL, forename, surname, date_of_birth)
  RETURNING id INTO l_customer_id;
  RETURN l_customer_id;
END add_customer;
```

Even if you are not familiar with Oracle's PL/SQL dialect, you should be able to understand what the add_customer() function does. It takes a forename, a surname, and a date of birth, and it inserts all these values into table customer to create a new customer. Afterward, it returns the ID of the newly created customer, which it got from the customer_id sequence.

The function's return type is PLS_INTEGER, although the appropriate column type is NUMBER(10). That's for performance reasons, because PLS_INTEGER is more efficient.

That all looks pretty nice and clean, but you might be wondering how you'd call the add_customer() function from your Ruby program. Here we go:

databases/stored_procedures/add_customer.rb

```
Line 1  require 'activerecord'
   -
   -    class Customer < ActiveRecord::Base
   -      set_table_name :customer
   5
   -      def self.create(params)
   -        cursor = self.connection.raw_connection.parse <<-PLSQL
   -        DECLARE
   -          new_id PLS_INTEGER;
```

```
10      BEGIN
 -        :new_id := add_customer(:forename, :surname, :date_of_birth);
 -      END;
 -      PLSQL
 -      cursor.bind_param('forename', params[:forename], String, 60)
15      cursor.bind_param('surname', params[:surname], String, 60)
 -      cursor.bind_param('date_of_birth', params[:date_of_birth])
 -      cursor.bind_param('new_id', nil, Fixnum)
 -      cursor.exec
 -      new_id = cursor['new_id']
20      cursor.close
 -      customer = Customer.new
 -      customer.id = new_id
 -      customer.forename = params[:forename]
 -      customer.surname = params[:surname]
25      customer.date_of_birth = params[:date_of_birth]
 -      customer
 -    end
 -  end
```

As usual, we derive our Customer class from ActiveRecord::Base, and in line 4, we set the table name to customer because otherwise ActiveRecord would assume that the table is named customers.

Then we define our own create() method, overwriting the one that has been defined by ActiveRecord. In line 7, we obtain a reference to the actual database connection through the raw_connection member. The connection is of type OCI8, because we are working with an Oracle database and the basis of ActiveRecord's Oracle support is the *ruby-oci8* library.[3] (Attention: You are leaving the vendor-independent sector! If you cannot stand to see nonportable code, you'd better leave the room now.)

After we have the database connection, we immediately call its parse() method, passing it another piece of PL/SQL. Here we declare a variable named new_id and set it to the return value of our add_customer() function. That's nearly the code you'd use in a PL/SQL program to call the add_customer() function. The only difference is that we have put a colon in front of every variable and argument name. This turns them into *bind variables* that we'll use later.

parse() returns a Cursor object, which is more or less Oracle's term for a *prepared statement*. Most databases support prepared statements. Instead of executing a SQL statement directly, the database creates

---

3. http://ruby-oci8.rubyforge.org/

Joe Asks...

What Is a Stored Procedure?

Since the beginning of relational databases, people always wanted more data types. It all started with numbers and strings, and today we can store arbitrary binary data, XML documents, or even complete object hierarchies. So, it came as no surprise that some vendors allowed their users to store and execute code in the database. Typically, the code has to be written in proprietary languages such as PL/SQL (Oracle) or Transact-SQL (Microsoft, Sybase), but some products support stored procedures written in Java or Perl.

Stored procedures were meant to speed up things in the database, but as with many technologies, they've been abused rather quickly. There are countless examples of companies that have implemented most of their business logic in stored procedures. That's a bad idea for many reasons; the most important one is vendor lock-in. You cannot easily port your application to any other database product. In addition, the design of such applications is often horrible, because data and business logic are coupled too tightly, and most stored procedure languages lack a lot of important features offered by other languages.

So, if you remember only one sentence from this book, it should be the following: *Thou shalt not store business logic in the database!*

only the query execution plan and returns a handle for the statement with placeholders for all its variable parts. If you actually want to execute the statement, you only have to pass the statement handle and the variable parts. This speeds up things tremendously, and it prevents SQL injection attacks. In a production version of our code, you'd call parse() only once and store the Cursor object.

Now that we have a Cursor object at hand, we only have to fill out its variable parts. This process is called *parameter binding* and is done with a method named bind_param(). It expects up to four arguments:

- The name or index of the parameter to be bound. If you prefer to reference parameters by index, keep in mind that counting starts at 1.

- The parameter value. For output parameters, this argument is set to nil. It can also be set to nil for input parameters, which results in a NULL value in the database.

- The parameter's type. Usually, the type of input arguments is derived from their value's type; that is, if you pass a String value, the parameter's type is String, too. Sometimes it's necessary to set the type explicitly. For example, you could set the type of an output parameter to Time and bind it to a DATE column in the database. OCI8 will convert it automatically then.

- The parameter's maximum length. Many database column types have a restricted length.

After we have bound all parameters, we can execute the statement by calling exec(), and in line 19, we read the result that has been returned by the PL/SQL function. Then we close the cursor to free resources, and finally we create a new Customer object. Here's a little sample run:

`databases/stored_procedures/add_customer.rb`

```ruby
ActiveRecord::Base.establish_connection(
  :adapter  => 'oracle',
  :username => 'maik',
  :password => 'tOp$ecret'
)

me = Customer.create(
  :forename      => 'Maik',
  :surname       => 'Schmidt',
  :date_of_birth => Time.mktime(1972, 9, 30)
)
puts "My ID is #{me.id}."

me_again = Customer.find(me.id)
puts "My name is #{me_again.forename}."
```

It prints the following:

```
mschmidt> ruby add_customer.rb
My ID is 1.
My name is Maik.
```

Our create() method behaves exactly like the original, and because we have derived our Customer class from ActiveRecord::Base, we still can use all its other methods such as find().

Despite all this, create() will never win a beauty contest. It's a classic example of database access from the 80s: get a connection, prepare a statement, bind parameters, execute, and read results. What could be more tedious? You might think "Hey, if ActiveRecord can map database tables to Ruby objects, why can't it map stored procedures to Ruby methods?" At the moment, it can't, and it probably never will; however, some alternative solutions work pretty well. One of them is *ruby-plsql*, a small library that maps stored procedures to Ruby methods automatically. At the time of this writing, it supports only a few data types (support for collection types such as VARRAY is missing completely, for example), but it's already sufficient to shorten our first implementation dramatically:

databases/stored_procedures/add_customer.rb

```
require 'ruby_plsql'
plsql.connection = ActiveRecord::Base.connection.raw_connection
new_id = plsql.add_customer('Jane', 'Rodriguez', Date.today)
```

That's how it should be: tell plsql where to find a database connection, then invoke stored procedures as if they were regular Ruby methods. We only had to assign the current Oracle connection to plsql.connection

Let's rewrite the first version of our Customer class using *ruby-plsql*. Instead of replacing the create() method directly, we will use the *activerecord-oracle_enhanced-adapter* library that adds useful extensions to ActiveRecord's Oracle adapter. Among others, it allows us to easily replace the default methods for creating, updating, and deleting objects. Here's how we replace ActiveRecord's original create() method:

databases/stored_procedures/enhanced_plsql.rb

```
Line 1   require 'activerecord'
    -    ActiveRecord::Base.establish_connection(
    -      :adapter  => 'oracle_enhanced',
    -      :username => 'maik',
    5      :password => 'tOp$ecret'
    -    )
    -    plsql.connection = ActiveRecord::Base.connection.raw_connection
    -
    -    class Customer < ActiveRecord::Base
   10      set_table_name :customer
    -
    -      set_create_method do
    -        plsql.add_customer(forename, surname, date_of_birth)
    -      end
   15    end
```

We connect to the database using the *oracle_enhanced* adapter, and as before we assign the current Oracle connection to plsql.connection. Then we define the Customer class and tell ActiveRecord that our table is named customer, not customers. In line 12, we use set_create_method()

to redefine the create() method. The new version does not execute an INSERT statement but calls our stored procedure instead. It can be used as follows:

`databases/stored_procedures/enhanced_plsql.rb`

```
maik = Customer.create(
  :forename     => 'Maik',
  :surname      => 'Schmidt',
  :date_of_birth => Time.mktime(1972, 9, 30)
)

jane = Customer.new
jane.forename = 'Jane'
jane.surname = 'Rodriguez'
jane.date_of_birth = Time.mktime(1973, 2, 21)
jane.save
```

The previous program creates two new database objects. One gets stored immediately by calling create(), while the other one (jane) is instantiated first by calling new() and is made persistent later with the save() method. In both cases, our stored procedure has been used to store the new customer objects. Similarly, ActiveRecord's update() and delete() methods can be changed using the set_update_method() and set_delete_method() methods. *activerecord-oracle_enhanced-adapter* comes with many more extensions, and to use it in a Rails application, simply use oracle_enhanced as the adapter name in config/database.yml.

Discussion

ActiveRecord is a great tool, but when it comes to specialties such as stored procedures, it doesn't help you much. You have to leave its warm and safe ecosystem and deal with real-world issues (redundant length definitions and proprietary interfaces, for example) manually. Use stored procedures only if you absolutely must.

Feed Rails Databases from the Outside

Problem

You have built an application with Rails, and you're managing its database completely with ActiveRecord. Because of some new requirements, you have to import bulk amounts of data from the outside; in other words, data will not be imported by the application but directly into the database.

In this recipe, you'll see how to achieve this with native database tools and with ActiveRecord.

Ingredients

- Install the ActiveRecord extensions:[4]

  ```
  $ gem install ar-extensions
  ```

Solution

Nearly all database products come with an import tool. Oracle calls it SQL*Loader, DB2 comes with DB2 LOAD, MySQL has the LOAD DATA statement, and so on. Their biggest advantages are that they are very fast and they usually have a lot of options to transform the data being imported in any imaginable way. But if you are using ActiveRecord, chances are good that you have defined a lot of your model constraints in Ruby and not in the database. To stay DRY,[5] you should use a custom importer to check all your validation rules. In this recipe, we'll look at both alternatives.

Let's say you have to import a list of locations weekly.

---

4. http://github.com/zdennis/ar-extensions/tree/master/
5. "Don't Repeat Yourself"; see *The Pragmatic Programmer* [HT00] to learn more about the DRY principle.

They are stored in a database table that has been created as follows:

`databases/dbload/dbload.rb`

```ruby
class CreateLocations < ActiveRecord::Migration
  def self.up
    create_table :locations, :force => true do |t|
      t.string :label, :street, :postal_code, :city, :country
    end
  end

  def self.down
    drop_table :locations
  end
end
```

The model class looks like this:

`databases/dbload/dbload.rb`

```ruby
class Location < ActiveRecord::Base
  validates_presence_of :label, :street, :postal_code, :city, :country
end
```

At the moment, we have defined only a single validation rule to make sure that none of a location's attributes is empty. The following CSV file contains two valid locations:

`databases/dbload/data.csv`

```
label;street;postal_code;city;country
Location 1;Musterstraße 42;12345;Musterstadt;DE
Location 2;1234 Sample Street;99887;Sample City;GB
```

In addition to the two data sets, the file contains a header line explaining which attributes are stored in the different columns. The following statement loads the CSV file into a MySQL database:

`databases/dbload/mysql_load.sql`

```sql
LOAD DATA LOCAL INFILE 'data.csv'
INTO TABLE locations
FIELDS TERMINATED BY ';'
LINES TERMINATED BY '\n'
IGNORE 1 LINES
(label, street, postal_code, city, country);
```

Because of the clean syntax, the statement should be self-explanatory. Here's how to use it:

```
mschmidt> mysql -u maik -p sample
Enter password:
Welcome to the MySQL monitor.  Commands end with ; or \g.
Your MySQL connection id is 29
Server version: 5.0.37-log MySQL Community Server (GPL)
```

Type 'help;' or '\h' for help. Type '\c' to clear the buffer.

```
mysql> source mysql_load.sql
Query OK, 2 rows affected (0.00 sec)
Records: 2  Deleted: 0  Skipped: 0  Warnings: 0
```

That works great, but what happens if we feed it some invalid data—data where mandatory fields are missing? Right: MySQL will happily load the invalid data, because it does not know about our application's constraints. All validation rules have been defined in the Location model, so if we do not want to violate the DRY principle, we have to write our own CSV importer, which is not difficult:

`databases/dbload/dbload.rb`

```
Line 1   class Location
     -     def self.load(filename)
     -       options = {
     -         :headers => true,
     5         :header_converters => :symbol,
     -         :col_sep => ';'
     -       }
     -
     -       begin
     10         Location.transaction do
     -           FasterCSV.foreach(filename, options) do |row|
     -             Location.create!(row.to_hash)
     -           end
     -         end
     15       rescue => ex
     -         $stderr.puts ex
     -       end
     -     end
     -   end
```

We have added a new class method named load() to the Location class, which uses FasterCSV to parse the data to be imported (see Recipe 17, *Manipulate CSV with Ruby*, on page 109 for more detailed information about parsing CSV with Ruby). Hence, the parsing could be reduced to a single foreach() call, and because the columns in the input files have the same names as the relevant database columns, we could use to_hash() in line 12 to create new Location objects.

The whole import process runs in a single transaction that starts in line 10. If the import file contains a single line that is not valid, the whole process will be stopped, all database changes will be rolled back, and an error message gets printed in line 16.

What About XML or YAML?

CSV is not the only data exchange format on this planet, so you might be asking yourself whether XML or YAML is a good choice for importing data. Short answer: no, they're not.

Both XML and YAML have been designed for serializing and deserializing complex data structures, and they are really good at it. Relational databases usually process large amounts of homogeneous data, and that's the main reason for their high performance. For importing data into a relational database, you should choose a format that closely meets a database's structure. So, you should use CSV or fixed-length records.

However, if you absolutely have to import XML or YAML files (maybe because a customer delivers data in one of these formats), you can import them by writing a custom script as we did for CSV in this recipe. Ruby has excellent support for both XML and YAML, and in the ActiveSupport (not ActiveRecord) class, you'll find a method named create_from_xml() that helps you turn XML documents into ActiveRecord objects easily.

It might well be that you want to choose a different import strategy; perhaps you'd like to ignore invalid input lines. To do so, remove the transaction block, and call create() instead of create!().

If you use a transaction, make sure the rollback segment of your database is sufficiently large (at least if you're using an Oracle database). Otherwise, the import process will run out of disk space if it reads really big files.

You can use the loader as follows:

`databases/dbload/dbload.rb`

```
ActiveRecord::Base.establish_connection(
    :adapter  => 'mysql',
    :database => 'sample',
    :username => 'maik',
    :password => 't0p$ecret'
)
Location.load(ARGV[0])
```

Now that we have two solutions available, let's compare them. To get representative results, we import a large input file containing 200,000 lines both with the MySQL loader and with our own solution. To be

as fair as possible, the transaction handling in the Ruby program has
been disabled temporarily. Here are the results:

```
mschmidt> time mysql -u maik -p sample < mysql_load_huge.sql
Enter password:

real  0m8.863s
user  0m0.010s
sys   0m0.035s

mschmidt> time ruby dbload.rb huge_file.csv
real  8m36.506s
user  3m48.672s
sys   0m21.995s
```

Scary, isn't it? Although this test isn't perfectly accurate (for example,
the time it took me to enter my password has been counted, too), it
should give you a good impression of the performance differences. Our
custom solution not only takes much longer, but it also puts a high
load on your database server. Under certain circumstances, the Ruby
importer would be no alternative.

A perfect solution would be a bridge between ActiveRecord and the
database's internal import features, wouldn't it? That's exactly what
the *ar-extensions* library gives us (among other useful features); we'll
use it now to find a better balance between speed and validation support.

We leave the migrations and the Location class as they are, but we have
to prepare the database access as follows:

databases/dbload/dbload_arext.rb

```ruby
require 'ar-extensions'
logger = Logger.new('import.log')
logger.level = Logger::INFO
ActiveRecord::Base.establish_connection(
  :adapter  => 'mysql',
  :database => 'sample',
  :username => 'maik',
  :password => 't0p$ecret'
)
ActiveRecord::Base.logger = logger
```

When using ActiveRecord outside Rails, it's always a good idea to initialize a Logger object. In our case, it is even more advisable, because if you
start an import process that crashes after it has loaded data for hours,
you certainly want to know what has happened. We set the log level to

INFO so the log file will not contain tons of boring debug messages, and now we can write the actual load() method:

`databases/dbload/dbload_arext.rb`

```
Line 1   def load(filename, chunk_size = 3_000, validate = true)
    -      options = {
    -        :headers => true,
    -        :header_converters => :symbol,
    5        :col_sep => ';'
    -      }
    -
    -      locations = []
    -      FasterCSV.foreach(filename, options) do |row|
    10       locations << Location.new(row.to_hash)
    -        if locations.size % chunk_size == 0
    -          Location.import locations, :validate => validate
    -          locations = []
    -        end
    15     end
    -      Location.import locations, :validate => validate if locations.size > 0
    -   end
```

The load() method gets the name of the CSV file to be imported, a chunk size, and a flag indicating whether the data should be validated while it is imported. The whole logic for reading the CSV file did not change noticeably compared to our first approach, but instead of importing every single location at once, we read chunks of a certain size and pass them to the import() method defined by *ar-extensions* in line 12.

In our first approach to writing a Ruby import script, we have used ActiveRecord's regular mechanism for creating objects in the database, which resulted in a separate INSERT statement for each object. *ar-extensions* is capable of *mass assignment statements*. As such, it can create multiple database objects with a single statement. To achieve this, it uses the database's internal mass assignment features, and the only method you need to know is import().

import() takes an array of ActiveRecord objects and imports them into the database. You might ask yourself why we did not load the whole CSV file into memory to import it in a single step. The main problem is that you cannot load every file imaginable into memory because some of them are too big. A more interesting point is that loading the whole file into memory will actually slow things down for big files, because they'd be managed by the operating system's virtual memory.

It's time for a first test run. Again, we will import 200,000 locations, and we will validate them, too (chunk_size has been set to 1,000):

```
mschmidt> time ruby dbload_arext.rb huge_file.csv
real    4m10.669s
user    4m0.778s
sys     0m1.343s
```

It's still much slower than MySQL's native import, but it's twice as fast as our first solution. And here are the results when the import process disables all validations:

```
real    2m8.000s
user    2m0.031s
sys     0m0.773s
```

Although the Location class does not have complex validations, the import process runs twice as fast, and two minutes for loading 200,000 objects is certainly sufficient for most purposes.

All in all, you have to find a healthy balance between checking constraints and performance. Often the best solution is to check constraints up front using a small script and then loading the data with the database's load tool. If performance doesn't matter, you can use a custom loader (preferably using *ar-extensions*), making sure all your constraints are met. That's especially important if you have to import complicated data affecting more than one table, for example.

Access Databases from Different Vendors Simultaneously

Your company migrates more and more legacy applications to Rails and MySQL. In the past, all applications were based on Oracle, so during the transition phase, you often have to access databases from different vendors simultaneously. For example, customer data is still stored in a legacy Oracle database, while new orders are already stored in a MySQL database.

In this recipe, you'll learn how to create database models that work together seamlessly, even though they are tied to completely different database products.

Solution

Before we start to operate on both the MySQL and Oracle databases, let's look at their structure. Orders are stored in a MySQL database, and the orders table has been created with the following migration:

`databases/multiple_db/shop/db/migrate/001_create_orders.rb`
```
create_table :orders do |t|
  t.column :customer_id, :int
  t.column :product_name, :string
  t.column :quantity, :int
  t.timestamps
end
```

Orders consist of a product name, a quantity of ordered products, and a reference to the customer who has placed the order.

Customers are defined as follows in an Oracle database:

databases/stored_procedures/create_db.sql

```
CREATE TABLE customer (
  id             NUMBER(10) NOT NULL PRIMARY KEY,
  forename       VARCHAR2(60),
  surname        VARCHAR2(60),
  date_of_birth DATE
);

CREATE SEQUENCE customer_id;
```

Each customer has a forename, a surname, a date of birth, and an ID that has been emitted by the customer_id sequence. Now we define the access parameters for both databases in Rails' database.yml file:

databases/multiple_db/shop/config/database.yml

```
development:
  adapter: mysql
  encoding: utf8
  database: shop
  username: maik
  password: t0p$ecret

customer_db:
  adapter: oracle
  username: maik
  password: t0p$ecret
```

Connection parameters of the MySQL database can be found in the development section, because it's the database where the current development actually happens. In addition, its name adheres to the Rails conventions, so it will actually be treated as the development database. The Oracle database parameters section is named customer_db, because we need it only for accessing customer data.

We have everything ready now to define our model classes, and the Order class is trivial:

databases/multiple_db/shop/app/models/order.rb

```
class Order < ActiveRecord::Base
  belongs_to :customer
end
```

Defining the Customer class is a bit more complicated, because we have to tell ActiveRecord that it should use our customer_db connection when mapping Customer objects.

To make this as easy and extensible as possible, we define a base class for all models that are mapped to the Oracle database:

databases/multiple_db/shop/app/models/customer_db.rb

```
class CustomerDatabase < ActiveRecord::Base
  self.abstract_class = true
  establish_connection(:customer_db) unless connected?
end
```

By setting the abstract_class member to true, we tell ActiveRecord that no instance of class CustomerDatabase will ever be created and that it's not necessary to map its attributes. Afterward, we call establish_connection(), passing it the access parameters for the customer_db database connection. From now on, all classes derived from CustomerDatabase will use this connection. We can easily define our Customer model now:

databases/multiple_db/shop/app/models/customer.rb

```
require 'customer_db'

class Customer < CustomerDatabase
  set_table_name :customer
  set_sequence_name :customer_id

  has_many :orders
end
```

Customer has been derived from CustomerDatabase, and because the objects in the Oracle database do not follow Rails' conventions, we have to explicitly set the name of the table to be mapped and the sequence to be used for generating new IDs. We declare that a customer potentially has many orders, and we are done. See our cross-database models in action:

```
mschmidt> ruby script/console
Loading development environment (Rails 2.1.0)
>> me = Customer.find_by_surname('Schmidt')
=> #<Customer id: 2, forename: "Maik", surname: "Schmidt",
   date_of_birth: "1972-09-30 00:00:00">
>> Order.create(
?>   :product_name => 'Ruby book',
?>   :quantity     => 5,
?>   :customer     => me
>> )
=> #<Order id: 2, customer_id: 2, product_name: "Ruby book",
   quantity: 5, created_at: "2008-05-12 15:32:12",
   updated_at: "2008-05-12 15:32:12">
>> me.orders.size
=> 1
```

```
>> me.orders.first.product_name
=> "Ruby book"
>> me.orders.first.quantity
=> 5
```

This console session looks absolutely harmless. First, we look up a customer who has a certain surname. Then, we create a new order placed by the customer. Behind the scenes a lot of magic happens, and without a single piece of SQL and without mentioning a vendor's name, we have placed a new order in the MySQL database and connected it to a customer in the Oracle database.

ActiveRecord's design makes it easy to access multiple database simultaneously. They do not have to be from different vendors; you can access multiple MySQL databases, too, for example. But don't be fooled by ActiveRecord's nice, clean interfaces. In the end there's always some dirty work to be done in the database server, and all products currently available differ in subtle and sometimes not so subtle details. For example, some products are capable of performing joins across different databases running on different servers, while others aren't. So, use this technique with caution.

ActiveRecord and Legacy Schemas

ActiveRecord works best with databases strictly adhering to its conventions, but it's still useful for legacy schemas that do not diverge too much from its expectations. Here's a list of common problems and their solutions:

- ActiveRecord expects all tables names to be in the plural form. For example, a table used for storing customers has to be named customers. If you prefer the singular form, execute the following statement after you've established a database connection:

```
ActiveRecord::Base.pluralize_table_names = false
```

- If you're working with table names that are neither singular nor plural forms of your models, you can set the table name explicitly:

```
class Customer < ActiveRecord::Base
  set_table_name 'cust'
end
```

- ActiveRecord assumes that all models have a primary ID column named id. To change this for a certain model, use the set_primary_key() method:

```
class Customer < ActiveRecord::Base
  set_primary_key 'customer_no'
end
```

- Sometimes you need to execute arbitrary and/or proprietary SQL statements. That's what execute() is for:

```
ActiveRecord::Base.connection.execute(
  'set current isolation = UR'
)
```

There are more methods making your life easier; for example, you can set prefixes and suffixes for table names (for details, refer to ActiveRecord's excellent API documentation).

Despite this, there are many problems that cannot be solved easily with ActiveRecord. For example, composite primary keys cannot be mapped adequately, but a plug-in exists that makes this task easier.*

---

*. http://compositekeys.rubyforge.org/

Manage Data with Subversion

You have to store text documents in a database and track all changes that have been made to them. That is, not only do you have to store each revision of the document, but you also have to store the name of the author of each change. In addition, you'd like to calculate the differences between two revisions.

Every mature version control system solves this problem with ease, so it's not too weird to think about using Subversion[6] as a database back end for your documents. In this recipe, you'll learn how to do this in an elegant and efficient way.

- Install the Ruby Subversion bindings.[7]

- The original bindings are far from being convenient, so we add another layer. Copy the file at http://www.oneofthewolves.com/svn_repos/svn_repos.rb to a place where your Ruby interpreter will find it. If you are developing a Rails application, copy it to the lib directory, for example.

Subversion internally uses a database to track all changes that have been made to documents stored in the repository. This database is based either on a regular file system or on Berkeley DB.[8] As a user, you won't notice the difference.

Usually, you don't access a Subversion repository directly but instead use its command-line clients or the appropriate features of your development tools.

---

6. http://subversion.tigris.org/
7. http://collaboa.org/docs/svnbindings/install/
8. http://www.oracle.com/database/berkeley-db/

For integrating Subversion with a Ruby application in principle, you have two choices:

- Execute Subversion's command-line client from your Ruby program, and parse its result. That would be an easy and straightforward solution, but it would be highly fragile, too. For example, if you depend on English messages to be returned by the command-line client, your software will not run in an environment that uses messages in another language. In addition, spawning a process for every access to the repository isn't efficient enough for many applications.
- Use the official bindings for Ruby that come with Subversion. They are fairly low-level, but they allow you to use Subversion's functionality in a stable, portable way, and they are pretty fast.

In this recipe, we'll use the second approach; we start simple and define a class that represents our documents and a minimal version of a DocumentStorage class:

databases/subversion/document_storage.rb

```
Line 1  require 'svn_repos'

        class Document
          attr_accessor :path, :content, :author, :revision
     5
          def initialize(path, content, author, revision)
            @path, @content, @author = path, content, author
            @revision = revision
          end
    10
          def to_s
            <<-"EOS".gsub(/^     /, '')
            path: #{@path}
            content: #{@content}
    15      author: #{@author}
            revision: #{@revision}
            EOS
          end
        end
    20
        class DocumentStorage
          attr_reader :repository

          DEFAULT_PATH = File.join('.', 'data', 'docstore')
    25
          def initialize(path = DEFAULT_PATH)
            @repository = if SvnRepos.repository_exists?(path)
              SvnRepos.open(path)
```

```
        else
30          SvnRepos.create(path)
        end
    end

    def add_document(path, content, author)
35      @repository.commit path => content, :author => author
    end
end
```

Every Document instance has a path where it can be found, some content, an author, and a revision number. The DocumentStorage class at the moment has only two methods: a constructor and a method to add new documents to the repository.

initialize() expects a path pointing to a Subversion repository in the local file system. In line 27, we check whether a repository already exists at the path specified. If it does, we open it; otherwise, we create a new one. In any case, @repository references an instance of class SvnRepos.

This instance is used in add_document() for the first time to add a new revision of a document to the repository. The method expects three arguments:

- The path that identifies the document in the repository, which is also the path you can use to get back the document later. If no document exists at this path, add_document() creates a new one. Otherwise, a new revision of the document is created.
- The content of the document, which can be both textual or binary.
- The name of the author who adds the document to the repository.

Line 35 contains the whole logic of the add_document() method and delegates all the work to the commit() method of class SvnRepos. It returns the current revision after the document has been stored.

Let's create a document storage and add some documents:

`databases/subversion/document_storage.rb`

```
ds = DocumentStorage.new
ds.add_document('/first/document', "Hello, world!\n", 'maik')
ds.add_document('/first/document', "Hello!\nHow are you?\n", 'jack')
ds.add_document('/another/document', "Yet another document.\n", 'maik')
```

The previous code adds two revisions of a document at /first/document (directories are created for you automatically). One has been edited by an author named *maik*; the other one has been contributed by *jack*.

In addition, *maik* has created another document that you can find at /another/document.

Until now we have not defined any methods for retrieving documents, so we cannot check immediately whether our new documents actually have been stored. But we can check whether a new Subversion repository has been created:

```
mschmidt> ls data/docstore
README.txt  conf    dav    db    format    hooks    locks
```

That's the typical content of a Subversion repository, and everything seems to be fine. We'll add the missing methods for getting back our documents:

databases/subversion/document_storage.rb

```
Line 1   class DocumentStorage
           def get_document(path, revision = nil)
             return nil unless @repository.path_exists?(path, revision)
             content = @repository.file_contents(path, revision)
     5       author = @repository.property(:author, revision)
             Document.new(path, content, author, revision)
           end

           def get_revisions(path)
    10       @repository.history(path)
           end

           def get_history(path)
             get_revisions(path).inject([]) do |h, r|
    15         h << get_document(path, r)
             end
           end
         end
```

get_document() is certainly the most important of our new methods, because it returns a document located at a certain path that has a particular revision number. Internally, it delegates most of its work to SvnRepos. First, it checks whether the requested document exists at all in line 3. If it doesn't, it returns nil immediately. In line 3, the document's content is read, and then the revision's author is determined. It is stored in a property named author.

To get the integer IDs of all revisions of a single document, you can call get_revisions(), passing it the document's path. get_history() returns an array containing all versions of a document stored in the database.

Here's how you use them:

`databases/subversion/document_storage.rb`

```
puts '--- Check for existence'
puts 'Does not exist.' if ds.get_document('/does/not/exist').nil?
puts '--- Get revision IDs'
puts "Revisions: #{ds.get_revisions('/first/document').join(',')}"
puts '--- Get document revision #1'
puts ds.get_document('/first/document', 1)
puts '--- Get document revision #2'
puts ds.get_document('/first/document', 2)
puts '--- Get document history'
puts ds.get_history('/another/document')
```

And here's the result:

```
--- Check for existence
Does not exist.
--- Get revision IDs
Revisions: 1,2
--- Get document revision #1
path: /first/document
content: Hello, world!

author: maik
revision: 1
--- Get document revision #2
path: /first/document
content: Hello!
How are you?

author: jack
revision: 2
--- Get document history
path: /another/document
content: Yet another document.

author: maik
revision: 3
```

Everything works as expected, and our DocumentStorage class is nearly finished. The only thing missing is a diff() method that calculates the difference between two documents. We won't define our own but use the one defined in SvnRepos:

`databases/subversion/document_storage.rb`

```
puts ds.repository.diff('/first/document', 1, '/first/document', 2)
```

This outputs the revision's differences in Subversion's diff format:

```
--- /first/document (rev 1)
+++ /first/document (rev 2)
@@ -1 +1,2 @@
-Hello, world!
+Hello!
+How are you?
```

Subversion together with its Ruby bindings can be a real time-saver when it comes to handling revisions of documents automatically. But in contrast to a relational database, you have to manage the repository's structure yourself. In a relational database, different entities are stored in separate tables, while in a Subversion repository they might be stored in the same directory. That makes them indistinguishable without looking at the files' contents, so plan carefully up front where to store data, and use only those models with a very simple structure.

You should also keep in mind that our solution works only on the local file system at the moment, so we do not have to care about user management, passwords, and so on. If you need a central storage, either you have to build a small server that wraps the DocumentStorage or you need to get familiar with Ruby's Subversion bindings, which is a good idea anyway.

Chapter 4

Tame File and Data Formats

Enterprise programming is about processing data, and data is a beast with a lot of different faces. It can be binary or textual, it can be structured or unstructured, it can be portable or not so portable, and so on. And the worst thing is that data never comes alone. It often comes in large amounts.

In this chapter, we will deal with all the data formats that are most popular in typical enterprise environments (except XML, which is covered in Chapter 5, *Process XML Documents the Ruby Way*, on page 133). If you have to process large amounts of nonhierarchical, homogeneous data, there are often better alternatives such as *comma-separated values* (CSV) or *fixed-length record* (FLR). They are fast, they do not waste a lot of space, and they are easy to parse and generate.

Often, you don't have a choice anyway. If you have to migrate thirty-year-old customer data to your newest Web 2.0 application, you'll probably have to deal with your forefather's data formats.

If you want to become a welcome visitor in the accounting department, CSV is the right format for you. For example, it's an excellent way to move data from a relational database to a spreadsheet application. In Recipe 17, *Manipulate CSV with Ruby*, on page 109, you'll see that it's a piece of cake to manipulate CSV with Ruby. You'll learn how to import and export CSV data meeting typical enterprise requirements.

Fixed-length record files may painfully remind you of your first computer science courses, but you probably encounter them over and over again in the real world. Because there's no standard library to process them in Ruby, you'll learn how to build one yourself in Recipe 18, *Read and Write Fixed-Length Records*, on page 115.

Although you won't find many JavaScript Object Notation (JSON)[1] files in a typical enterprise environment, it might well happen that you have to integrate your programs with one of those new and fancy Web 2.0 applications over a network. They often offer HTTP interfaces based on JSON documents, and Recipe 19, *Harness JSON in Ruby*, on page 123 shows you how to use them in your Rails application.

Countless proprietary formats were created in ancient times when storage was much more expensive than today. A lot of them are still in use in many companies, because it would be too expensive to spend valuable developer time to change them and all the applications that are based on them. In Recipe 20, *Master Binary Data*, on page 127, you'll learn what to do if you have to process binary data with Ruby.

---

1. http://json.org/

Manipulate CSV with Ruby

Problem

Today's web applications often have a nice interface, but a lot of tasks still can be processed much easier with a spreadsheet application. People working in accounting departments especially love spreadsheets, and they will love you, too, if you provide them with CSV data that can be imported into Microsoft Excel or Apple's Numbers.

But CSV data is important for developers and members of the operations department, too, because it is an excellent format for exporting and importing complete database tables. In this recipe, you'll learn how to manipulate CSV with Ruby.

Ingredients

* If you are using Ruby version 1.8.7 or older, you have to install the *fastercsv* gem:[2]

```
$ gem install fastercsv
```

Solution

Let's assume your company provides worldwide weather services to thousands of customers. Surprisingly, there are many microclimates on this planet, so it might well be that the weather is fine where you live but only a few kilometers away a blizzard is raging (at least that's what your boss will tell you when he's not coming to the office today).

The data is gathered from weather stations all over the world and is stored in a local database. It's your job to build the import and export functions for CSV files. Specifically, you have to create functions that import a CSV file into the database and that export the whole database as a CSV file.

---

2. http://fastercsv.rubyforge.org/

The database table has been created with the following migration:

```
create_table :weather_information do |t|
  t.string  :location, :cond_day, :cond_night
  t.date    :date
  t.float   :temp_max, :temp_min
  t.integer :rain_probability
  t.timestamps
end
```

We've shamelessly stolen our database column names from the headers in our CSV files, which look as follows:

```
LOCATION;DATE;COND_DAY;COND_NIGHT;TEMP_MAX;TEMP_MIN;RAIN_PROBABILITY
"Duisburg";20080721;"Sunny";"Cloudy";27.8;19.1;0
"Duisburg";20080722;"Showers";"Showers";25.2;19.9;70
"Duisburg";20080723;"Mostly sunny";"Showers";25.2;16.4;20
"Duisburg";20080724;"Mostly sunny";"Showers";25.3;16.5;0
"Duisburg";20080725;"Late shower";"Late shower";25.7;19.2;70
"Duisburg";20080726;"Mostly sunny";"Cloudy";25.2;18.4;40
"Duisburg";20080727;"Late shower";"Late shower";27.3;20.8;60
```

Every line describes the weather (minimum temperature, maximum temperature, day condition, night condition, rain probability in percentage) on a certain day and in a certain location.

Like most CSV files, it looks pretty harmless, but before processing it, you have to carefully examine its structure. First, you should know its character set encoding. Second, you have to determine the data type of each column. In our case, it's pretty easy: the DATE column contains Date objects; TEMP_MIN, TEMP_MAX, and RAIN_PROBABILITY contain Float objects; and the rest will be String objects. Oh, the separation character is a semicolon, not a comma (that's why I prefer that it be called "character-separated values" and not "comma-separated values").

First we'll write a view for uploading a new file:

```
<% form_for :weather_data, @weather_data,
  :url  => { :action    => 'import' },
  :html => { :multipart => true } do |f| %>

  <label for='weather_data_file_data'>Import File:</label>
  <%= f.file_field :file_data %><br/>
  <%= submit_tag 'Import' %>
<% end %>
```

We do not use anything special here, and we allow the user to upload a file using a browser's regular file upload mechanism. The data is transferred to the server in parameter weather_data.

Now that we can upload CSV files to our application, we have to process them by loading their content into our database. The files can become quite large, so we'd better choose the right tool for the job. It should be fast, it should not consume much memory, and it should allow us to perform some simple transformations (type conversions, for example) on the input data while importing it. The *fastercsv* library[3] does all this and even a bit more. It is a replacement for Ruby's standard CSV library, and as its name suggests, it's significantly faster, but it also has a slightly better interface. Here's the import() method:

data_formats/csv/weather_app/app/controllers/weather_controller.rb

```
class WeatherController
  def import
    parser = FasterCSV.new(
      params[:weather_data][:file_data],
      :headers => true,
      :header_converters => :symbol,
      :col_sep => ';'
    )
    parser.convert do |field, info|
      case info.header
        when :date
          Date.parse(field)
        when :rain_probability
          field.to_i
        when :temp_max, :temp_min
          field.to_f
        else
          field
      end
    end

    WeatherInformation.delete_all
    parser.each do |row|
      WeatherInformation.create(row.to_hash)
    end
  end
end
```

---

3. In Ruby 1.9 the former CSV library has been replaced by *fastercsv*, so it no longer has to be installed separately. If you're working with Ruby 1.9 already, you have to replace *fastercsv* with CSV in all samples.

Is There Any CSV Standard?

A lot of people still think that there's no CSV standard, but that's not exactly true: since October 2005, RFC 4180* tries to define how CSV files should look and, in addition, even defines a MIME type (text/csv). *fastercsv* is compliant with this RFC.

---

*. http://www.ietf.org/rfc/rfc4180.txt

FasterCSV has a nice interface for simple tasks consisting solely of class methods. For enterprise requirements, this rarely is sufficient, so we'll create a FasterCSV instance in line 3, pass it the data to be processed, and add all options we need before we parse a single line of CSV data.

With the headers option, we tell FasterCSV that the first line of our input data contains a list of column headers. header_converters defines what should be done with the headers; we decided to turn them into symbols (the column header names will be turned into lowercase strings first!) that can be used to index our columns later. Finally, we tell FasterCSV that our column separator is a semicolon (the default is comma) by setting col_sep.

In line 9, we install some converters for our input columns that get called automatically during the import. The convert() method expects a code block that gets passed two parameters: the current field value and a FieldInfo object containing the column index, the column header, and the current line in the input file. Depending on the column name, convert() returns a converted field or the original value (for more elaborate filters, FasterCSV has a filter() method).

The only thing left to do is to parse every single line of the uploaded CSV file. We start in line 23, and in good old Ruby tradition, it does not need more than a call to each(). For the sake of simplicity, we'll always load the whole weather information. In other words, we delete the weather information in the database completely before we read new information. In line 24, we convert the current CSV input row into a Hash object and pass it to ActiveRecord's create() method. To make all this work in such an elegant way, you have to make sure that the database columns have the same names as the headers in the CSV file.

Now that we can import data into our system, it should be easy to export it, too.

And it is:

`data_formats/csv/weather_app/app/controllers/weather_controller.rb`

```
Line 1    require 'fastercsv'

          class WeatherController < ApplicationController
            def export
     5        output = FasterCSV.generate do |csv|
                csv << %w(
                  LOCATION DATE COND_DAY COND_NIGHT
                  TEMP_MAX TEMP_MIN RAIN_PROBABILITY
                )
    10          WeatherInformation.find(:all).each do |wi|
                  csv << [
                    wi.location, wi.date.strftime('%Y%M%d'), wi.cond_day,
                    wi.cond_night, wi.temp_max, wi.temp_min,
                    wi.rain_probability
    15            ]
                end
              end
              send_data(
                output,
    20          :type => get_content_type(request.user_agent),
                :filename => "weather_#{Time.now.strftime('%Y%M%d')}.csv"
              )
            end

    25      private

            def get_content_type(user_agent)
              user_agent =~ /windows/i ? 'application/vnd.ms-excel' : 'text/csv'
            end
    30    end
```

For generating the CSV data, we use FasterCSV's generate() method in line 5. It expects a code block and passes it a FasterCSV object. With the <<() operator, we can add new lines to it, and we immediately use it to write the header line to the output.

Beginning in line 10, we iterate over all the weather information we currently have in our database and convert each table row into a line of CSV data. Finally, in line 18, we send back all exported data using Rails' send_data() method. We set the content type depending on the client's user agent, so if the client has Microsoft Excel installed, it will open automatically and display the CSV file.

Read and Write Fixed-Length Records

You have a file containing a list of credit card transactions that has to be imported by your company's payment gateway. The file looks like this:

`data_formats/flr/creditcards.flr`

```
10112012010hdzNOEyP62uyhTYiignW8Q==                    Maik Schmidt
019950820098MxbHUfW/Z8Wv1WLZeeO231rH5BKos/FasPFcHxYQMc=John Doe
00300122009DkiZJkx9uNkBN2n1JwuQxM26ueVYQOrtodP94T8Zcj8=Jane Rodriguez
```

The file consists of fixed-length records (FLRs); that is, the attributes of all data records have a constant width. For example, the first five characters of each row contain the amount (in cents) to be charged from a credit card.

Fixed-length records are popular, which comes as no surprise if you think about the internals of a relational database for a second. Whenever you define a new column, you have to restrict its size somehow, so exporting or importing data in fixed-length record format is an obvious choice.

Ruby does not have a standard library for processing FLR files, and there does not seem to be any complete library available at all. In this recipe, we write a library ourselves, which is not too difficult.

The complete format description of our file looks like this:

- 1–5: Amount in cents

- 6–11: Credit card valid until the end of (mmyyyy)

- 12–55: Primary account number (Base64, encrypted with AES-256-CBC)

- 56–95: Name of card holder

That's all information we need, so we start with a reader:

`data_formats/flr/flrfile.rb`

```
Line 1  class FixedLengthRecordFile
   -      include Enumerable
   -
   -      def initialize(source, field_sizes)
   5        if field_sizes.nil? or field_sizes.empty?
   -          raise ArgumentError, 'Please, pass field sizes!'
   -        end
   -        @file = source
   -        @field_pattern = get_pattern(field_sizes)
  10      end
   -
   -      def each
   -        @file.each_line do |line|
   -          record = line.chomp.unpack(@field_pattern)
  15          record.map { |f| f.strip! }
   -          yield record
   -        end
   -      end
   -
  20      private
   -
   -      def get_pattern(field_sizes)
   -        'A' + field_sizes.join('A')
   -      end
  25    end
   -
   -    FLR = FixedLengthRecordFile # Saves some typing.
```

Ah, I know what you're thinking: this class looks so harmless! But I can assure you; it will be everything you need whenever you have to read fixed-length records (at least if the data you have to read consists solely of character data).

When initializing a new FixedLengthRecord object, you have to pass two things: the input source to be processed and an array containing the width of each column in the file. We merely store this information for further use, and we build up a format string for the unpack() method, which splits a string into an array according to a format description. For our file, it's "A5A6A44A40," and it tells us that each line consists of four components. The first one is five characters wide, the second comprises six characters, and so on (see the sidebar on the next page for more details).

The definition of the each() method in line 12 is more interesting. It iterates over each line using IO's each_line() method and splits each line

pack and unpack

pack() turns an Array into a String that has a certain format, and unpack() does the opposite. Both methods look a bit arcane at first, but they are invaluable when manipulating data of nearly any kind. They are similar to the printf() family of functions: they expect a format string describing the data to be packed or unpacked.

The following sample turns an array containing three integer numbers and a string into a null-terminated string:

data_formats/flr/pack_sample.rb

```
name = [ 72, 111, 109, 'er' ]
name.pack('c3 A2x') # => "Homer\000"
```

pack()'s format string is built using a little language with a simple structure. In our case, the format string expands to three characters represented by integer values (c3), two ASCII characters (A2), and a null byte (x)—blanks in the format string are ignored.

Both pack() and unpack() support a large list of data types that are all identified by a single letter (these letters are called *directives*, and you definitely should take a look at their documentation). Some of them may be followed by a count, as we used in the previous example. If the count is *, it extends to the end of the array. We use this feature in the following sample to convert a string to Base64 with the m directive:

data_formats/flr/pack_sample.rb

```
['Homer'].pack('m*') # => "SG9tZXI=\n"
"SG9tZXI=\n".unpack('m*')[0] # => "Homer"
```

Because it is so easy to manipulate Base64 data with pack() and unpack(), the *base64* library has been removed from Ruby's standard library.

into its components, with unpack() using the format string we created in initialize(). Finally, we pass the array of components to a code block in line 16. As you might know already, it's always a good idea to include Enumerable when you define an each() method. We did it in line 2, and it will pay off later.

After all this explanation, let's try to process our credit card data:

data_formats/flr/read_flr_file.rb

```
Line 1    require 'date'
    -     require 'flrfile'

    -     parser = FLR.new(File.new(ARGV[0]), [5, 6, 44, 40])
    5     parser.each do |row|
    -       amount = row[0].to_f / 100
    -       valid_to = Date.parse(row[1][0, 2] + '/' + row[1][2, 4]) >> 1
    -       number, holder = row[2], row[3]
    -       puts "Charge #{amount} from #{holder}."
    10      puts "Credit card: #{number}"
    -     end
```

This short program produces the following output if we pass it our original input file:

```
mschmidt> ruby read_flr_file.rb creditcards.flr
Charge 101.12 from Maik Schmidt.
Credit card: hdzNOEyP62uyhTYiignW8Q==
Charge 19.95 from John Doe.
Credit card: 8MxbHUfW/Z8Wv1WLZeeO231rH5BKos/FasPFcHxYQMc=
Charge 3.0 from Jane Rodriguez.
Credit card: DkiZJkx9uNkBN2n1JwuQxM26ueVYQOrtodP94T8Zcj8=
```

In line 4, we create a new FixedLengthRecord object using the FLR abbreviation. We pass it our input file and the widths of our input columns. Then we iterate over each line using the each() method. In the code block we can access each column by indexing the row array accordingly. We haven't decrypted the credit card number yet, because that's a topic for another recipe (see Recipe 1, *Protect Information with Symmetric Ciphers*, on page 5).

Programming the writer is a bit more complicated, because we have to open and close the file to be generated, but it's still easy:

data_formats/flr/flrfile.rb

```
Line 1    class FixedLengthRecordFile
    -       def self.open(path, mode, field_sizes)
    -         file = File.open(path, mode)
    -         begin
    5           flr_file = new(file, field_sizes)
```

```
     yield flr_file
   ensure
     file.close
   end
end

def <<(record)
  @file.puts(record.map { |x| x.to_s}.pack(@field_pattern))
end
end
```

To emulate the regular behavior of Ruby's file access methods, we store the output file's current state in our open() method. The we create a FixedLengthRecord object in line 5 and pass this to a code block afterward. To ensure that the file gets closed in any case, we have put everything into a begin ... ensure statement.

It's certainly useful that we can open fixed-length record files for writing, but it would be great if we could actually write to them, too. That's where the <<() operator comes into play. It is defined in line 12, and it uses the pack() method to turn an array into a string of fixed-length columns (before an element is packed, it is converted into a string using to_s()). Unsurprisingly, pack() is the inverse method belonging to unpack().

Let's use the open() method to create a file containing the status of each credit card transaction. Our record description looks like this:

- 1–3: Transaction ID, which is the line number where the transaction appeared in the input file.

- 4–5: Status code. 0 means the transaction has been processed successfully. All other codes indicate an error.

- 6–45: Card holder's name.

Here's the code to write the (faked) results of our credit card transactions to a file:

`data_formats/flr/write_flr_file.rb`

```
require 'flrfile'

FLR.open('/tmp/results.flr', 'w', [3, 2, 40]) do |flr|
  flr << [1, 0, 'Maik Schmidt']
  flr << [2, 0, 'John Doe']
  flr << [3, 9, 'Jane Rodriguez']
end
```

After running the program, the content of /tmp/result.flr looks like this:

```
mschmidt> cat /tmp/results.flr
1   0 Maik Schmidt
2   0 John Doe
3   9 Jane Rodriguez
```

Discussion

You might have noticed that we have silently made an important design decision: our class processes files, not strings. This absolutely makes sense when working with big files, because it saves a lot of memory, but what if you get your data not from a file system but via a network or something similar? Then you have to process a string, and Ruby's StringIO class makes it easy to add file behavior to a string:

data_formats/flr/from_string.rb

```ruby
require 'stringio'
require 'flrfile'

content = <<CONTENT
10112012010hdzNOEyP62uyhTYiignW8Q==                    Maik Schmidt
019950820098MxbHUfW/Z8Wv1WLZeeO231rH5BKos/FasPFcHxYQMc=John Doe
00300122009DkiZJkx9uNkBN2n1JwuQxM26ueVYQOrtodP94T8Zcj8=Jane Rodriguez
CONTENT

parser = FLR.new(StringIO.new(content), [5, 6, 44, 40])
puts parser.inject(0) { |total, row| total += row[0].to_f / 100 }
```

Our program prints the total amount of money (124.07) that will be charged when processing the input file. As promised earlier, now it pays off that we have included the Enumerable module, because we can use the inject() method that makes our program look so cool. Please note that we did not have to modify the FixedLengthRecord class to achieve this. Everything is managed behind the scenes, because StringIO behaves exactly like a File object.

Writing fixed-length records to a string is a bit more difficult. I have always wanted to write something like "This is left as an exercise for the reader," but I couldn't resist:

data_formats/flr/flrfile.rb

```ruby
Line 1   require 'stringio'
  -
  -      class FixedLengthRecordFile
  -        def self.generate(field_sizes)
  5          buffer = StringIO.new
  -          flr_file = new(buffer, field_sizes)
```

```
      yield flr_file
      buffer.close
      buffer.string
10    end
   end
```

This solution is similar to the one that writes to a file: generate() expects an array of column widths and a code block. In line 5, we create a new StringIO object and pass it to FixedLengthRecord's constructor. Then we invoke the code that has been passed to generate(). Finally, we close the string buffer and return its content as a string. We can use this method as follows:

data_formats/flr/write_flr_file.rb

```
result = FLR.generate([3, 2, 40]) do |flr|
  flr << [1, 0, 'Maik Schmidt']
  flr << [2, 0, 'John Doe']
  flr << [3, 9, 'Jane Rodriguez']
end
puts result
```

And it produces the following:

```
1  0 Maik Schmidt
2  0 John Doe
3  9 Jane Rodriguez
```

Only one important thing is missing now: converters. Just like the converters you can install when using FasterCSV, it should be possible, for example, to automatically convert column data into the right format or type. Oh, and setting header names would be a great idea, too, so we could use them instead of numerical indices, and.... No, this time it's really left as an exercise for the reader!

Harness JSON in Ruby

JavaScript Object Notation (JSON)[4] might not be as popular as XML, but it is not an esoteric data format either. It has been standardized for a long time, and there's even a request for comments (RFC).[5] Ruby has excellent support for JSON, and in this recipe you'll learn how to use it in a real-world situation (to learn more about JSON, see the sidebar on page 125).

- Since Ruby 1.9, the *json* library is bundled with Ruby. For older versions, install Ruby's JSON library[6] as a gem:

```
$ gem install json
```

Let's face it: this world is far from being perfect, and if you run a commercial web service, you'll probably know that there are nearly as many scoundrels as honest customers out there. You should do everything to protect yourself from being cheated. *E-scoring* has become an important technology for many e-commerce websites.

An e-score numerically describes a customer's creditworthiness. The higher the e-score, the more creditworthy a customer is. Usually, an e-score is derived from a customer's address, from his credit history, and from a lot of statistical data. E-scoring has become an important business, so it comes as no surprise that you have to integrate with an e-scoring application, too.

The service you have to use expects a list of persons to be scored, and it returns a list of scores, one for each person. It is accessed via HTTP, and the documents that are exchanged are encoded with JSON.

---

4. http://json.org/
5. http://www.ietf.org/rfc/rfc4627.txt
6. http://json.rubyforge.org/

As a Ruby programmer, you can ignore the JSON details for the moment and concentrate on the actual data structure. Our customer list looks as follows:

`data_formats/json/client.rb`

```ruby
customers = [
  {
    :id => 42,
    :name => {
      :forename => 'Maik', :surname => 'Schmidt'
    },
    :address => {
      :street  => 'Musterstraße 42',
      :city    => 'Musterstadt',
      :country => 'Germany'
    },
    'bank-account' => {
      'bank-code' => '11122233', :bac => '987654321'
    }
  }
]
```

Coincidentally, it's the same structure that is expected by the e-scoring service. The list contains only one customer, and this customer has all the attributes we'd usually expect: there's an ID, a name, an address, and a bank account consisting of a bank code and a bank account number.

Now we have to convert the customers array into a JSON document and send it to the e-scoring service via HTTP. In Ruby, both HTTP and JSON are simple. Here we have an example that sends a single person to be scored to a local test server:

`data_formats/json/client.rb`

```ruby
require 'rubygems'
require 'json'
require 'net/http'

payload = customers.to_json
puts JSON.pretty_generate(customers)
http = Net::HTTP.new('localhost', 8080)
response = http.post('/e-score', payload)
scores = JSON.parse(response.body)
scores.each do |score|
  puts "Customer #{score['id']}: #{score['escore']}"
end
```

It really is that easy. In line 5, we convert our array containing customer data into a JSON string by calling to_json(). Then we create an HTTP

What Is JSON?

JavaScript Object Notation is a text format for data exchange. If you are familiar with JavaScript, then you'll already know how to work with it, because it looks exactly like JavaScript's literals for strings, arrays, hashes, and so on.

Instead of explaining the format by showing you tons of boring BNF grammars, let's look at an example:

```
{
  "price": 32.95,
  "title": "Enterprise Integration with Ruby",
  "tags": ["ruby", "XML", "database", "LDAP"]
}
```

In Ruby, the same structure looks like this:

```
{
  "price" => 32.95,
  "title" => "Enterprise Integration with Ruby",
  "tags"  => ["ruby", "XML", "database", "LDAP"]
}
```

Can you spot the differences? Only the => pieces have been replaced by colons. The rest is completely the same (in Ruby 1.9 you can even use colons when your keys are symbols). Interestingly, it's nearly the same in Perl and Python, and that's probably the reason for JSON's popularity among programmers who use dynamic languages.

connection to our local server and send the JSON document to the /e-score path using the POST method.

We get back a result array that is encoded in JSON, too. Consequently, we parse it in line 9 to get the scores belonging to our customers.

Here's the output you get if you run the program:

```
mschmidt> ruby client.rb
[
  {
    "name": {
      "forename": "Maik",
      "surname": "Schmidt"
    },
    "bank-account": {
      "bank-code": "11122233",
      "bac": "987654321"
    },
    "id": 42,
```

```
      "address": {
        "street": "Musterstra\u00dfe 42",
        "city": "Musterstadt",
        "country": "Germany"
      }
    }
  ]
Customer 42: 0
```

We have transmitted a perfect JSON document, and the pretty printer of the JSON class did a really good job (please note that the German eszett ß has been properly encoded as \u00df). Oh, and with a 0 e-score, I'd suggest you'd insist that your customer pay up front....

Discussion

Rails directly supports JSON, so to render the customers data structure used in our example, you'd use the following statement in your Rails action:

```
render :json => customers
```

It's certainly a good idea to play around with JSON because it's a lightweight alternative for XML and integrates perfectly with Ruby's dynamic nature. It's also perfect for integrating with JavaScript applications in your web front ends, so the next time you have to invent a new data format that's going to be emitted by a back-end service, give JSON a chance.

Master Binary Data

You need to know how to manipulate bits and bytes directly using Ruby.

In this recipe, we look at the graphics formats supported by mobile devices, because playing around with computer graphics is always a lot of fun and gives us an excellent opportunity to learn a lot about handling binary data with Ruby.

The most popular graphics format for mobile devices is the Wireless Bitmap Format (WBMP).[7] It's part of the WAP standard,[8] and it is as simple as a graphics format could be, because it supports only monochrome images and no animation. Consequently, its internal structure is simple, too:

- Each monochrome WBMP image starts with two 0 bytes. The first byte indicates the image's type (0 means monochrome, uncompressed), and the second byte can be used for extension headers. If it is set to 0, no extension headers are transmitted.

- The width and height of the image (measured in pixels) follow and are stored as variable-length unsigned integers[9] (the WAP specification calls them *multibyte* integers). That's a really awkward format that was invented when bandwidth was a valuable good. Each integer value is encoded as a sequence of octets, and for every octet, the most significant bit (MSB) indicates whether there is another octet following (MSB is 1; MSB is 0). To calculate the resulting integer, concatenate the list of 7-bit values in big-endian order[10] (don't be scared—it's only five lines of Ruby code).

- Finally, the image data is transmitted as a matrix arranged in rows (1 bit per pixel). A 0 represents a black pixel, and a white pixel is denoted by 1. Where the row length is not divisible by 8, the row is padded with 0 bits to the byte boundary.

---

7. http://en.wikipedia.org/wiki/Wireless_Application_Protocol_Bitmap_Format
8. http://en.wikipedia.org/wiki/Wireless_Application_Protocol
9. http://en.wikipedia.org/wiki/Variable_length_unsigned_integer
10. http://en.wikipedia.org/wiki/Big-endian

When working with binary data, it's indispensable to actually take a look at the data. The best tool for doing this is a good old hex viewer. Use whatever you like, but I prefer xxd,[11] because it is so simple and is installed on many systems by default (many text editors such as TextPad have a hex mode, too). Here's the content of the test image we are going to use:

```
mschmidt> xxd example.wbmp
0000000: 0000 2020 fff0 0fff ff80 01ff fe0f f07f  ..  ............
0000010: fc7f fc3f f8ff ff1f f1ff ff8f e3ff ffc7  ...?............
0000020: c7ff ffe3 cfcf f3f3 8f87 e1f1 9f03 c0f9  ................
0000030: 9f03 c0f9 3f87 e1fc 3fcf f3fc 3fff fffc  ....?...?...?...
0000040: 3fff fffc 3fff fffc 3eff ff7c 3eff ff7c  ?...?...>..|>..|
0000050: 3e7f fe7c 9f7f fef9 9f3f fcf9 9f9f f1f1  >..|.....?......
0000060: cfc1 83f3 c7e0 07e3 e3f8 1fc7 f1ff ff8f  ................
0000070: f8ff ff1f fc7f fe3f fe0f f07f ff80 01ff  .......?........
0000080: fff0 0fff                                 ....
```

The file starts with two 0 bytes followed by two 0x20 bytes. That means the image we are going to read is an uncompressed, monochrome image and is 32 pixels wide and 32 pixels high (if you can even imagine how the image looks, your geek code[12] is probably infinitely high).

Before we do anything else, we create a storage class that encapsulates all the necessary attributes—an image's width, its height, and its pixel data encoded as a two-dimensional byte array:

data_formats/binary/image_demo/lib/wbmp_image.rb
```ruby
class WbmpImage
  attr_reader :width, :height, :image_data

  def initialize(width, height, image_data)
    @width, @height, @image_data = width, height, image_data
  end
end
```

That was trivial, but now we will create the core of our little demo application, the WBMP reader. By the way, we do this only for educational purposes, because there are excellent tools already for manipulating WBMP data.[13]

---

11. http://linuxcommand.org/man_pages/xxd1.html
12. http://www.geekcode.com/
13. http://rmagick.rubyforge.org/

Here's our implementation:

data_formats/binary/image_demo/lib/wbmp_image.rb

```
Line 1   class WbmpImage
    -      def self.from_raw_data(raw_data)
    -        type, header = raw_data.slice!(0, 2)
    -        unless type == 0 && header == 0
    5          raise 'Unsupported image type!'
    -        end
    -        width = get_multibyte_integer(raw_data)
    -        height = get_multibyte_integer(raw_data)
    -        image_data = get_image_data(width, height, raw_data)
    10         WbmpImage.new(width, height, image_data)
    -      end
    -
    -      def self.get_multibyte_integer(raw_data)
    -        multi_int = 0
    15         while raw_data[0][7] == 1
    -          multi_int = (multi_int << 7) | (raw_data.shift & 0x7f)
    -        end
    -        (multi_int << 7) | raw_data.shift
    -      end
    20
    -      def self.get_image_data(width, height, raw_data)
    -        bytes_per_row = width / 8
    -        bytes_per_row += 1 if (width % 8) != 0
    -        image_data = []
    25         height.times { image_data << raw_data.slice!(0, bytes_per_row) }
    -        image_data
    -      end
    -    end
```

These three methods are all we need to convert a stream of bytes representing a WBMP image into a WbmpImage object. We start with from_raw_data(), which expects a byte array containing the image data and returns the according WbmpImage object. First we extract the type and the extension headers in line 3.

When working with chunked data, it's convenient to have a method that cuts a piece of data from a stream. We use Array#slice!(start,length) for this task. It returns the first length bytes from raw_data starting at index start and removes them from the array. In our case, we get back the first two bytes, which contain the type and the extension headers of the image.

Then we extract the width and height of the image using get_multi_int(). This method reads a variable-length unsigned integer from a byte stream and uses one of Ruby's nicest features regarding bit handling: you can index Fixnum objects with the []() operator to get the value of a certain bit. In line 15, we check whether the most significant bit of the first byte of raw_data is set. In addition, we use a lot of the regular bit manipulation operators that you can find in nearly every modern programming language: bitwise AND (&), bitwise OR (|), and left shift (<<).

Finally, we convert the image data into a two-dimensional array. Therefore, we calculate the amount of bytes used by every row and use our old friend slice!() to copy the image data row by row.

That's all we had to do to create a reader that fully supports the WBMP specification. Wouldn't it be fun to actually display our test image? Let's write a small Rails application that renders an arbitrary WBMP image using ASCII characters. Here's a method that returns a string representation of a WbmpImage:

data_formats/binary/image_demo/lib/wbmp_image.rb
```ruby
class WbmpImage
  def to_ascii_art
    ascii_art = ''
    @image_data.each do |line|
      line.each do |byte|
        7.downto(0) { |i| ascii_art << (byte[i] == 1 ? '*' : '.') }
      end
      ascii_art << "\n"
    end
    ascii_art
  end
end
```

Black pixels are represented by the asterisk (*); for white pixels we use a period (.). Now we need a form for uploading WBMP files to our Rails application:

data_formats/binary/image_demo/app/views/image/index.html.erb
```erb
<% form_for :image, @image_data,
  :url  => { :action  => 'convert' },
  :html => { :multipart => true } do |f| %>

  <label for='image_data_file_data'>Convert Image:</label>
  <%= f.file_field :file_data %><br/>
  <%= submit_tag 'Convert' %>
<% end %>
```

There is nothing special about this, and we can see that the form expects our application to provide an image controller and a convert() method. Here it is:

> data_formats/binary/image_demo/app/controllers/image_controller.rb

```
Line 1    require 'wbmp_image'

          class ImageController < ApplicationController
            def convert
5             raw_data = params[:image][:file_data].string.unpack('C*')
              image = WbmpImage.from_raw_data(raw_data)
              @ascii_art = image.to_ascii_art
            end
          end
```

When a file is transmitted to the application, we get a StringIO object that encapsulates the file's content. In line 5, we turn the StringIO into a string with the string() method and convert the resulting string into an array of unsigned bytes using unpack(). Now we have the image's binary representation and create a WbmpImage from it, which gets rendered in the most trivial way:

> data_formats/binary/image_demo/app/views/image/convert.html.erb

```
<pre>
<%= @ascii_art %>
</pre>
```

As you can see in Figure 4.1, on the following page, we are done! We have implemented a viewer for binary WBMP images in plain Ruby.

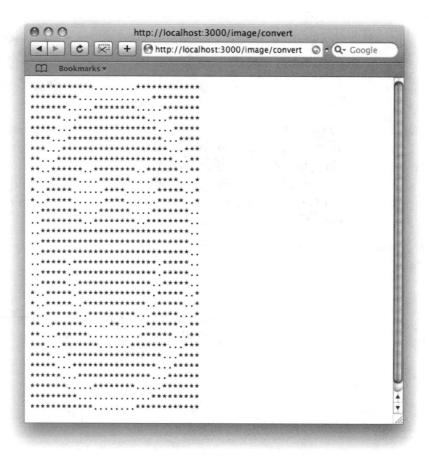

Figure 4.1: WBMP AS ASCII ART

Chapter 5

Process XML Documents the Ruby Way

Extensible Markup Language (XML) has become one of the most important enterprise technologies in the past decade. Not all enterprises use message queues and not all have a service-oriented architecture, but it's hard to imagine any company that does not use XML.

If you've worked with platforms like Java or .NET before, you may be surprised about the, um, compactness of Ruby's standard XML support. But don't be misled by its simplicity. Combined with Ruby's elegance, it's highly convenient, and if you need raw processing power, you have some alternative libraries right at hand.

In this chapter, we'll address specific problems that occur when processing XML documents in an enterprise environment.

Sometimes building complete object hierarchies from an XML document is a bit over the top and you're better off turning your document into a mix of hashes and arrays. Recipe 21, *XML Data Binding on Steroids*, on page 135 shows you how to achieve this.

In Recipe 22, *Use XML Files as Models*, on page 139, you'll learn how to bind XML documents to Ruby objects using REXML, Ruby's standard XML parser.

Scarce resources (both RAM and CPU) are a problem even in the biggest enterprise, and Ruby sometimes is a bit greedy. In Recipe 23, *Handle Large XML Documents*, on page 147, you'll learn to process documents of nearly arbitrary size, and in Recipe 24, *High-Performance Parsing*, on page 153 you'll see how fast a Ruby solution actually can be.

As you might know, XML has some ugly relatives, such as HTML and its nicer cousin XHTML. Like grouchy uncle Albert, you have to meet them once in a while, so in Recipe 25, *Work with HTML and Microformats*, on page 159, you'll learn how to get back home as quickly as possible.

Generating XML documents with Ruby and Rails normally is a piece of cake, as you'll see in Recipe 26, *Build Plain-Vanilla XML Documents*, on page 167. But it can be a tough challenge if the recipient insists on weird formatting and character set encodings. In Recipe 27, *Build Arbitrary XML Documents*, on page 169, you'll see how to satisfy even the strangest requirements.

You'd face most of these problems in any enterprise environment regardless of the programming language you have to use. But as you'll see, Ruby can be a strong ally in such situations, and, even more important, it will be more fun....

XML Data Binding on Steroids

You have to read data from XML files, but you do not want to parse them manually or map them to a sophisticated object hierarchy. You are interested only in their content, and you want it *now*!

- Rails comes with XmlSimple[1] already, but if you want to use it in a regular Ruby application, you have to install the *xml-simple* gem separately:

```
$ gem install xml-simple
```

More often than not, you are not interested in all the information that is stored in an XML document, and consequently you do not want to put a lot of effort into parsing and mapping it. Additionally, it's sometimes inappropriate to create tons of objects that represent only a configuration file or a single order.

Let's say you want to display the content of order documents that look like this:

xml/data_binding/xmlsimple_demo/data/orders/47110815.xml

```
<?xml version='1.0'?>
<order id='47110815' date='2008-07-27'>
  <customer-no>94429999</customer-no>
  <items>
    <item product-id='42-007-x'>
      <name>Beer</name>
      <quantity>6</quantity>
    </item>
    <item product-id='16-666-x'>
      <name>Nuts &amp; Gum</name>
      <quantity>1</quantity>
    </item>
  </items>
</order>
```

---

1. http://xml-simple.rubyforge.org/

For this purpose, we use XmlSimple, a Ruby library that turns an XML document automatically into a mix of hashes and arrays. It already comes with Rails (it's part of ActiveSupport), so you do not have to install it separately. You do not even have to require it.

First we create a model based on XML files:

xml/data_binding/xmlsimple_demo/app/models/order.rb

```ruby
class Order
  ORDER_DIR = File.join('data', 'orders')

  def self.find(order_id)
    XmlSimple.xml_in(
      File.join(ORDER_DIR, "#{order_id}.xml"),
      'force_array' => ['item'],
      'group_tags' => { 'items' => 'item' }
    )
  end
end
```

The find() method reads a single XML document from the data/orders directory and returns its XmlSimple representation. Ignore the options right now; I'll explain them later.

Let's examine the results in the Rails console (p()'s output has been reformatted for better clarity):

```
mschmidt> ruby script/console
Loading development environment (Rails 2.1.0)
>> p Order.find('47110815')
{
  "items" => [
    {
      "name" => "Beer",
      "quantity" => "6",
      "product-id" => "42-007-x"
    },
    {
      "name" => "Nuts & Gum",
      "quantity" => "1",
      "product-id" => "16-666-x"
    }
  ],
  "date" => "2008-07-27",
  "customer-no" => "94429999",
  "id" => "47110815"
}
=> nil
```

As you can see, our document's element and attribute names have been mapped to hash keys quite naturally. XmlSimple's magic is performed by the xml_in() method, which accepts two arguments: an XML data source (a filename, an XML string, or an IO object) and a hash of options that controls how the document's pieces are mapped.

In our example, we have used a filename and only two of XmlSimple's many options:

- force_array allows you to specify a list of element names that should always be forced into an array representation. In our case, this option is interesting for <*item*> elements, because we do not know up front how many items an order will have. If we did not set this option, we'd get back a single element if there was only one <*item*> element. But we'd get an array if there were two or more <*item*> elements. By setting force_array, we can rely on getting back an array, which makes it much easier to write processing code.

- group_tags eliminates extra levels of indirection in the resulting Ruby data structure. By default, XmlSimple will create a new Array or Hash object for every new element hierarchy in the XML document. For the <*item*> element, we do not want this additional level; we prefer to have an array of items referenced by the key items.

To fully understand these options, it's best to play around with them. Remove the group_tags option in the controller, for example, and see what happens.

With a single statement you can turn a complex XML document into a native Ruby structure; that is, accessing the document's content is as natural as it can be. But XmlSimple has many more options, it has an additional object-oriented interface, and it can output Ruby structures as XML documents, too:

`xml/data_binding/xmlsimple_demo/app/models/order.rb`

```
Line 1   class Order
    -      def self.to_xml(order)
    -        builder = XmlSimple.new(
    -          'root_name'  => 'order',
    5          'group_tags' => {
    -            'customer-no' => 'content',
    -            'items'       => 'item',
    -            'name'        => 'content',
    -            'quantity'    => 'content'
   10          }
    -        )
    -        builder.xml_out(order)
    -      end
    -    end
```

The previous to_xml() method turns the result of the find() method into the original XML document. Because Hash and Array objects have no name, XmlSimple uses <*opt*> by default as the root element's tag. We override this in line 4, so our root element is named <*order*> again.

By default, XmlSimple turns hash keys into attributes, but in our original document we have mostly worked with elements. In the following lines, we use the group_tags option for turning potential attributes into elements. The content element has a special meaning and stands for the textual content of every element. If needed, it can be configured using XmlSimple's content_key option.

All in all, XmlSimple is a convenient way of working with XML. Additionally, it can be fast, too, if you have to select different elements often, because after the document has been parsed, which is one-time overhead, you're working with plain Ruby arrays and hashes. If you're working with REXML, for example, a lot of XPath expressions would be evaluated otherwise.

Use XML Files as Models

In nearly every company the most critical information is stored in relational databases, but often only a few privileged processes are allowed to access it directly. All other processes and services get exported only as XML files. For example, all information needed to create invoices may be stored in a database that gets exported periodically as a set of XML files so they can be sent to a print shop or the files can be displayed online.

Rails is a database-centric framework, and usually that's a good thing, because nearly every serious web application needs a database. But if you have to read your model data from a different data source—for example, from an XML file—you can easily do that, too.

Let's assume you have to display invoices, but instead of reading the corresponding model data from a database, you have to read it from XML files. All files are stored in a directory named data/invoices, and the filenames follow a simple pattern: <customer-no>.xml. The documents we have to process potentially contain a list of invoices and look like this:

`xml/data_binding/invoice_app/data/invoices/94429999.xml`

```xml
<?xml version='1.0'?>
<invoices>
  <invoice invoice-no='47110815'>
    <invoice-date>2008-09-15</invoice-date>
    <due-date>2008-10-01</due-date>
    <customer customer-no='94429999'>
      <name>Maik Schmidt</name>
      <address>
        <street>Musterstraße 42</street>
        <city>Musterstadt</city>
        <postal-code>12345</postal-code>
      </address>
    </customer>
    <net-amount currency='USD' amount='7.73'/>
    <gross-amount currency='USD' amount='8.97'/>
```

```
      <vat rate='16.0' currency='USD' amount='1.24'/>
      <items>
        <item product-id='42-007-x'>
          <name>Beer</name>
          <unit-price currency='USD' amount='0.99'/>
          <quantity>6</quantity>
          <net-amount currency='USD' amount='5.94'/>
          <gross-amount currency='USD' amount='6.89'/>
          <vat rate='16.0'/>
        </item>
        <item product-id='16-666-x'>
          <name>Nuts &amp; Gum</name>
          <unit-price currency='USD' amount='1.79'/>
          <quantity>1</quantity>
          <net-amount currency='USD' amount='1.79'/>
          <gross-amount currency='USD' amount='2.08'/>
          <vat rate='16.0'/>
        </item>
      </items>
    </invoice>
</invoices>
```

<item> elements contain all the information you would typically expect in an invoice, such as a due date, customer data, a list of invoice line items, lots of money amounts, and VAT rates. Note that all these amounts come with a currency, and we do not have to perform any calculations ourselves. We have to display the data only.

Although we do not read any data from a database, we need to create a model for our invoices. Typically, models are built using Rails' Active-Record module, which insists on model data coming from a database. This time, we will read our model data from an XML file and parse it using Ruby's standard XML parser, Ruby Electric XML (REXML).[2]

First we map the XML document's elements and attributes to a hierarchy of business objects. Ruby's Struct class makes this easy:

xml/data_binding/invoice_app/app/models/invoice.rb

```ruby
Money = Struct.new(:currency, :amount)
Address = Struct.new(:street, :postal_code, :city)
Customer = Struct.new(:customer_no, :name, :address)
Vat = Struct.new(:rate, :amount)
Item = Struct.new(
  :product_id, :name, :unit_price, :quantity,
  :net_amount, :gross_amount, :vat
)
```

---

2. http://www.germane-software.com/software/rexml/

```
class Invoice
  attr_accessor :invoice_no, :invoice_date, :due_date, :customer
  attr_accessor :net_amount, :gross_amount, :vat, :items
end
```

We did not declare any types explicitly, but you can easily guess that the address attribute of a Customer object will be an instance of class Address, for example.

These simple storage classes are all we need to proceed, so now we are going to map some real XML documents to our new classes using REXML. Let's begin with the *<invoice>* element:

```
xml/data_binding/invoice_app/app/models/invoice.rb
```

```
Line 1  require 'rexml/document'
    -   class Invoice
    -     INVOICES_DIR = File.join('data', 'invoices')
    -
    5     def self.find(customer_no)
    -       filename = File.join(INVOICES_DIR, "#{customer_no}.xml")
    -       invoice_doc = REXML::Document.new(File.new(filename))
    -       invoice_node = invoice_doc.root.elements[1]
    -       invoice = Invoice.new
   10       invoice.invoice_no = invoice_node.attributes['invoice-no']
    -       invoice.invoice_date = invoice_node.elements['invoice-date'].text
    -       invoice.due_date = invoice_node.elements['due-date'].text
    -       invoice.customer = get_customer(invoice_node)
    -       invoice.net_amount = get_money(invoice_node.elements['net-amount'])
   15       invoice.gross_amount = get_money(
    -         invoice_node.elements['gross-amount']
    -       )
    -       invoice.vat = get_vat(invoice_node)
    -       invoice.items = get_items(invoice_node)
   20       invoice
    -     end
    -   end
```

We require REXML first, so in line 7, we load and parse an XML document by calling the constructor of REXML::Document. If the file cannot be found or the document cannot be parsed for any reason, this action raises an exception. Otherwise, invoice_doc refers to a tree representing our document.

To get the root of the tree, we call the document's root() method in line 8. Remember that our root node is an *<invoices>* element, which has one or more *<invoice>* children. For the sake of simplicity we read only the first *<invoice>* child. Every element node in a REXML tree has a member named elements that can be indexed with a numerical position

> ## XPath
>
> One of the most useful features of REXML is its integrated XPath 1.0* support. XPath is a domain-specific language that makes it easy to access every single piece of an XML document. XPath expressions look a bit like file paths, but they are much more powerful and can contain function calls and logical operators.
>
> REXML allows you to index the elements member of an REXML::Element object with an XPath expression, for example:
>
> xml/data_binding/xpath_sample.rb
>
> ```
> doc = REXML::Document.new(File.new('invoices/94429999.xml'))
> doc.elements['//items/item[1]/name'].text # -> 'Beer'
> doc.elements['//net-amount/@amount']      # -> '7.73'
> ```
>
> As you can see, the XPath is not related to the element; that is, you can fetch any element of a document through any other element.
>
> A full introduction of XPath is beyond the book's scope, but the Internet is full of excellent tutorials.†
>
> * .   http://www.w3.org/TR/xpath
> † .   See http://www.w3schools.com/xpath/default.asp, for example.

or with an XPath pointing to a child element. We use the position 1 to refer to the first child element (yes, the index starts at 1, not 0!).

In line 10, we copy content for the first time using the attributes member. You can treat it as a regular Ruby Hash object (although it isn't one). In other words, you can get the value of a particular attribute by indexing attributes with the attribute's name.

Getting the textual content belonging to an element is different: you have to call text() on the element, as you can see in line 12. If your element contains more than one text node, call texts() to get an array of all text nodes belonging to the element.

XPath, elements, and attributes are the most important tools when working with REXML, and we use them frequently in several helper methods such as get_money() or get_customer().

Those methods are defined as follows:

`xml/data_binding/invoice_app/app/models/invoice.rb`

```ruby
class Invoice
  private

  def self.get_money(node)
    Money.new(node.attributes['currency'], node.attributes['amount'])
  end

  def self.get_customer(invoice_node)
    customer_node = invoice_node.elements['customer']
    Customer.new(
      customer_node.attributes['customer-no'],
      customer_node.elements['name'].text,
      get_address(customer_node)
    )
  end

  def self.get_address(customer_node)
    address_node = customer_node.elements['address']
    Address.new(
      address_node.elements['street'].text,
      address_node.elements['postal-code'].text,
      address_node.elements['city'].text
    )
  end

  def self.get_vat(invoice_node)
    Vat.new(
      invoice_node.elements['vat'].attributes['rate'],
      get_money(invoice_node.elements['vat'])
    )
  end

  def self.get_items(invoice_node)
    items = []
    invoice_node.elements.each('items/item') do |item|
      items << Item.new(
        item.attributes['product-id'],
        item.elements['name'].text,
        get_money(item.elements['unit-price']),
        item.elements['quantity'].text.to_i,
        get_money(item.elements['net-amount']),
        get_money(item.elements['gross-amount']),
        item.elements['vat'].attributes['rate']
      )
    end
    items
  end
end
```

All these methods do not contain anything special in that they copy the XML document's content using only the elements and attributes members. The only exception is the iterator code in line 35. Here we use elements not to access a single element but to iterate over all <item> children of an <items> node.

If we copy our parsing code to app/models/invoice.rb, we can look up invoices like regular database models using find() in a Rails controller:

```
xml/data_binding/invoice_app/app/controllers/invoice_controller.rb
class InvoiceController < ApplicationController
  def show
    @invoice = Invoice.find(params[:id])
  end
end
```

A bit of view code turns our object into a nice and printable invoice document, as you can see in Figure 5.1, on the facing page. The HTML code to render the inner table looks like this:

```
xml/data_binding/invoice_app/app/views/invoice/show.html.erb
<table width="100%" id="invoicetable">
  <tbody>
    <tr>
      <th> Product ID </th>
      <th> Product Name </th>
      <th> Unit Price </th>
      <th> Quantity </th>
      <th> Net Amount </th>
      <th> VAT </th>
      <th> Gross Amount </th>
    </tr>
    <% for item in @invoice.items %>
    <tr class="<%= cycle('odd', 'even') %>">
      <td><%= item.product_id %></td>
      <td><%= item.name %></td>
      <td><%= number_to_currency(item.unit_price.amount) %></td>
      <td><%= item.quantity %></td>
      <td><%= number_to_currency(item.net_amount.amount) %></td>
      <td><%= item.vat %>%</td>
      <td><%= number_to_currency(item.gross_amount.amount) %></td>
    </tr>
    <% end %>
    <tr class="divider">
      <td colspan="6"> </td>
      <td> </td>
    </tr>
    <tr class="total">
      <td colspan="6" align="right"><b>Total</b></td>
```

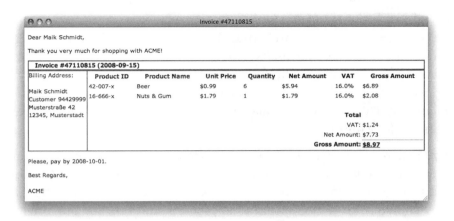

Figure 5.1: THE RENDERED INVOICE

```
        <td> </td>
      </tr>
      <tr class="total">
        <td colspan="6" align="right">VAT: </td>
        <td><%= number_to_currency(@invoice.vat.amount.amount) %></td>
      </tr>
      <tr class="total">
        <td align="right" colspan="6">Net Amount: </td>
        <td><%= number_to_currency(@invoice.net_amount.amount) %></td>
      </tr>
      <tr class="total">
        <td align="right" colspan="6"><b>Gross Amount: </b></td>
        <td style="border-top: 1px dotted black">
          <u>
            <b>
              <%= number_to_currency(@invoice.gross_amount.amount) %>
            </b>
          </u>
        </td>
      </tr>
    </tbody>
</table>
```

Rails strictly follows the Model-View-Controller (MVC) pattern, so it comes as no surprise that our view does not differ from a view that uses a regular database model. The view and model are completely separated, and only the controller knows our little secret: the model data has been read from an XML file, not from a database table.

Experienced developers are probably familiar with this kind of XML data binding. On platforms like Java, for example, it's supported by a lot of tools. Because of the dynamic nature of Ruby, additional tools aren't necessary, and we can easily map XML documents to classes manually. This way, we can also add more business logic such as validations, for example.

By using only a few methods of the REXML-API, we have turned a complex XML document into a hierarchy of business objects. REXML offers many more functions to conveniently manipulate XML documents, and you should take a close look at its documentation. For our original purpose, the few methods described earlier are sufficient.

But you have to keep some shortcomings in mind:

- REXML supports all modern character set encodings for both input and output, but internally it encodes all text nodes with the UTF-8 character set encoding. Be careful if you manipulate text.

- Currently, REXML does not support any validation standards such as Document Type Definition (DTD) or XmlSchema. There's basic support for RELAX NG, but it's far from version 1.0.

- REXML is slow, and you should use it only when programmer convenience is more important than performance.

- See Recipe 21, *XML Data Binding on Steroids*, on page 135 to learn how to serialize XML documents automatically.

Handle Large XML Documents

RAM gets cheaper and cheaper every day, but it's still severely limited, especially if you're creating a web application that is used concurrently by a lot of users. It's not a good idea to slurp really large XML documents into main memory.

Interestingly, it happens often that people generate XML documents without thinking about the size of the result file. Maybe five years ago the file contained only 20KB, but as the business grew, the files grew, too, and now they are monsters. That's mostly because those people who create the files rarely have to process them, so it might happen that an application that ran seamlessly for years crashes unexpectedly.

In this recipe, you'll learn how to bring the memory footprint of your XML parsing code to a minimum.

Solution

We'll assume you are working for a telecom company that generates large XML documents containing call detail records (CDRs)[3] every day.

In principle, a CDR describes who called whom and for how long. There is no official standard, and probably every telecom company on this planet has invented its own data format to store this vital information. The data files are way too big to be loaded into RAM completely, and it's your job to visualize all records belonging to a particular phone number. Our data files looks like this:

xml/pull_parser/demo/data/cdr/20080719.xml

```
<?xml version="1.0"?>
<cdr-list date='2007-09-27'>
  <cdr from='+42111111111' timestamp='00:23:39'
       to='+4912345678'   duration='720'/>
  <cdr from='+32012345678' timestamp='00:23:40'
       to='+4912345678'   duration='907'/>
```

---

3. http://en.wikipedia.org/wiki/Call_detail_record

```
<cdr from='+4912345678' timestamp='00:24:02'
     to='+42111111111'  duration='808'/>
<cdr from='+019999999' timestamp='00:25:00'
     to='+32012345678' duration='1051'/>
<!-- ... -->
<cdr from='+019999999' timestamp='23:02:17'
     to='+4912345678'  duration='574'/>
<cdr from='+4912345678' timestamp='23:02:18'
     to='+42111111111'  duration='880'/>
<cdr from='+4912345678' timestamp='23:43:29'
     to='+4912345678'   duration='1137'/>
<cdr from='+42111111111' timestamp='23:44:15'
     to='+4912345678'    duration='214'/>
</cdr-list>
```

These files look harmless, because they consist only of *<cdr>* elements that have four attributes: from= tells us who initiated the phone call, to= contains the recipient's phone number, timestamp= determines the call's start time, and duration= contains the duration of the call measured in seconds. Typically, such a file comprises several million records and can quickly grow larger than 2GB.

REXML—Ruby's standard XML parser—comes with a powerful *pull parser* API that allows us to read XML documents piece by piece. We can use it to read the CDR files incrementally without consuming noticeable amounts of memory:

xml/pull_parser/demo/app/models/call_detail_record.rb

```
Line 1   require 'rexml/parsers/pullparser'
  -
  -      class CallDetailRecord
  -        CDR_DIR = File.join('data', 'cdr')
  5        attr_accessor :from, :to, :timestamp, :duration
  -
  -        def initialize(from, to, timestamp, duration)
  -          @from, @to, @timestamp, @duration = from, to, timestamp, duration
  -        end
  10
  -        def self.find_all(from, date = Time.now)
  -          input_file = CDR_DIR + '/' + date.strftime('%Y%m%d') + '.xml'
  -          parser = REXML::Parsers::PullParser.new(File.new(input_file))
  -          cdrs = []
  15        while parser.has_next?
  -            event = parser.pull
  -            if event.start_element? and event[0] == 'cdr'
  -              attributes = event[1]
  -              if attributes['from'] == from
  20              cdrs << CallDetailRecord.new(
  -                  attributes['from'],
```

```
                    attributes['to'],
                    attributes['timestamp'],
                    attributes['duration']
25              )
          end
        end
      end
      cdrs
30    end
  end
```

The first part of our CallDetailRecord class is pretty straightforward. We merely declare accessors for all the attributes we have found in the XML document. It gets more interesting in line 13. Here we initialize the pull parser for our input file. Please note that we only create a new File object and do not read the file immediately.

A pull parser turns an XML document into a stream of events, and in line 15, we check whether there are still events left in our input file. Whenever we get a new event, we extract it from the stream in line 16. But what is an event?

A new event is generated if the parser finds something interesting such as the start tag of a new element or a new text node. You can check what type of event has been encountered by calling one of the following methods: attlistdecl?(), cdata?(), comment?(), doctype?(), elementdecl?(), end_element?(), entity?(), entitydecl?(), instruction?(), notationdecl?(), start_element?(), text?(), or xmldecl?().

We are interested only in <cdr> elements, so in line 17, we use the start_element?() method to check whether we have found the start of a new element. If yes, we use event[0] to check whether the element is named cdr. REXML does not implement an inheritance hierarchy for the different event types. Instead, you have to use the ()() operator to get more information about an event object. Depending on the event type, the number of attributes you can look up varies (take a look at the REXML documentation[4] for the details).

In the case of a start element, you'll find the name of the element in event[0] and a Hash object containing its attributes in event[1]. We use this in line 18, and whenever we find an element that has the right from= attribute, we create a new CallDetailRecord object and append it to the cdrs array.

---

4. http://www.ruby-doc.org/stdlib/libdoc/rexml/rdoc/classes/REXML/Parsers/PullEvent.html

So if the NSA ("No Such Agency") wants to know which numbers have been dialed from +4912345678 on July 19, 2008, run the following statement on your Rails console:

```
mschmidt> ruby script/console
Loading development environment (Rails 2.1.0).
>> who = '+4912345678'; ts = Time.utc(2008, 7, 19)
=> Sat Jul 19 00:00:00 UTC 2008
>> CallDetailRecord.find_all(who, ts).each do |cdr|
?>    puts cdr.timestamp + ": #{cdr.to}"
>> end
00:24:02: +42111111111
23:02:18: +42111111111
23:43:29: +4912345678
=> [#<CallDetailRecord:0x34574ac @duration="808", @to="+42111111111",
     @from="+4912345678", @timestamp="00:24:02">,
    #<CallDetailRecord:0x34562c8 @duration="880", @to="+42111111111",
     @from="+4912345678", @timestamp="23:02:18">,
    #<CallDetailRecord:0x3455d3c @duration="1137", @to="+4912345678",
     @from="+4912345678", @timestamp="23:43:29">]
```

We use CallDetailRecord as if it were a regular database model. It does not have all the convenience methods you'd get from an ActiveRecord object, but at least it hides all the ugly XML parsing details (an important detail you should not forget about is that REXML encodes all texts as UTF-8 internally).

Discussion

Our solution works best with homogeneous documents that contain large lists of equally structured elements. Whenever you have such a document and whenever you have to process it sequentially—that, is element by element—you should consider using pull parsing.

For many years developers have used only two XML parsing strategies: *tree parsing* and *event parsing*. The most popular APIs are the Document Object Model (DOM) for tree parsing and the Simple API for XML (SAX) for event parsing.

With DOM, you have to read every XML document completely into main memory, which is definitely not an option if the string representation of your document exceeds a certain size. Usually, a DOM tree consumes several times more memory than the same document on a hard disk.

The memory footprint of a SAX parser is much better, but its programming model is more complicated, because it somehow inverses control: the parser tells you what to do and when to do it.

Pull parsers have been developed to make XML parsing possible even in highly restricted environments such as cell phones. They use a hybrid approach; they do not read an input document completely but piece by piece. But instead of waiting for the parser to tell you what it has found, you ask it whether it has something interesting for you whenever you need more information. This way, the memory footprint of a pull parser is minimal, and you are still in control.

Pull parsers have some disadvantages, too: they work on a very low level, and you have to take care of every tiny detail. Additionally, error handling becomes more complicated. For example, it's possible to realize your document is not well-formed right after you've read the last character, and therefore you have to roll back all the things you have done until then.

Eventually, you shouldn't forget that RAM is not the only scarce resource. If the documents you'd like to process are really big, it might well happen that you can still process them without running out of memory, but processing could take far too long.

Also See

- See Recipe 24, *High-Performance Parsing*, on page 153 if you want to save not only memory but also CPU cycles when parsing XML documents.

High-Performance Parsing

Problem

Ruby is an interpreted language, which means it's not as fast as its compiled counterparts. By the time you read this, several Ruby compilers will be available, but none of them will automatically solve the problems described in this recipe. Usually, this is not a problem, but it could happen that you create a Ruby program for parsing an XML document that is too slow. Maybe you have developed it in record time, but that doesn't count much if it does not fulfill your customer's needs.

In this recipe, you'll learn how to increase the performance of your XML parsing code tremendously.

Ingredients

- Install the *LibXML*[5] gem:

  ```
  $ gem install libxml-ruby
  ```

  At the time of this writing, installing *LibXML* as a gem does not work out of the box on the Microsoft Windows platform.

Solution

Let's assume you have to create a Rails application that scans through an XML file containing credit card transactions and displays all transactions belonging to a particular credit card. The file might look like this:

`xml/libxml2/ccdemo/data/cc_xactions/20080729.xml`

```
<?xml version='1.0'?>
<cc-xactions date='20080729'>
  <cc-xaction id='100001' cc-ref='2537403' type='credit' amount='12.00'>
    <text>Monthly bill.</text>
  </cc-xaction>
  <!-- ... -->
  <cc-xaction id='400224' cc-ref='95932' type='purchase' amount='19.99'>
    <text>A new book.</text>
  </cc-xaction>
</cc-xactions>
```

---

5. http://libxml.rubyforge.org/

Each transaction has a unique identifier that can be found in the id= attribute. All credit cards are identified by a reference ID, which is stored in the cc-ref= attribute (using the credit card number to identify a credit card is not allowed, which is why we use an artificial identifier).

If you get money from your customer, the type= attribute is purchase; otherwise, it's credit. amount= tells us how much money has been transferred, and the content of the *<text>* element appears on the customer's credit card bill.

The input files contain several thousand credit card transactions, and you've tried all traditional methods already, but your application is still too slow. You've measured performance and have come to the conclusion that more CPU cycles are needed in the XML parsing code.

To solve this problem, we'll use the *LibXML* library. It is a C extension and embeds the GNOME *libxml2* library[6] into the Ruby interpreter. Like REXML, it uses XPath wherever possible. Our model looks like:

xml/libxml2/ccdemo/app/models/credit_card_transaction.rb

```
Line 1   require 'xml/libxml'

         class CreditCardTransaction
           XACTION_DIR = File.join('data', 'cc_xactions')
      5
           attr_reader :xaction_id, :cc_ref, :type, :amount, :text

           def initialize(xaction_id, cc_ref, type, amount, text)
             @xaction_id, @cc_ref, @type = xaction_id, cc_ref, type
     10      @amount, @text = amount, text
           end

           def self.find_all(cc_ref)
             xactions = []
     15      input_file = "#{XACTION_DIR}/xactions.xml"
             doc = XML::Document.file(input_file)
             doc.find('//cc-xactions/cc-xaction').each do |node|
               if node['cc-ref'] == cc_ref
                 xactions << CreditCardTransaction.new(
     20            node['id'],
                   node['cc-ref'],
                   node['type'],
                   node['amount'],
                   node.find_first('text')
     25          )
               end
             end
```

---

6. http://xmlsoft.org/

```
            xactions
        end
30   end
```

That does not differ much from our REXML solution, because both libraries have a similar API, and they even use UTF-8 for encoding characters internally.

In line 16, we read and parse our input file in a single step. The result is a tree representation of our XML document. In line 17, we iterate over all *<cc-xaction>* elements using the find() method. As with REXML's iterators, we can use an XPath expression to select the nodes we're interested in (see Recipe 22, *Use XML Files as Models*, on page 139). In line 20, we copy the content of an attribute, and in line 24, we copy an element's content. The controller action for finding all credit card transactions is trivial:

xml/libxml2/ccdemo/app/controllers/credit_card_transaction_controller.rb

```ruby
class CreditCardTransactionController < ApplicationController
  def show
    @xactions = CreditCardTransaction.find_all(params[:id])
  end
end
```

The view looks as follows, and its result can be seen in Figure 5.2, on the following page:

xml/libxml2/ccdemo/app/views/credit_card_transaction/show.html.erb

```erb
<% if @xactions.size == 0 %>
  <p>Currently, there are no transactions.</p>
<% else %>
  <table>
    <tr>
      <th>Transaction ID</th>
      <th>Credit Card Reference</th>
      <th>Amount</th>
      <th>Text</th>
    </tr>
    <% for xaction in @xactions %>
      <tr>
        <td><%= xaction.xaction_id %></td>
        <td><%= xaction.cc_ref %></td>
        <% sign = (xaction.type == 'purchase') ? '+' : '-' %>
        <td><%= sign + number_to_currency(xaction.amount) %></td>
        <td><%= xaction.text %></td>
      </tr>
    <% end %>
  </table>
<% end %>
```

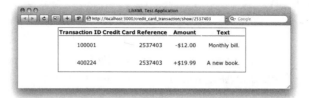

Figure 5.2: LIST OF CREDIT CARD TRANSACTIONS

Although we have read model data from an XML file and although we have parsed the files using a C extension, we could still use Rails' regular MVC pattern. By looking at the view, you cannot see where the data came from.

Discussion

So far, so good, but our solution does not differ much from a REXML solution. Why should it be so much faster?

The secret ingredient is the raw power of C, but you cannot determine how much faster your program runs by looking at the code. I have provided a little benchmark that compares three functions that do the same but use different parsers. The first one uses *LibXML*:

`xml/libxml2/performance_test.rb`

```
require 'xml/libxml'
def libxml_parse(xml_string)
  xactions = []
  parser = XML::Parser.new
  parser.string = xml_string
  doc = parser.parse
  doc.find('//cc-xactions/cc-xaction').each do |node|
    xactions << CreditCardTransaction.new(
      node['id'],
      node['cc-ref'],
      node['type'],
      node['amount'],
      node.find('text').to_a.first.content
    )
  end
  xactions
end
```

That looks exactly like the code we used in the CreditCardTransaction class. The only difference starts in line 4. Here we read our input document from a string and not from a file to create fair testing conditions for all approaches. Here's a solution that uses REXML:

xml/libxml2/performance_test.rb

```
Line 1  require 'rexml/document'
   -    def rexml_parse(xml_string)
   -      xactions = []
   -      doc = REXML::Document.new(xml_string)
   5      doc.elements.each('//cc-xactions/cc-xaction') do |node|
   -        xactions << CreditCardTransaction.new(
   -          node.attributes['id'],
   -          node.attributes['cc-ref'],
   -          node.attributes['type'],
   10         node.attributes['amount'],
   -          node.elements['text'].text
   -        )
   -      end
   -      xactions
   15   end
```

This function should not contain any surprises, and for the sake of completeness we'll look at an *Hpricot* version, too (see Recipe 25, *Work with HTML and Microformats*, on page 159 to learn more about *Hpricot*):

xml/libxml2/performance_test.rb

```
Line 1  require 'hpricot'
   -    def hpricot_parse(xml_string)
   -      xactions = []
   -      doc = Hpricot.XML(xml_string)
   5      (doc/'//cc-xactions/cc-xaction').each do |node|
   -        xactions << CreditCardTransaction.new(
   -          node['id'],
   -          node['cc-ref'],
   -          node['type'],
   10         node['amount'],
   -          (node/'text').inner_html
   -        )
   -      end
   -      xactions
   15   end
```

Hpricot was always meant to be an HTML parser, but its XML() method makes it possible to parse XML documents, too.

As you can see, the three solutions differ only in a few characters, and now we use Ruby's *Benchmark* module to compare them.

xml/libxml2/performance_test.rb

```ruby
require 'benchmark'
xml_string = IO::read(input_file)
label_width = 8
Benchmark.bm(label_width) do |x|
  x.report('rexml:  ') { rexml_parse(xml_string) }
  x.report('libxml: ') { libxml_parse(xml_string) }
  x.report('hpricot:') { hpricot_parse(xml_string) }
end
```

First, we feed our two functions with an example document containing 1,000 credit card transactions (I've run those tests on an Apple MacBook Pro):

```
mschmidt> ruby performance_test.rb 1000
              user      system      total        real
rexml:     3.110000    0.040000    3.150000  (  3.189711)
libxml:    0.050000    0.010000    0.060000  (  0.060367)
hpricot:   0.510000    0.000000    0.510000  (  0.523038)
```

That's pretty impressive already, but let's see what happens when we parse 10,000 elements:

```
mschmidt> ruby performance_test.rb 10000
              user      system      total        real
rexml:   218.810000    1.640000  220.450000  (222.433778)
libxml:    2.020000    0.110000    2.130000  (  2.168987)
hpricot:   6.600000    0.060000    6.660000  (  6.727825)
```

Wow! As you can see, not only is *LibXML* much faster than REXML, but it is really fast! Regarding this figures, it would be completely impossible to provide a satisfying user experience using REXML, but the performance of *LibXML* is still acceptable. *Hpricot* has excellent performance, too, but when you have to install a separate library anyway, you should install the fastest one. In addition, *LibXML* fully implements the XML standard (and some of its relatives), while *Hpricot* does not.

Despite all this, you have to consider some shortcomings: although *LibXML* is probably one of the most complete XML implementations available, its Ruby binding is still in an early stage of development, and as with all C extensions, you have to test your software intensely. You especially have to check for memory leaks!

REXML is convenient and an adequate solution for small XML documents. But the API of *LibXML* is nice, too, and it's currently the only library that enables you to handle really big documents sufficiently fast.

Work with HTML and Microformats

Problem

It happens often that you have to extract information from websites by actually parsing their HTML code. Usually, you use a mixture of regular expressions and methods for string manipulation, but this approach does not scale well, because it leads to ugly and fragile solutions.

In this recipe, you'll learn how to parse HTML.

Ingredients

- Install the *hpricot*[7] gem:

  ```
  $ gem install hpricot
  ```

- Install the *mofo*[8] library:

  ```
  $ gem install mofo
  ```

Solution

Microformats[9] are a perfect way to embed snippets of structured information into an ordinary website. Simply put, a microformat is only a naming convention for Cascading Style Sheets (CSS)[10] classes. For example, there's a microformat for storing address information as an *hCard*, which is the microformat representation of a vCard defined in RFC-2426.[11]

An hCard's full name is always stored in an XHTML element that has the CSS class fn (*full name*), an email address is stored in an element that has the class email, and so on. The type of the element doesn't matter. Currently, nine microformats have been specified, and draft specifications exist for another eleven.

---

7. http://code.whytheluckystiff.net/hpricot/
8. http://mofo.rubyforge.org/
9. http://microformats.org/
10. http://www.w3.org/Style/CSS/
11. http://www.ietf.org/rfc/rfc2426.txt

If the microformat document you are interested in is embedded in an XHTML document, everything is fine, because you can use an XML parser to extract it. Otherwise, you have to parse HTML, which is a lot more complex.

Although XML and HTML look similar, they are different beasts from a technical point of view. Still, they get mixed often, and you can find XHTML documents that have been embedded into HTML files, for example. Here we have such a document:

`xml/microformats/vcard_demo/public/hcard/maik.html`

```
Line 1  <html>
   -      <head>
   -        <title>Maik Schmidt&apos;s Vcard</title>
   -      </head>
   5    <body>
   -        Here's some content that is not even well-formed!
   -        <p>
   -        <div id="hcard-Maik-Schmidt" class="vcard">
   -          <a class="url"
   10             href="http://maik-schmidt.de">Maik Schmidt</a><br/>
   -          <span class="fn" style="display:none">Maik Schmidt</span>
   -          <div class="adr">
   -            <div class="street-address">Musterstra&szlig;e 42</div>
   -            <span class="locality">Musterstadt</span><br/>
   15           <span class="postal-code">12345</span>
   -            <span class="country-name">Germany</span>
   -          </div>
   -          Phone: <span class="tel">+49123456789</span><br/>
   -          Email: <a class="email"
   20                  href="mailto:foo@example.com">foo@example.com</a>
   -        </div>
   -      </body>
   -  </div>
```

That's a perfectly valid HTML page (see a rendered version in Figure 5.3, on the facing page), and although it looks pretty normal, it still contains something special: a microformat hCard.

Plug-ins are available for some web browsers that automatically extract microformat information and allow you to use it in other applications. In Figure 5.4, on the next page, you can see one for Apple's Safari browser.[12] I've opened the page containing my vCard, and the plug-in offers to add it to the address book automatically. If a page contains hCalendar elements (that's a microformat for calendar entries), they can be added to iCal automatically, and so on.

---

12. http://zappatic.net/safarimicroformats/

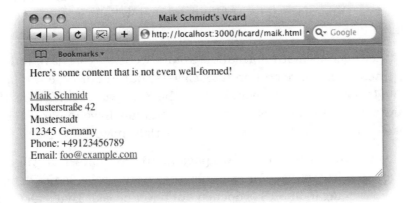

Figure 5.3: MAIK'S VCARD

Figure 5.4: A BROWSER PLUG-IN FOR MICROFORMATS

This kind of information exchange works for web applications, too, and you can give your customers the opportunity to import their vCard data encoded as a microformat hCard from another website instead of entering them manually.

To extract microformat information from a website, you have to identify elements that have certain CSS classes, but in our case the target website is not an XHTML document, so the XML parser complains that the site's content is not well-formed. You actually have to parse HTML, but it's much easier than you might think right now.

When you feed our sample HTML page to an XML parser, it will complain about a few things. For example, the entity ß is not defined, and the *
* tag in line 18 is opened but never closed. That's all OK for HTML documents, but it is not allowed in an XML document. Anyway, the embedded microformat hCard is encoded as XHTML, and we'd like to map it to a Vcard object that has the following structure:

```
xml/microformats/vcard_demo/app/models/vcard.rb
class Vcard
  attr_accessor :name, :street, :postal_code, :city, :email
  attr_accessor :phone, :url, :country
end
```

Parsing HTML is usually much more difficult than parsing XML, but Ruby programmers can use one of the most convenient HTML parsers ever: *Hpricot.* We use it in this recipe to map the profile data manually:

```
xml/microformats/vcard_demo/app/controllers/vcard_controller.rb
Line 1  require 'hpricot'
     -  require 'open-uri'
     -
     -  class VcardController < ApplicationController
     5    def import
     -      external_url = params[:external_url]
     -      doc = Hpricot(open(external_url))
     -      @vcard = Vcard.new
     -      @vcard.url = doc.at('//a[@class="url"]')['href']
    10      @vcard.name = classified_node(doc, 'fn')
     -      @vcard.street = classified_node(doc, 'street-address')
     -      @vcard.city = classified_node(doc, 'locality')
     -      @vcard.postal_code = classified_node(doc, 'postal-code')
     -      @vcard.country = classified_node(doc, 'country-name')
    15      @vcard.phone = classified_node(doc, 'tel')
     -      @vcard.email = classified_node(doc, 'email')
     -    end
     -
```

```
     private

 def classified_node(doc, class_name)
   doc.at("//[@class='#{class_name}']").inner_html
 end
end
```

We find the URL to read the vCard data from in params[:external_url]. To parse our customer's vCard, we read the document from the remote location in line 7 and pass it to Hpricot (see Recipe 29, *Find Solutions Quickly with open-uri*, on page 183 for more information about *open-uri*). In line 9, we search for an <a> element that has the class url using the at() method. It expects an XPath expression identifying the node we are interested in, and we access the node's href= attribute with the ()() operator.

In the following example, we use the classified_node() method to extract the missing information from the input document. classified_node() builds an XPath expression dynamically to find an element that has a certain class name. It returns its content calling inner_html(), which creates an HTML fragment consisting of all children's contents. There's a method named inner_text(), too, which returns only text nodes, but in our case inner_html() is an adequate choice, because it preserves HTML entities (we use ß in the street name, for example).

After we've copied the content to our Vcard object, we can render it as follows (see the result in Figure 5.5, on the next page):

xml/microformats/vcard_demo/app/views/vcard/import.html.erb

```
<% if @vcard.nil? %>
  <p>We could not import you Vcard.</p>
<% else %>
  <p>Your Vcard has been imported successfully:</p>
  <p>
    <%= link_to @vcard.name, @vcard.url %><br/>
    <%= @vcard.street %><br/>
    <%= @vcard.postal_code %> <%= @vcard.city %><br/>
    <%= @vcard.country %><br/>
  </p>
  <p>
    Email: <%= @vcard.email %><br/>
    Phone: <%= @vcard.phone %>
  </p>
<% end %>
```

Now, you might think it'd be a great idea to build a library that extracts microformats automatically from HTML documents.

Figure 5.5: THE IMPORTED VCARD

But it'd be better to spend your time building a better mousetrap, because the *mofo* library already hides the nitty-gritty details and supports all microformats currently available. Here's an alternative version of our import() action:

`xml/microformats/vcard_demo/app/controllers/vcard_controller.rb`

```ruby
require 'mofo'

class VcardController
  def import_mofo
    @vcard = hCard.find :first => params[:external_url]
  end
end
```

That's nice, isn't it? With a single line of code we've extracted the whole vCard, and its attributes are encapsulated in an HCard object already. Attributes of these objects can be mapped directly to the microformat class names, and they can be used in a view like this:

`xml/microformats/vcard_demo/app/views/vcard/import_mofo.html.erb`

```erb
<% if @vcard.nil? %>
  <p>We could not import you Vcard.</p>
<% else %>
  <p>Your Vcard has been imported successfully:</p>
  <p>
    <%= link_to @vcard.fn, @vcard.url %><br/>
    <%= @vcard.adr.street_address %><br/>
    <%= @vcard.adr.postal_code %> <%= @vcard.adr.locality %><br/>
    <%= @vcard.adr.country_name %><br/>
  </p>
  <p>
    Email: <%= @vcard.email %><br/>
    Phone: +<%= @vcard.tel %>
  </p>
<% end %>
```

All CSS classes have been cleanly mapped to attribute names, and *mofo* does it not only for hCard objects but also for all the other microformats that have been specified already.

Parsing HTML documents is needed more often than you might think. A lot of companies still offer services not in the form of sophisticated SOAP or REST interfaces but instead force you to read information directly from their websites. Because this technology is so popular, it even has a name: it's called *screen scraping*[13] (see Recipe 31, *Scrape Screens with WWW::Mechanize*, on page 193 to learn more about it). The structure of the embedded data is often completely proprietary (sometimes the information is embedded as CSV in HTML comments), but if you are lucky, the provider uses a microformat or at least XHTML. In these cases, *Hpricot* or *mofo* is everything you need to build a solution quickly.

---

13. http://en.wikipedia.org/wiki/Screen_scraping

Build Plain-Vanilla XML Documents

Problem

Nearly every enterprise application has to generate XML documents sooner or later, so in this recipe you'll learn how to do this in the most elegant way with Ruby.

Ingredients

- Builder[14] comes with Rails automatically, but if you want to create XML documents outside a Rails application, you have to install it as a separate gem:

```
$ gem install builder
```

Solution

Rails comes with an excellent XML generator named Builder::XmlMarkup, and usually that is all you need. For example, here's how you turn a typical customer object (with a name, an address, and so on) into an XML document (the @customer variable could have been initialized in a Rails controller, for example):

`xml/build_xml/demo/app/views/customer/show.xml.builder`

```
Line 1   xml.instruct! :xml, :version => '1.0', :encoding => 'utf-8'
    -    xml.customer('customer-no' => @customer.customer_no) do
    -      xml.name(
    -        :forename => @customer.forename,
    5        :surname => @customer.surname
    -      )
    -      xml.street(@customer.street)
    -      xml.city(@customer.city)
    -      xml.tag!('postal-code', @customer.postal_code)
    10   end
```

Builder is really a great tool, and although its usage is highly intuitive, we'll walk through our example.

---

14. http://builder.rubyforge.org/

Being good citizens we generate an XML prolog in line 1. The following line, then, uses nearly all of Builder's features. Whenever you invoke a method on a Builder instance, an element with the same name as the method is created. In our case, a *<customer>* element gets emitted. We pass the method a Hash object, and its key/value pairs automatically become attributes of the *<customer>* element. Then it gets a bit more interesting, because we also pass the customer() message a code block. Within the code block, we get a reference to the customer element, so we can add child elements to it.

The only method left to be explained is tag!() in line 9. Many characters that are allowed in XML elements and attribute names are not allowed in Ruby method names. For example, a Ruby method cannot be named postal-code(). In such cases you have to use tag!().

To see what is returned by our application, we use the curl[15] command:

```
mschmidt> curl -i http://localhost:3000/customer/show/1
HTTP/1.1 200 OK
Content-Type: application/xml; charset=utf-8
Content-Length: 231

<?xml version="1.0" encoding="utf-8"?>
<customer customer-no="94429999">
  <name surname="Schmidt" forename="Maik"/>
  <street>Musterstra&#223;e 42</street>
  <city>Musterstadt</city>
  <postal-code>12345</postal-code>
</customer>
```

For the sake of brevity we have removed all the HTTP headers that we are currently not interested in. Everything is OK: the document is well-formed, and the character set encoding is correct. Usually, that's all you need to produce XML documents.

---

15. http://curl.haxx.se/

Build Arbitrary XML Documents

Problem

Far too many people do not use an XML parser for processing XML documents. Some of them still parse XML documents using Java's indexOf( ) method and think that all character set encodings other than Windows-1251[16] are from Hell. That's not too clever, but if you have to interact with a system that expects all incoming documents to have the same encoding or some weird formatting, you have to create your documents accordingly.

You might be tempted to ignore such issues on your new project, but you might have to integrate with a nonliberal application. (Unfortunately, it's not one of those monsters that disappears if you stop believing in it.) Not too long ago, for example, it made a big difference if you sent <br/> or <br /> to a popular web browser (did you notice the blank before the second slash?).

You can rarely control all details with typical XML generators, so in this recipe you'll learn how to create even the strangest XML documents.

Solution

XML is a rather liberal standard regarding formatting issues. For example, there are several ways to encode empty elements:

```
<empty-element/>
<empty-element></empty-element>
```

Usually, the order of attributes doesn't matter, and it doesn't matter whether you use single or double quotes. The following elements are all equal:

```
<name forename="Maik" surname="Schmidt"/>
<name surname="Schmidt" forename="Maik"/>
<name surname='Schmidt' forename='Maik'/>
```

---

16. http://en.wikipedia.org/wiki/Windows-1251

If you actually have to control such details, it's best if you take things into your own hands and create the documents from a regular template instead of using a generator. So, let's assume we have a reference to a typical customer object in an instance variable named @customer (a customer has the usual attributes: forename, surname, and so on). The following template file turns it into an XML document:

xml/build_xml/demo/app/views/customer/show_flexible.xml.erb
```
<?xml version='1.0' encoding='iso-8859-15'?>
<customer customer-no='<%= @customer.customer_no %>'>
  <name surname='<%= @customer.surname %>'
        forename='<%= @customer.forename %>'/>
  <street><%= @customer.street %></street>
  <city><%= @customer.city %></city>
  <postal-code><%= @customer.postal_code %></postal-code>
</customer>
```

It should be fairly obvious that we can do whatever we want now regarding formatting issues. We can arrange elements and attributes in any way we like, we can use either double quotes or single quotes, and so on. But we also have to be careful about many things ourselves. For example, the previous view code silently assumes that the attributes of our customer object do not contain special characters such as &. Otherwise, we would have to encode them accordingly.

What if you have to create XML documents in another character set encoding such as ISO-8859-15? Then you have to convert the resulting document accordingly, and because we may need the conversion method more than once, we add a convenience method to the ApplicationController:

xml/build_xml/demo/app/controllers/application.rb
```
require 'iconv'

class ApplicationController < ActionController::Base
  def convert(to_char_set = 'iso-8859-15')
    converter = Iconv.new(to_char_set, 'utf-8')
    response.body = converter.iconv(response.body)
    content_type = "application/xml; charset=#{to_char_set}"
    response.headers['content-type'] = content_type
  end
end
```

convert() converts the response body from UTF-8 to ISO-8859-15 and sets the HTTP header content-type correctly. Now we install convert() with Rails' after_filter() mechanism.

`xml/build_xml/demo/app/controllers/customer_controller.rb`

```ruby
class CustomerController < ApplicationController
  after_filter :convert, :only => [:show_flexible]

  def show_flexible
    @customer = Customer.find(params[:id])
    respond_to do |format|
      format.xml
    end
  end
end
```

After the show_flexible() method has finished its job, convert() gets called, turns our result document into the right encoding, and sets all necessary HTTP headers correctly. Here's a sample run (executed in a terminal using the ISO-8859-15 encoding):

```
mschmidt> curl -i http://localhost:3000/customer/show_flexible/1
HTTP/1.1 200 OK
Content-Type: application/xml; charset=iso-8859-15
Content-Length: 240

<?xml version='1.0' encoding='iso-8859-15'?>
<customer customer-no='94429999'>
  <name surname='Schmidt'
        forename='Maik'/>
  <street>Musterstraße 42</street>
  <city>Musterstadt</city>
  <postal-code>12345</postal-code>
</customer>
```

There's one important thing left to remember: we assume that our application uses UTF-8 internally, and if your element or attribute names contain special characters themselves, you have to save the template file in the right character set encoding.

Iconv

In version 1.8, Ruby's native support for different character set encodings is currently far from being complete, but with the GNU libiconv[17] project we have a strong ally in an international environment. This library supports nearly every important character set on the planet and converts data encoded in a particular character set into another (if you'd like to see which languages are supported on your system, run iconv -l on your command line).

---

17. http://www.gnu.org/software/libiconv/

Its Ruby binding is named Iconv and can be used like this:

```
require 'iconv'
converter = Iconv.new('utf-8', 'iso-8859-1') # to, from
puts converter.iconv('Über-Programmer')
```

This program converts the text "Über-Programmer" from the character set ISO-8859-1 to the Unicode character set UTF-8. You have to make sure that your input string actually has the right encoding, so if you read data from a database or from a file, make sure you know its encoding.

The situation has changed dramatically. Since version 1.9, Ruby supports different character set encodings for source files, objects, and IO streams. See *Programming Ruby* [TFH08] to learn all about it.

Part III

Networking & Messaging Recipes

## Chapter 6

Perform Basic
Networking Tasks with Ease

As the Internet gets bigger and bigger, nearly every application needs to access network resources somehow. Sometimes it's as simple as checking for updates of an application at startup, but often programs have to interact with complex web services or even allow their users to work concurrently on shared data.

In enterprise environments, network programming is a common task, too. For example, the different components of a distributed application usually communicate via networks. Although network programming in an enterprise environment does not differ much from network programming in the outside world, you still have to take care of some important requirements. Every request should have a timeout to prevent applications from hanging, and you often have to use proxy servers instead of accessing foreign hosts directly, for example.

Sockets are still the basis for most networked applications, and therefore you'll learn how to use them in Recipe 28, *Harness the Power of Sockets*, on page 177. Then we will deal with higher-level application protocols such as HTTP, HTTPS, and FTP. We start in Recipe 29, *Find Solutions Quickly with open-uri*, on page 183, where you'll learn how to request network resources with a single line of code. In Recipe 30, *Get the Most Out of HTTP*, on page 187, you'll see how to control even the tiniest details of HTTP conversations, and you'll even learn how to implement new HTTP commands. Eventually, in Recipe 31, *Scrape Screens with WWW::Mechanize*, on page 193, we have some fun and learn how to control websites programmatically without using a web browser.

Harness the Power of Sockets

Sockets are the basis of nearly all networked applications, but usually you do not have to use them directly, because application protocols such as HTTP hide all the details from you. Still, from time to time you have to use them on both the server side and the client side.

In enterprise environments you often find many legacy socket servers, so in this recipe you'll learn how to replace one of them with a shiny new Ruby server. You'll learn how to write a client, too.

The server we are going to replace implements a minimal service repository. No one knows who wrote the server, and the source code has disappeared, too. Some changes are needed, so it has to be replaced by a new server with the same interface.

For every service that is running in your company's service-oriented architecture, the server contains a basic set of information. For example, it tells you where a particular service is running, which version has been deployed, and how many instances of the service have been started. All service information is stored in a single database table:

```
mysql> select * from service_infos;
+---------+---------+-------------+-------+-----------+
| name    | version | host        | port  | instances |
+---------+---------+-------------+-------+-----------+
| billing | 2.13    | prodhost    | 4711  |         2 |
| order   | 8.01    | staginghost | 11223 |         5 |
+---------+---------+-------------+-------+-----------+
2 rows in set (0.00 sec)
```

As you can see, version 2.13 of a service named billing runs on host prodhost. It listens on port 4711 and 4712, because two instances of the service have been started.

Currently, the server understands only an info command, which expects a service name and returns all service information as a list of key/value pairs. The first line starts with OK if everything is OK, and it starts with ERROR if something went wrong.

A typical conversation using the telnet command looks like this:

mschmidt> **telnet localhost 12345**

⇒   Trying ::1...
      telnet: connect to address ::1: Connection refused
      Trying 127.0.0.1...
      Connected to localhost.
      Escape character is '^]'.
⇐   **info billing**
⇒   OK
      name: billing
      instances: 2
      port: 4711
      version: 2.13
      host: prodhost
      Connection closed by foreign host.

The old server works as specified, so let's write a new one that behaves
the same way:

basic_networking/socket/basic_server.rb

```
Line 1   require 'gserver'
    -    require 'activerecord'
    -
    -    class ServiceInfo < ActiveRecord::Base; end
    5
    -    class ServiceInfoServer < GServer
    -      def initialize(port = 12345, logger = $stdout)
    -        super(port, GServer::DEFAULT_HOST, Float::MAX, logger, true)
    -      end
   10
    -      def serve(client)
    -        begin
    -          command = client.gets.chomp
    -          log "Got command: #{command}"
   15         if command =~ /info\s+(.+)/
    -            service_name = $1
    -            if si = ServiceInfo.find_by_name(service_name)
    -              client.puts 'OK'
    -              si.attributes.each { |k,v| client.puts "#{k}: #{v}" }
   20           else
    -              client.puts "ERROR: service #{service_name} is unknown."
    -            end
    -          else
    -            client.puts 'ERROR: command #{command} is unknown.'
   25         end
    -        rescue => ex
    -          log "An error occurred: #{ex.message}"
    -          client.puts 'ERROR'
    -        end
   30     end
    -    end
```

Ruby comes with *gserver*, which is an excellent library for creating multithreaded socket servers. To build a new server, you have to derive from GServer and implement a method named serve() that gets called for every new client connection in a separate thread.

That's exactly what we do, but first we initialize the server in line 8. GServer's initialize() method expects a lot of parameters:

- port and host (defaults to 127.0.0.1) determine on which host the server is running and on which port it is listening.
- maxConnections sets the maximum amount of connections that will be handled in parallel (defaults to 4).
- stdlog (defaults to $stderr) can be used to set a logger and audit controls if logging should be enabled or not (the default).
- debug (the default is false) sets the server into a debugging mode in which it logs more detailed error messages.

In line 13, we read the data the client has sent and check whether it contains a valid command. If yes, we try to read service information from the database and send it back in line 18 together with an OK status. In case of an error, we send an error status to the client, and if we detect an unexpected exception, we write a log message in line 27. The only thing left to do is start the server:

basic_networking/socket/basic_server.rb

```
ActiveRecord::Base.establish_connection(
    :adapter  => 'mysql', :database => 'services',
    :username => 'admin', :password => 't0p$ecret'
)
server = ServiceInfoServer.new(12345)
server.start
server.join
```

After initializing the database connection, we create an instance of class ServiceInfoServer and invoke its start() method. The server is started in a separate thread, and to prevent it from terminating immediately, we call join(), which waits for all running threads to complete. Currently, we don't care about pooling the database connection, but all the other concurrency issues are handled by GServer.

If we send the server the info billing command from earlier, it will return the same information as the old server, and it will print the following on the console:

```
[Sun Jul 20 16:09:23 2008] ServiceInfoServer 127.0.0.1:12345 start
[Sun Jul 20 16:09:31 2008] ServiceInfoServer 127.0.0.1:12345 client:6527
  localhost<127.0.0.1> connect
```

```
[Sun Jul 20 16:09:35 2008] Got command: info billing
[Sun Jul 20 16:09:35 2008] ServiceInfoServer 127.0.0.1:12345 client:6527
  disconnect
```

We are done! A less responsible developer would spend the rest of the day at the beach, but we will add some final touches. Servers should always write a log file, and GServer has some basic logging support. To be honest, it is very basic, so we will replace it with something more sophisticated, namely, Ruby's Logger class:

> basic_networking/socket/service_info_server.rb

```ruby
require 'logger'

class ServiceInfoServer
  def log(message, level = Logger::INFO)
    @stdlog.add(level) { message } if @stdlog
  end

  def debug(message) log(message, Logger::DEBUG); end
  def info(message) log(message); end
  def warn(message) log(message, Logger::WARN); end
  def fatal(message) log(message, Logger::FATAL); end
end
```

We override log() and use GServer's @stdlog attribute, which refers to the logger object that has been passed to initialize().

Now we can use methods such as debug(), info(), or warn() to write messages that have a certain level to a log file. But we have to create a Logger object before we start the server:

> basic_networking/socket/service_info_server.rb

```ruby
logger = Logger.new('server.log')
logger.formatter = proc { |severity, datetime, progname, msg|
    "#{datetime.strftime('%Y-%m-%d %H:%M:%S')} #{severity} - #{msg}\n"
}
server = ServiceInfoServer.new(12345, logger)
```

When you use ActiveRecord, the behavior of Logger slightly changes, so we set its log line format explicitly.

Let's use our new log methods to write a message to the log file whenever we get a new request. Instead of adding this to the server() method, we'll use event handlers, another nice GServer feature.

basic_networking/socket/service_info_server.rb

```ruby
class ServiceInfoServer
  def connecting(client)
    hostname = client.peeraddr[2] || client.peeraddr[3]
    info "Got a request from #{hostname}."
  end

  def stopping
    info 'Shutting down server.'
    @stdlog.close if @stdlog
  end
end
```

You can add up to four event handlers that get called when a client connects (connecting()), when it disconnects (disconnecting()), when the server is started (starting()), and when it is stopped (stopping()). We have implemented connecting() to write a short message to the log file for every incoming request, and in stopping() we clean up a bit.

The server is complete now, but testing it manually using telnet is a bit tedious. A Ruby client will help:

basic_networking/socket/client.rb

```ruby
Line 1  require 'socket'

        class ServiceInfoClient
          def initialize(port, host = 'localhost')
    5       @port, @host = port, host
          end

          def get_service_info(name)
            socket = TCPSocket.open(@host, @port)
    10      socket.write("info #{name}\n")
            service_info = socket.read
            socket.close
            lines = service_info.split(/\n/)
            status = lines.shift
    15      raise status unless status == 'OK'
            lines.inject({}) do |result, line|
              key, value = line.chomp.split(':')
              result[key] = value.strip
              result
    20      end
          end
        end
```

Using a socket server is even simpler than building it.

If you run the client like this:

`basic_networking/socket/client.rb`

```
require 'pp'
client = ServiceInfoClient.new(12345)
pp client.get_service_info('order')
```

it will output the following to the console:

```
{"name"=>"order",
 "instances"=>"5",
 "port"=>"11223",
 "version"=>"8.01",
 "host"=>"staginghost"}
```

In the server log file, you will find something like this:

```
2008-07-20 19:43:36 INFO - ServiceInfoServer 127.0.0.1:12345 start
2008-07-20 19:43:41 INFO - Got a request from localhost.
2008-07-20 19:43:41 INFO - Got command: info order
2008-07-20 19:43:41 INFO - ServiceInfoServer 127.0.0.1:12345 client:6542
  disconnect
2008-07-20 19:44:00 INFO - Shutting down server.
```

The whole socket handling happens in lines 9 to 12. We open a TCP socket, write data to it, read the response, and close the socket. That's all there is to it; the rest of the code deals with parsing the response and checking the status of the operation.

GServer's API consists of only a few methods, but it's sufficient to create socket servers that can handle small to medium traffic in record time. It's also possible to add industrial-strength logging to it and to handle important events such as new connections separately. On the client side, we can benefit from Ruby's excellent socket support, which is covered in full detail in *Programming Ruby* [TFH08].

Find Solutions Quickly with open-uri

You often find yourself writing tedious networking code when you just want to fetch some data via HTTP or FTP. You think it doesn't have to be so complicated. In this recipe, you'll learn that you're right and that *open-uri* is what you need.

To quickly access data on a network, Ruby's *open-uri* is an excellent choice. Basically, *open-uri* adds new functionality to Ruby's original open() method in the Kernel module. If the first argument passed to open() starts with a protocol specifier such as http://, https://, or ftp://, then it reads data from a network resource. Otherwise, it falls back to the original version of open().

Here's how you read some information about new Ruby books from your favorite publisher's website:

`basic_networking/open-uri/read_pragprog.rb`

```ruby
require 'open-uri'

ruby_count = 0
options = { 'user-agent' => "Ruby/#{RUBY_VERSION}" }
open('http://www.pragprog.com', options) do |f|
  f.each_line { |line| ruby_count += 1 if line =~ /Ruby/ }
  puts f.base_uri
  puts f.content_type
  puts f.charset
  if f.content_encoding.size > 0
    puts content_encoding.join(',')
  else
    puts 'Missing content encoding.'
  end
  puts f.last_modified || 'Missing last-modified header.'
  puts f.status.join(': ')
end
puts "#{ruby_count} lines contain the word 'Ruby'."
```

That's the output you get when you run this program (yours may vary depending on Ruby's current popularity):

```
mschmidt> ruby read_pragprog.rb
http://www.pragprog.com
text/html
utf-8
Missing content encoding.
Missing last-modified header.
200: OK
5 lines contain the word 'Ruby'.
```

In our program, we invoke open(), passing it a URL and the HTTP header user-agent, which gets sent with the request. You can provide as many headers as you need, and it's possible to set some additional options we'll talk about later. open() accepts a code block, which itself is passed a File object (a Tempfile object to be concise). You can use all regular methods to read from it, and the object has been enriched by a few methods related to the network protocol used such as content_type() or status().

It's also possible to get all the information directly, that is, without passing a code block:

basic_networking/open-uri/read_pragprog2.rb

```ruby
require 'open-uri'

result = open("http://www.pragprog.com")
if result.status[0] == '200'
  lines = result.read.split(/\n/)
  ruby_count = lines.select { |line| line =~ /Ruby/ }.size
  puts "The web site was encoded using #{result.charset}."
  puts "#{ruby_count} lines contain the word 'Ruby'."
else
  puts "We've got an unexpected result: #{result.status.join('/')}"
end
```

And it works for FTP, too:

basic_networking/open-uri/ftp_test.rb

```ruby
require 'open-uri'
require 'digest/md5'

filename = 'ruby-1.8.6-p111.tar.gz'
response = open("ftp://ftp.ruby-lang.org/pub/ruby/1.8/#{filename}")
content = response.read
digest = Digest::MD5.hexdigest(content)
if digest != 'c36e011733a3a3be6f43ba27b7cd7485'
  puts "Wrong digest: #{digest}!"
```

```
else
  puts 'Everything is fine!'
  File.open(filename, 'wb') { |f| f.write(content) }
end
```

This program downloads a certain version of the Ruby interpreter and checks its validity by calculating its MD5 digest and comparing it to the one that is noted on the website. The call to open() does not differ from the HTTP version; we only pass a URL starting with ftp://.

In enterprise applications, you often have to access network resources using proxies. By default *open-uri* considers the content of the environment variables http_proxy, https_proxy, and ftp_proxy. That is, you can use them to specify a proxy for a particular protocol. The following shell command sets your HTTP proxy host to *myproxyhost* and the proxy port to 8080 (run it before starting your program):

```
mschmidt> export http_proxy=http://myproxyhost:8080
```

If you want to disable proxies explicitly, set the :proxy option to nil:

```
response = open('http://www.pragprog.com/', :proxy => nil)
```

When you are trying the examples with Ruby 1.8, you might run into some problems depending on your firewall settings and depending on the URLs you are trying to fetch. *open-uri* is under active development, and Ruby 1.9 brings some new and useful options that fix all these problems. For example, HTTP redirections can be followed automatically now with the :redirect option, and it's possible to specify a timeout with the :read_timeout option. Timeouts are extremely important in an enterprise environment, because a hanging network call can have severe consequences and bring many dependent applications to an unexpected halt. In Ruby 1.9, you can set a timeout of two seconds like this:

```
response = open('http://www.pragprog.com/', :read_timeout => 2)
```

Thanks to the *timeout* module, you can achieve the same result in Ruby 1.8:

basic_networking/open-uri/timeout_test.rb

```
require 'open-uri'
require 'timeout'

begin
  timeout(2) do
    response = open('http://www.pragprog.com')
    puts response.status.join('/')
  end
```

```
rescue Timeout::Error
  puts 'The open call timed out.'
rescue => ex
  puts "An unexpected exception occurred: #{ex}."
end
```

This works for all potentially blocking calls, so in principle *timeout* is a nice tool. But it has a severe bug,[1] so be careful, or use the *terminator* gem[2] instead.

Support for HTTPS has gotten much better, too. In Ruby 1.8, *open-uri* insists on verifying a peer certificate, which is often not what you want if you are writing a one-off script only. At the moment, you actually have to patch *open-uri* to circumvent this. If you are using a more recent version of Ruby already, you can set the :ssl_verify_mode option to OpenSSL::SSL::VERIFY_NONE.

Finally, you can set your FTP connections to passive mode by setting :ftp_active_mode to false.[3] But because it's the new default anyway, you probably won't do that very often.

All in all, *open-uri* is a highly productive tool (especially in recent versions of Ruby), but you have to keep its shortcomings in mind. For example, it supports only GET requests and does not give access to HTTP headers. In Recipe 30, *Get the Most Out of HTTP*, on the next page and Recipe 33, *Use REST Services*, on page 209, you can learn how to overcome these limitations.

---

1. http://headius.blogspot.com/2008/02/rubys-threadraise-threadkill-timeoutrb.html
2. http://codeforpeople.com/lib/ruby/terminator/
3. Read http://slacksite.com/other/ftp.html if you do not know what active and passive modes are.

Get the Most Out of HTTP

You often have to implement clients for services based on HTTP, and you need a library that allows you to control every single aspect of requests, responses, and connections. In this recipe, you'll learn about Net::HTTP, Ruby's standard HTTP client library.

Net::HTTP is the basis of most specialized Ruby network libraries, due to the fact that it belongs to the Ruby standard and has a convenient API. For example, you can use it for quickly sending GET requests and printing their results. The following program prints the HTTP standard to your console (if you have downloaded it, read it; it really contains a bunch of useful information):

`basic_networking/net-http/get_sample.rb`

```ruby
require 'net/http'
Net::HTTP.get_print 'www.ietf.org', '/rfc/rfc2616.txt'
```

Posting form data is easy, too, and in the following program we'll post a request to the publisher's website, search for the term *Enterprise*, and print all links on the result page:

`basic_networking/net-http/enterprise_search.rb`

```ruby
Line 1   require 'net/http'
    -    require 'hpricot'
    -
    -    response = Net::HTTP.post_form(
    5      URI.parse('http://www.pragprog.com/search'),
    -      { 'q' => 'Enterprise' }
    -    )
    -
    -    case response
   10      when Net::HTTPSuccess
    -        puts 'Your search succeeded.'
    -        doc = Hpricot(response.body)
    -        (doc/'//a').each { |a| puts a.attributes['href'] }
    -      when Net::HTTPRedirection
   15        puts "The search form has moved to #{response['location']}."
    -      else
    -        response.error!
    -    end
```

To post a form on the fly, post_form() is an excellent choice. It expects an URI object pointing to the location we'd like to post form data to and a Hash object containing all form parameters we'd like to post (the only parameter we send is named q). All encoding and header issues are handled behind the scenes, and we get back a Net::HTTPResponse object.

To be concise, we get back an object whose class has been derived from Net::HTTPResponse, because that's how Net::HTTP indicates the response status. We check the status beginning in line 9, and if everything went fine—that is, if response is an instance of Net::HTTPSuccess—we parse the response's body and print all the links it contains. If you do not understand how we extract all anchor tags using *Hpricot*, take a look at Recipe 25, *Work with HTML and Microformats*, on page 159.

If our request has been redirected, we print its new location (HTTP header elements can be accessed with the response object's []() operator), and if we have an error, we print an error message and raise an exception using error!().

That's all nice, but if you need to just quickly download a document or post some form data, you could also use *open-uri* (see Recipe 29, *Find Solutions Quickly with open-uri*, on page 183) or *WWW::Mechanize* (see Recipe 31, *Scrape Screens with WWW::Mechanize*, on page 193). They are even slightly more convenient, so we will concentrate on the more advanced features of Net::HTTP.

Net::HTTP is a good choice if you need full-blown support for HTTPS, such as if you have to control aspects such as timeouts and proxies or if you need some of the more esoteric features of HTTP such as the OPTIONS or TRACE verbs. In Net::HTTP, every HTTP verb is represented by its own class; you can create an object representing a certain HTTP command and initialize it step-by-step. The first example in this recipe could be rewritten as follows:

```
basic_networking/net-http/get_sample2.rb
```

```
Line 1  require 'net/http'

        url = URI.parse('http://www.ietf.org/rfc/rfc2616.txt')
        request = Net::HTTP::Get.new(url.path)
     5  response = Net::HTTP.start(url.host, url.port) do |http|
          http.request(request)
        end
        puts response.body
```

You might ask yourself why you should use a more complicated solution, but believe me: we're building up to something. In line 4, we create a Net::HTTP::Get object representing a GET request. We do not send it immediately and could still set some request headers, for example. Then we start an HTTP connection, and in line 6, we eventually send the request to the server. At the end, we print the response's body, and we're done.

The representation of HTTP commands as classes is one of the most interesting features of Net::HTTP, because it makes the library highly extensible. Right now it already implements HTTP and WebDAV,[4] but you can easily add new verbs. For example, you could write a library for CalDAV.[5] Both WebDAV and CalDAV are HTTP extensions; in other words, they add new verbs to the regular set of GET, POST, and so on. For example, CalDAV adds MKCALENDAR that can be used to create new calendars on a central web server.

We'll start small and will implement a new HTTP command only for demonstration purposes. Our command is named UNDO, and it could be used to undo changes that happened to a particular web resource.

First we implement an HTTP server that supports an UNDO command:

basic_networking/net-http/undo.rb

```ruby
require 'webrick'
include WEBrick

class UndoServlet < HTTPServlet::AbstractServlet
  def do_UNDO(request, response)
    response.status = 200
    response.body = "Changes to #{request.path} have been undone.\n"
  end
end

server = HTTPServer.new(:Port => 4200)
server.mount('/', UndoServlet)
%w(INT TERM).each do |signal|
  trap(signal) { server.shutdown }
end
server.start
```

Yes, that's all. Instead of GET or POST, our web server supports only UNDO. It does not actually do anything, but if you start it, you can send it an UNDO command and get a response.

---

4.   http://www.webdav.org/specs/rfc4918.html

5.   http://www.webdav.org/specs/rfc4791.html

```
mschmidt> telnet localhost 4200
```

⇒
```
Trying ::1...
Connected to localhost.
Escape character is '^]'.
```
⇐   **UNDO /resource HTTP/1.0**
⇒

```
HTTP/1.1 200 OK
Connection: close
Content-Length: 39

Changes to /resource have been undone.
Connection closed by foreign host.
```

OK, the server is working fine, but we are interested in a client for our completely proprietary HTTP extension. Here it is:

basic_networking/net-http/undo_client.rb

```ruby
Line 1  require 'net/http'

        module Net
          class HTTP
    5       class Undo < HTTPRequest
              METHOD = 'UNDO'
              REQUEST_HAS_BODY = false
              RESPONSE_HAS_BODY = true
            end
    10    end
        end

        url = URI.parse('http://localhost:4200/my-resource')
        request = Net::HTTP::Undo.new(url.path)
    15  response = Net::HTTP.new(url.host, url.port).start do |http|
          http.request(request)
        end

        case response
    20    when Net::HTTPSuccess
            puts response.body
          else
            response.error!
        end
```

Lines 3 to 11 contain everything we need to define the UNDO command. We set its name, and we determine whether the request and/or response carries data in the body. That's all we have to do, and if you think about it, everything makes sense. HTTP defines a tight framework where the requests and responses of new commands can have a body or not, but everything else is fixed.

Alternative HTTP Client Libraries

Net::HTTP is probably the most popular HTTP client library, because it belongs to Ruby's standard distribution and has a nice, clean interface. But it also lacks some important features, and for some purposes it's not as convenient as it could be. You can choose from several alternative libraries:

- *HttpClient** supports cookies, digest authentication, automatic redirections, asynchronous requests, and much more.

- *RFuzz*† was developed mainly to test HTTP services. It gives you a lot of control over even the tiniest details, and it's extremely fast. It has rudimentary cookie support and can be extended easily.

- *WWW::Mechanize*‡ helps automate typical website interactions and makes it possible to script user interactions. It is covered in Recipe 31, *Scrape Screens with WWW::Mechanize*, on page 193.

---

*.   http://dev.ctor.org/http-access2/
†.   http://rfuzz.rubyforge.org/
‡.   http://mechanize.rubyforge.org/

In line 14, we create our new command for the first time, and the rest of the program looks like our previous examples, which is exactly what we wanted. We have just invented a new HTTP command, and its usage does not differ from any of the standard commands.

UNDO is certainly a command you'd like to protect using basic authentication, and maybe your server can be accessed only via HTTPS and through a proxy? No problem, the following program has it all:

`basic_networking/net-http/undo_client_safe.rb`

```
require 'net/https'
proxy = Net::HTTP::Proxy(
  proxy_host, proxy_port, proxy_user, proxy_pass
)
connection = proxy.new('localhost', 4200)
connection.use_ssl = true
connection.verify_mode = OpenSSL::SSL::VERIFY_NONE
request = Net::HTTP::Undo.new('/my-resource')
request.basic_auth 'maik', 't0p$secret'
response = connection.request(request)
puts response.body
```

Instead of creating a connection directly, we create a Proxy object first and use it to create a connection in line 5 (if the proxy host is nil, you'll get back a regular connection). Then we put the connection into SSL mode and tell it to not verify certificates. We create a new Undo request object (our example works for all other HTTP commands as well), and in line 9, we set the username and password for HTTP basic authentication. Finally, we send the request and print the response's body.

There are a lot of convenience libraries out there dealing with protocols based on HTTP such as XML-RPC or SOAP. If you're working with these protocols, you should use specialized libraries. But if you need access to every single detail of HTTP, you should consider using Net::HTTP. It allows you to start small and grow with your needs.

Also See

- See Recipe 5, *Create Strong and Convenient Passwords*, on page 23 if you need to know how to verify certificates.

Scrape Screens with WWW::Mechanize

Today many websites are applications too, but their interfaces usually consist of a bunch of HTML pages, which rarely can be processed easily by other applications. The situation is getting better and better, with more new web applications offering both an HTML interface and a REST interface, but there are still countless interesting applications that you cannot use out of the box.

And wouldn't it also be nice if you could test your legacy web applications automatically just as you test your new and shiny Rails applications? Maybe there's a website whose content you'd like to use in a totally different context but it's hidden in the gory details of some HTML pages. Or maybe you want to add an RSS feed to a site that doesn't have one.

Screen scraping[6] is a technology that deals with exactly these problems, and in this recipe you'll learn how to control websites with Ruby.

- Install *WWW::Mechanize*,[7] a screen-scraping library:

  ```
  $ gem install mechanize
  ```

In the beginning it's easy to download web pages programmatically using an arbitrary HTTP client and to "parse" HTML pages using spiffy regular expressions. Sooner or later you'll realize this approach does not scale well and is overly fragile. You'll quickly have to deal with cookies, with session IDs, and with subtle changes in the HTML pages on a daily basis. It will pay off quickly to use a grown-up solution from the

---

6. http://en.wikipedia.org/wiki/Screen_scraping
7. http://mechanize.rubyforge.org/

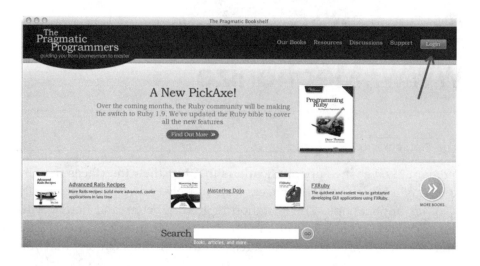

Figure 6.1: PRAGMATIC BOOKSHELF HOME PAGE

beginning. Ruby programmers can use *WWW::Mechanize*, which is not only powerful but also convenient. *WWW::Mechanize* is a library that was built to automate the interaction with websites. Instead of clicking a link on a website manually, you tell *WWW::Mechanize* to do it and get back the resulting page. *WWW::Mechanize* takes care of all details such as cookie handling, redirections, and so on.

As a first exercise, we will visit the publisher's website,[8] log in to the shop, and look how often the words *Ruby* and *Rails* are mentioned on the welcome page. To do that with a regular web browser, you have to point it to the website and click the "Login" button (see it in Figure 6.1). Then you are transferred to a page containing the login form you can see in Figure 6.2, on the next page (secured by SSL, of course). By inspecting the page's source code, you can see how the different elements of the form are named. The email field is named email, the password field is named password, and the checkbox's name is remember_me. Input your credentials (you are a registered customer already, aren't you?), then click the "Login" button, and you'll be directed to the welcome page.

---

8. http://www.pragprog.com/

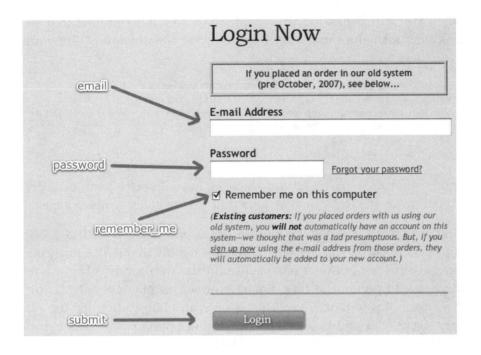

Figure 6.2: PRAGMATIC BOOKSHELF LOGIN FORM

Now that we have explained what we want to do in epic prose, let's take
a look at the Ruby solution:

`basic_networking/screen-scraping/pp_login.rb`

```
Line 1  require 'logger'
        require 'mechanize'

        agent = WWW::Mechanize.new { |a| a.log = Logger.new('scrape.log') }
     5  agent.user_agent_alias = 'Mac Safari'
        page = agent.get('http://www.pragprog.com')
        page = agent.click page.links.text('Login')

        login_form = page.forms.first
    10  login_form.email = ARGV[0]
        login_form.password = ARGV[1]
        agent.log.debug "Logging in with email address #{ARGV[0]}."
        login_form.checkboxes.name('remember_me').check
        page = agent.submit(login_form, login_form.buttons.first)
    15
        page.links.each { |link| puts link.text if link.text =~ /Ruby|Rails/ }
        agent.click page.links.text('Log Out')
```

When you run it passing your credentials, you'll get output that will look like this (yours may vary depending on the amount of Ruby and Rails links on your welcome page):

```
mschmidt> ruby pp_login.rb you@example.com t0p$ecret
Advanced Rails Recipes: 72 New Ways to Build Stunning Rails Apps
Agile Web Development with Rails: Second Edition
Agile Web Development with Rails, 1st Edition
Rails for PHP Developers
Payment Processing with PayPal and Ruby
```

That's amazing, isn't it? All the steps we have described can be represented by simple Ruby instructions that we are going to dissect now.

First we create a *WWW::Mechanize* agent, providing it with a Logger object. Our client will log all interesting details about the forthcoming conversation between our client and the web server. Then we tell the agent to pretend to be a Safari browser on Mac OS X by setting user_agent_alias to Mac Safari. This is only an abbreviation for the real user agent that will be sent; a mapping of popular browsers can be found in WWW::Mechanize::AGENT_ALIASES.

In line 6, we tell our client to read the Pragmatic Programmer's home page by calling get(). This method call actually does a lot: it requests the page specified by our URL, it automatically follows redirections (no matter whether the new target location is accessed via HTTP or HTTPS), it handles cookies, and it parses the HTML page we get back using *Hpricot* (see Recipe 25, *Work with HTML and Microformats*, on page 159 to learn more about it).

Then we simulate a click on the link named "Login" to get to the login page. All links that *WWW::Mechanize* could find are stored in an attribute named links. You can treat it as an array, but you can look up links by name as well by using text(). Here we have some magic again, because the definition of the link we are clicking looks as follows:

```
<a href="http://www.pragprog.com/login/" class="login-button">
  <img alt="Login" height="27"
      src="http://www.pragprog.com/images/login-button.gif?12037268"
      title="" width="72" />
</a>
```

The link referring to the login page does not have a name, because it is a button represented by an image. But we still can refer to it by the name "Login," because *WWW::Mechanize* is clever enough to get the text from the <*img*> tag's alt= attribute.

Corresponding to the links attribute there is a forms attribute containing all forms of an HTML page. From inspecting the page's source code, we know that the login form is the first one, so we obtain a reference to it in line 9. *WWW::Mechanize* automatically turns all form members into attributes, so text and password fields can be initialized by setting the appropriate members of the form. Checkboxes are treated differently, and we activate the remember_me checkbox using the check() method in line 13 (you can uncheck it with uncheck(), and you can toggle its status with click()).

In line 12, we demonstrate how to write custom messages to the log file, which is possible but rarely needed, because *WWW::Mechanize* writes a lot of useful information itself. For example, the log file contains all request and response headers, all cookies and their values, all redirections, and so on.

Eventually, we submit the form using submit(), passing it the form and the button we'd like to click, and we get back the shop's welcome page. We iterate over all links in the page, print their text, and as good citizens log out.

WWW::Mechanize comes with many more useful options that are especially important in enterprise environments. For example, the following program sets the timeout for opening a connection to two seconds and the timeout for reading from a connection to five seconds. In addition, it specifies a proxy server including the username and password.

basic_networking/screen-scraping/mechanize_options.rb

```
agent = WWW::Mechanize.new
agent.open_timeout = 2
agent.read_timeout = 5
agent.set_proxy('myproxy', 8080, 'proxy_user', 'proxy_password')
```

Another interesting feature is that the agent remembers all pages it has visited in an internal history. For example, you can use visited?() to check whether a certain URL has been visited already, and you can use visited_page() to get a page you have seen before:

basic_networking/screen-scraping/crawler.rb

```
agent = WWW::Mechanize.new
index_page = 'http://www.pragprog.com'
page = agent.get(index_page)
puts agent.visited?(index_page)          # -> true
puts agent.visited_page(index_page).title # -> The Pragmatic Bookshelf
```

It gets even better: *WWW::Mechanize* supports transactions; that is, you can visit a page, then follow some links on it in a separate transaction, and finally return to your starting point as if nothing happened. The following script visits the publisher's home page, follows all links that have the word *titles* in it (these are the links that point to a book's page), and prints their title:

`basic_networking/screen-scraping/crawler.rb`

```
Line 1   class LinkCrawler < WWW::Mechanize
  -        def process
  -          home_page = get 'http://www.pragprog.com'
  -          home_page.links.with.href(/titles/).each do |link|
  5            begin
  -              transact do
  -                book_page = click link
  -                # Now we are on a new page.
  -                print book_page.title
  10             end
  -              # We are on the home page again.
  -            rescue => ex
  -              puts ex
  -            end
  15            puts " (#{visited?(link.href)})"
  -          end
  -        end
  -      end
  -
  20   LinkCrawler.new.process
```

For the first time we've created a class for our web agent that is derived from *WWW::Mechanize*. This allows us to use all methods directly, which results in really beautiful code. Look at line 4, for example, where we iterate over all links containing the word *titles*. Isn't that lyrical? *Hpricot* makes this possible.

When you run this script, it will probably visit some links more than once, so it prints the title of some books more than once, too. That's because on the home page every book is typically linked more than once ("Don't Repeat Yourself, eh?"). You might ask whether we could prevent this by using visited?(). You have to keep in mind that our visit runs in a transaction, and because the agent's history will be reset after the transaction is over, the agent will not remember that we have followed a particular link already. Hence, visited?() will always return false.

There are many more powerful features in *WWW::Mechanize* we cannot cover in this short recipe. You should have learned that screen scraping is an useful technique and that it can be easily implemented in Ruby.

Chapter 7

Use and Build Web Services

Web services are an exciting technology and have a lot of advantages over more traditional application architectures. Suddenly you can build great mashups and connect applications in ways no one would have thought of a few years ago.

But why should you care about them when writing enterprise software? Well, the term *web services* is a bit misleading. You are not limited to the Web when you want to use and implement them. They use only standard web technology, and their underlying protocols are exactly what you need when implementing a *service-oriented architecture* (SOA) in a modern enterprise infrastructure.

Simply put, you can choose between two different architectures today: Representational State Transfer (REST) and SOAP. There are a lot of flame wars raging on the Internet about which way is superior, but in this book we will not take sides and will follow a more pragmatic approach. We use whatever makes our life easier, because Ruby and Rails have excellent support for both SOAP and REST.

You'll learn how to build your own REST services using Rails in record time in Recipe 32, *Publish Resources with REST*, on page 201, and Recipe 33, *Use REST Services*, on page 209 shows you how to manipulate resources with Ruby.

We use *soap4r* below in Recipe 34, *Build Your Own SOAP Services*, on page 215 to implement a pure Ruby SOAP server, and in Recipe 35, *Use SOAP Services with WSDL*, on page 219 you'll learn how to access such a server if you have a description of its interface written in WSDL.

Publish Resources with REST

Problem

You want to expose some of your company's applications as REST services, because they need only a minimal set of infrastructural overhead and can be used by all clients that have access to an HTTP library. In addition, you can quickly add an HTML user interface to them if you need one.

In this recipe, you'll learn how to build such services using the Rails framework.

Solution

Let's say your company has access to an SMS gateway but its interface is somewhat complicated, so you decide to hide it behind a REST interface. Not only will the service send the SMS, but it will also store it in a database. Consequently, it provides endpoints for reading messages, but it does not allow you to update or delete them.

We'll build the service in several steps, and before we write any RESTful code, we design the resources, their representations, and their URIs. Then we build the server, and finally we write a small test client.

The REST service can be used by different applications that we call *mandators*. Every mandator has a name and a message limit that defines how many messages it is allowed to send in a certain period of time (-1 means "no limit"). Mandators are represented in the database as follows:

`web_services/rest/rest-sample/db/migrate/001_create_mandators.rb`

```ruby
create_table :mandators do |t|
  t.column :name,          :string
  t.column :message_limit, :int
  t.timestamps
end
```

In addition, we need an XML representation of our mandator resource. The following document describes a mandator named "Application Monitor" that is currently not allowed to send any messages:

`web_services/rest/mandator.xml`

```xml
<mandator name='Application Monitor' message_limit='0'/>
```

HTTP Verb	URI	Action
GET	/message-service/mandators	index
GET	/message-service/mandators/{mandatorname}	show
POST	/message-service/mandators	create
PUT	/message-service/mandators/{mandatorname}	update
DELETE	/message-service/mandators/{mandatorname}	destroy

Figure 7.1: MAPPING REST RESOURCES TO ACTIONS

To manipulate mandators "the REST way," we have to write an application that responds to certain combinations of HTTP commands and URIs that we have listed in Figure 7.1 (variable URI components are set in curly braces).

A DELETE command should be mapped to a destroy() action, a POST command should be mapped to create(), and so on. Wouldn't it be great if we could automatically map these commands to the actions of a class named, let's say, MandatorsController? You guessed it already: Rails has a mechanism to do this:

```
web_services/rest/rest-sample/config/routes.rb
```

```
Line 1   ActionController::Routing::Routes.draw do |map|
   -        base = '/message-service'
   -        map.resources :mandators, :path_prefix => base
   -        map.resources :messages,
   5                    :path_prefix => base + '/mandators/:mandatorname'
   -      end
```

This configuration maps HTTP commands to methods of class MandatorsController as we have defined them in Figure 7.1. If, for example, we get a DELETE request pointing to /message-service/mandators/billing, the destroy() action gets invoked, and params[:id] contains billing. In this context, id is quite a misnomer, but that's Rails' standard behavior, because in Rails resource URIs typically contain the primary keys of all resources involved. For example, instead of using a name such as billing to identify a mandator, you would use a number such as 42. You'll find readable resource names a much better style to use, so we'll create an application that supports readable resource names. In line 4, we define how our message resources are represented, but you can safely ignore this for now.

After this little preparation, we can implement the create() method of our controller that gets invoked for POST requests and creates a new mandator resource:

web_services/rest/rest-sample/app/controllers/mandators_controller.rb

```
Line 1   class MandatorsController < ApplicationController
           skip_before_filter :verify_authenticity_token

           # POST /message-service/mandators
      5    def create
             mandator = Mandator.find_or_create_by_name(
               :name => params[:mandator][:name],
               :message_limit => params[:mandator][:message_limit]
             )
     10      headers[:location] = mandator_path(mandator)
             render :nothing => true, :status => '201 Created'
           end
         end
```

Before we do anything else, we disable the verify_authenticity_token filter in line 2, which is used to prevent cross-site request forgery.[1] In our internal application, we don't need it, and in fact it would make life a bit more complicated, because we had to authenticate ourselves when using most of the HTTP commands.

REST services should be *idempotent*; that is, if a client tries to create a resource that already exists, it gets back a URL pointing to the existing resource. That's why we use the find_or_create_by_name() method to create a new mandator resource.

In line 7, we profit again from some Rails magic. Although we have sent an XML document to our action, we do not have to parse it explicitly. Rails has already done this for us and converted the document into a hash using XmlSimple (see Recipe 21, *XML Data Binding on Steroids*, on page 135). If you absolutely want to parse the request body yourself, you can get it by calling request.body.read.

After we have stored the new mandator in the database, we set the location header in line 10 so that our clients know how to reference the newly created resource. To build the resource URI, we use mandator_path(), which has been generated by Rails behind the scenes. We have to pass it only the variable part of our resource URI, and it returns the complete URI. Please note that we do not check whether a mandator already exists before we create it. We can safely send the same XML document twice, which is the valid behavior for a REST service, and

---

1. http://en.wikipedia.org/wiki/Cross-site_request_forgery

it's called *idempotence* (to be honest, we should have checked that all attributes of the new resource are equal—not only the name but also the message limit).

Finally, we can add our application monitor to the list of mandators by posting its XML representation to our application:

```
mschmidt> curl -i -d@mandator.xml \
> -H 'content-type: application/xml' \
> http://localhost:3000/message-service/mandators
HTTP/1.1 201 Created
location: /message-service/mandators/Application%20Monitor
```

We have skipped most of the HTTP headers for brevity, but you can see that the status code and the location header have been set correctly. On the request side, it's important to set the right content-type header. By the way, if you've ever asked yourself when to use application/xml for the content-type header and when to use text/xml, you should take a look at the official W3C standard.[2]

When working with resources, you always have to be prepared for missing resources, too. The REST way of telling your client that something is missing is to send back the HTTP status code 404. Because we need this often, we add a new method to the ApplicationController:

web_services/rest/rest-sample/app/controllers/application.rb

```
class ApplicationController
  def if_found(obj)
    if obj
      yield
    else
      render :text => 'Not found.', :status => '404 Not Found'
      false
    end
  end
end
```

Adding the missing methods to MandatorsController is easy:

web_services/rest/rest-sample/app/controllers/mandators_controller.rb

```
Line 1  class MandatorsController
   -      # GET /message-service/mandators
   -      def index
   -        mandators = Mandator.find(:all)
   5        if_found(mandators) { render :xml => mandators.to_xml }
   -      end
```

---

2. http://www.w3.org/TR/xhtml-media-types/

```
       # GET /message-service/mandators/{mandatorname}
       def show
10       mandator = Mandator.find_by_name(params[:id])
         if_found(mandator) { render :xml => mandator.to_xml }
       end

       # PUT /message-service/mandators/{mandatorname}
15     def update
         mandator = Mandator.find_by_name(params[:id])
         if_found mandator do
           current_name = mandator.name
           attributes = {
20           :name => params[:mandator][:name],
             :message_limit => params[:mandator][:message_limit]
           }
           if mandator.update_attributes(attributes)
             if mandator.name == current_name
25             render :nothing => true, :status => '200 OK'
             else
               headers[:location] = mandator_path(mandator)
               render :nothing => true,
                       :status => '301 Moved Permanently'
30           end
           else
             render :xml => mandator.errors.to_xml,
                     :status => '400 Bad Request'
           end
35       end
       end

       # DELETE /message-service/mandators/{mandatorname}
       def destroy
40       mandator = Mandator.find_by_name(params[:id])
         if_found mandator do
           mandator.messages.each { |m| m.destroy }
           mandator.destroy
           render :nothing => true, :status => '200 OK'
45       end
       end
     end
```

Rails takes care of all the technical details; it routes incoming requests
to the right action, but it's still the application's task to adhere to the
REST principles. For example, we send back a 404 status code whenever a resource is missing, and we send back a 301 (Moved Permanently)
when a mandator is renamed in line 28.

We use ActiveRecord's to_xml() method to convert database objects into
XML strings, but usually, this method does not return what you want,
so you are better off overwriting it in your model class.

```
web_services/rest/rest-sample/app/models/mandator.rb
```

```ruby
class Mandator < ActiveRecord::Base
  has_many :messages
  validates_uniqueness_of :name

  def to_xml(options = {})
    options[:indent] ||= 2
    xml = options[:builder] ||= Builder::XmlMarkup.new(
      :indent => options[:indent]
    )
    xml.instruct! unless options[:skip_instruct]
    xml.mandator(
      'name' => self.name,
      'message_limit' => self.message_limit
    )
  end
end
```

We are done with the mandator resource, so now it's time to take care of the messages we'd like to send and store. In the database they look as follows:

```
web_services/rest/rest-sample/db/migrate/002_create_messages.rb
```

```ruby
create_table :messages do |t|
  t.column :mandator_id, :int
  t.column :sender,      :string
  t.column :receiver,    :string
  t.column :content,     :string
  t.column :status,      :string, :default => 'in-transmission'
  t.timestamps
end
```

And as XML documents they look like this:

```
web_services/rest/message.xml
```

```xml
<message created-at='2008-10-18T13:40:00'>
  <sender phone-number='12345678'/>
  <receiver phone-number='987654321'/>
  <content>Hello, world!</content>
</message>
```

We have defined the routing for this resource already in the routes.rb file at the beginning of this recipe. The MessagesController class will look similar to the MandatorsController class. Most of its method depend on the existence of a mandator in the database. Hence, we add a method to ApplicationController that makes sure we get a valid mandator reference with every request and that loads the referenced mandator from the database.

web_services/rest/rest-sample/app/controllers/application.rb

```ruby
class ApplicationController
  def must_specify_mandator
    if params[:mandatorname]
      @mandator = Mandator.find_by_name(params[:mandatorname])
      if_found(@mandator) { params[:mandator_id] = @mandator.id }
      return false unless @mandator
    end
    true
  end
end
```

We will install must_specify_mandator() using before_filter(), so it's easy to implement the missing methods:

web_services/rest/rest-sample/app/controllers/messages_controller.rb

```ruby
Line 1  class MessagesController < ApplicationController
   -      skip_before_filter :verify_authenticity_token
   -      before_filter :must_specify_mandator
   -
   5      # GET /message-service/{mandatorname}/messages
   -      def index
   -        messages = @mandator.messages
   -        messages = nil if messages.empty?
   -        if_found(messages) { render :xml => messages.to_xml }
  10      end
   -
   -      # GET /message-service/{mandatorname}/messages/{id}
   -      def show
   -        message = Message.find(params[:id])
  15        if_found(message) { render :xml => message.to_xml }
   -      end
   -
   -      # POST /message-service/{mandatorname}/messages
   -      def create
  20        limit = @mandator.message_limit
   -        if limit != -1 and @mandator.messages.size >= limit
   -          render :nothing => true, :status => '400 Bad Request'
   -        else
   -          sms = params[:message]
  25          status = send_message(sms)
   -          message = Message.create(
   -            :mandator => @mandator,
   -            :receiver => sms[:receiver][:phone_number],
   -            :sender   => sms[:sender][:phone_number],
  30            :content  => sms[:content],
   -            :status   => status
   -          )
   -          headers[:location] = message_path(@mandator.name, message)
   -          render :nothing => true, :status => '201 Created'
  35        end
   -      end
   -
```

```
     def update
       render :nothing => true, :status => '405 Method Not Allowed'
40   end

     def destroy
       render :nothing => true, :status => '405 Method Not Allowed'
     end
45
     private

     def send_message(sms)
       # Add your code to send short messages here.
50     'in-transmission'
     end
   end
```

There are not many unusual things in the controller. The most complex method is create(), but that's mainly because we store several attributes and because we check whether a mandator's message limit has been exceeded. From a technical point of view, line 33 is interesting. Here we create a resource URI comprising two variable parts: a mandator name and a message identifier.

It's not allowed to update or delete messages, so we send back the HTTP status code 405 (Method Not Allowed) when update() or destroy() is called.

In this recipe we have implemented a REST service for nontrivial nested resources that have readable URIs that can be manipulated by various HTTP commands. Our service sends back reasonable status codes and strictly adheres to the HTTP standard. Using Rails we could follow a step-by-step approach—that is, we could develop the service incrementally for every URI and for every HTTP command that should be supported. Take a look at *RESTful Web Services* [RR07] if you want to learn more about REST.

Use REST Services

Problem

REST services are becoming more and more popular on the Web and in enterprise infrastructures, so it's a good idea to learn how to use them from your Ruby application.

In this recipe, we'll develop a client library for the short message service we built in Recipe 32, *Publish Resources with REST*, on page 201. All its commands and their resources are listed in Figure 7.1, on page 202, and our client will fully support all methods related to the manipulation of mandators. As you probably remember, all applications that want to use the message service have to register as a mandator, which is characterized by its name and a message limit that determines how many messages it is allowed to send in a certain period of time.

Ingredients

• Install the *rufus-verbs*[3] gem:

```
$ gem install rufus-verbs
```

Solution

Before you manipulate resources on a server, it's always a good idea to implement a local resource abstraction yourself. Here's ours:

`web_services/rest/mandator.rb`

```ruby
require 'rexml/document'

class Mandator
  attr_accessor :name, :message_limit

  def initialize(name, message_limit)
    @name, @message_limit = name, message_limit
  end

  def to_s
    "#{@name}: #{@message_limit}"
  end

  def to_xml
```

---

3. http://rufus.rubyforge.org/rufus-verbs/

```
      doc = REXML::Document.new
      doc.add_element('mandator',
        'name' => @name, 'message_limit' => @message_limit
      )
      xml_string = ''
      doc.write(xml_string)
      xml_string
    end

    def Mandator.from_xml(xml_string)
      mandators = []
      doc = REXML::Document.new(xml_string)
      doc.each_element('//mandator') do |element|
        mandators << Mandator.new(
          element.attributes['name'],
          element.attributes['message_limit']
        )
      end
      mandators
    end
  end
end
```

That's all we need to represent a mandator and to map it to XML documents, and vice versa (learn more about XML processing in Chapter 5,
Process XML Documents the Ruby Way, on page 133). Such documents
look like this:

web_services/rest/mandator.xml

```
<mandator name='Application Monitor' message_limit='0'/>
```

Now we can start to implement the REST client. All RESTful web services are based on HTTP, and in principle you can use them with any
library that supports all HTTP commands such as Net::HTTP. But there
are more convenient solutions that support caching, automatic com-
pression, and other nice things, for example. One of them is *rufus-verbs*,
and we use it as follows:

web_services/rest/message_service_rufus.rb

```
Line 1  require 'rubygems'
     -  require 'rufus/verbs'
     -  require 'uri'
     -  require 'mandator'
     5
     -  include Rufus::Verbs
     -
     -  class MessageService
     -    def initialize(host, port)
    10      @base_url = "http://#{host}:#{port}/message-service"
     -    end
```

```
      def get_mandators
        response = get "#{@base_url}/mandators"
15      return [] if response.code.to_i == 404
        assert_response_code(response, 200)
        Mandator.from_xml(response.body)
      end

20    def get_mandator(mandatorname)
        response = get mandator_path(mandatorname)
        return nil if response.code.to_i == 404
        assert_response_code(response, 200)
        Mandator.from_xml(response.body).first
25    end

      def mandator_path(mandatorname)
        "#{@base_url}/mandators/#{URI.encode(mandatorname)}"
      end
30
      def assert_response_code(response, code)
        if response.code.to_i != code
          raise "Got unexpected response code: #{response.code}"
        end
35    end
    end
```

In initialize(), we determine the base URL needed to identify all the resources we'd like to manipulate. Then in get_mandators(), we actually access the REST service for the first time. In line 14, we send a GET request and get back the expected response. The method we call is actually named get(), because Rufus::Verbs defines a method for all HTTP commands. These methods return an object that has been derived from Net::HTTPResponse, because under the hood Rufus::Verbs uses Net::HTTP.

If no mandators could be found (we get back the HTTP status 404), we return an empty array. Otherwise, we make sure we've gotten the status code 200 and then convert the response body into an array of Mandator objects. Because we often have to check for a certain HTTP status, we have added the assert_response_code() method. It checks whether we have gotten a particular status code and raises an exception if we haven't.

get_mandator() works similarly; the only thing worth noting is a little convenience method named mandator_path(), which creates a resource identifier for a mandator that has a particular name. We can thus use our client to get a list of all mandators or to get a mandator with a certain name.

```
web_services/rest/message_service_rufus.rb
```

```ruby
service = MessageService.new('localhost', 3000)
service.get_mandators.each { |m| puts m }
puts service.get_mandator('foo')
```

We still have to add methods that actually create and modify resources on the server, but adding the missing functionality is easy, because *rufus-verbs* also implements a put() method, a post() method, and a delete() method:

```
web_services/rest/message_service_rufus.rb
```

```ruby
Line 1  class MessageService
    -     XML_TYPE = 'application/xml'
    -
    -     def create_mandator(mandator)
    5       response = post("#{@base_url}/mandators") do |req|
    -         req['content-type'] = XML_TYPE
    -         mandator.to_xml
    -       end
    -       assert_response_code(response, 201)
   10       response['location']
    -     end
    -
    -     def update_mandator(mandatorname, mandator)
    -       options = { :no_redirections => true }
   15       response = put(mandator_path(mandatorname), options) do |req|
    -         req['content-type'] = XML_TYPE
    -         mandator.to_xml
    -       end
    -       if !([200, 301].include?(response.code.to_i))
   20         raise "Could not update mandator: #{response.code}"
    -       end
    -     end
    -
    -     def delete_mandator(mandatorname)
   25       response = delete(mandator_path(mandatorname)) do |req|
    -         req['content-type'] = XML_TYPE
    -       end
    -       assert_response_code(response, 200)
    -     end
   30   end
```

All these methods accept a code block that gets passed the current request object (it's an instance of class Net::HTTPRequest), so we can set the right content-type header before sending the request to the server. The content that's eventually sent is the value returned by the code block.

The rest is business as usual; in other words, we check the status code of the response and raise an exception wherever it is appropriate.

Line 14 is a bit more interesting, because there we set the no_redirections option to true. The reason for this is simple: by default, *rufus-verbs* follows redirects, and when updating a mandator resource, it might well happen that we get back a 301 status (Moved Permanently) (such as if we change its name). Setting no_redirections prevents our client from following such a redirection. Here you can see how to use it:

web_services/rest/message_service_rufus.rb

```
service = MessageService.new('localhost', 3000)

# Create a new mandator named 'foo'.
mandator = Mandator.new('foo', 42)
service.create_mandator(mandator)
puts service.get_mandator('foo')

# Change the mandator's message limit to 1,000.
mandator.message_limit = 1000
service.update_mandator('foo', mandator)
puts service.get_mandator('foo')

# Change the mandator's name to 'bar'.
mandator.name = 'bar'
service.update_mandator('foo', mandator)
puts service.get_mandator('foo') # Does no longer exist!
puts service.get_mandator('bar')
```

That's it! We have written a client for our REST service that handles all possible return codes and even comes with a class that deals with the whole XML serialization in fewer than 100 lines of code.

Alternative REST Client Libraries

REST is a popular technology among Ruby programmers, so it should come as no surprise that more than one client library exists. *rest-client*[4] and *HTTParty*[5] are interesting products, for example.

rest-open-uri[6] is interesting, too, because it adds some code to Ruby's *open-uri* library (see Recipe 29, *Find Solutions Quickly with open-uri*, on page 183 for more details) and turns it into a full-blown REST client

---

4. http://rest-client.heroku.com/
5. http://httparty.rubyforge.org/
6. http://rest-open-uri.rubyforge.org/

library. Here's an alternative implementation of the get_mandators() and create_mandator() methods using *rest-open-uri*:

`web_services/rest/message_service_rest_uri.rb`

```
Line 1   def get_mandators
    -       response = nil
    -       begin
    -         response = open "#{@base_url}/mandators"
    5       rescue OpenURI::HTTPError => ex
    -         return [] if ex.message =~ /^404/
    -       end
    -       assert_response_code(response, 200)
    -       Mandator.from_xml(response.read)
    10   end
    -
    -   def create_mandator(mandator)
    -       response = open(
    -         "#{@base_url}/mandators",
    15        :method => :post,
    -         :body => mandator.to_xml,
    -         'content-type' => XML_TYPE
    -       )
    -       assert_response_code(response, 201)
    20      response.meta['location']
    -   end
    -
    -   def assert_response_code(response, code)
    -       if response.status[0].to_i != code
    25        raise "Got unexpected response code: #{response.code}"
    -       end
    -   end
```

As you can see, there are only a few subtle differences. *rest-open-uri* raises an exception whenever a resource cannot be found, so we have to check for this condition explicitly in line 5. Instead of defining a method for each HTTP command, the open() method accepts a :method option that we set to POST in line 15.

Handling responses is slightly different. The objects that are returned by open() have a property named meta that contains meta-information such as response headers. We use it in line 20 to get the location header. To get the HTTP status of a response, we have to use the status attribute, a two-element array. The first element contains the status code, and the second element contains the status message.

Also See

- Read Recipe 32, *Publish Resources with REST*, on page 201 first to learn how to create REST services.

Build Your Own SOAP Services

For big companies it's often a problem to define services and interfaces in a standardized manner. SOAP addresses this problem (and solves others too), and Ruby is an excellent platform for rapidly developing new services.

Perhaps many applications in your company need to verify bank accounts. This is a nontrivial task, because nearly every banking institution uses its own proprietary algorithm to generate new account numbers. You decided to pay for an external web service that provides this functionality. It expects the bank identification code (BIC) and the international bank account number (IBAN) of the bank account to be checked (despite its full-bodied name, the IBAN is currently limited to European countries). It returns the verification result (true or false) and the name of the bank belonging to the BIC. If the BIC is invalid, the name will be empty.

In this recipe, we build a bank account verification service based on SOAP that has the interface described earlier.

- Since Ruby 1.9, *soap4r*[7] is no longer part of Ruby's standard library and has to be installed as a gem:

```
$ gem install soap4r
```

Instead of tying each application directly to the service, we'd like to implement a SOAP service that hides its interface. This way, we have to implement it only once, all clients can access it in standardized manner, and if the external services' interface changes someday, we have to change only a single component (for an overview of our architecture, see Figure 7.2, on the next page).

---

7. http://dev.ctor.org/soap4r/

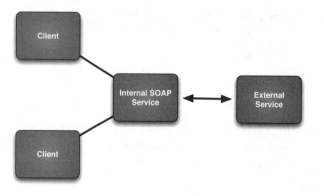

Figure 7.2: SOAP ARCHITECTURE

Before dealing with any SOAP details, we will build our own account checker service:

```
web_services/soap/account_checker.rb
class AccountChecker
  def check_account(bic, iban)
    if iban.to_i % 2 == 0
      ['National Bank', true]
    else
      [nil, false]
    end
  end
end
```

This is only a dummy service for demonstration purposes; a real solution would probably send the input parameters to a web service via HTTPS or something similar. But for our rapid prototyping approach, it does everything we need, and its interface is realistic. Now we have to expose the check_account(bic,iban) method; we can choose from at least three different SOAP libraries:

- Although *Action Web Service*[8] has been removed from the Rails core, it's still a powerful tool. It supports both SOAP and its simpler sibling, XML-RPC.
- The *WSO2 Web Services Framework for Ruby*[9] is a rather new project depending on a web services library written in C.

---

8. http://aws.rubyforge.org/
9. http://wso2.org/projects/wsf/ruby/

- The standard library *soap4r* has always been an excellent choice.

We use *soap4r* to implement our service, because it does not have to be installed separately and because it is very convenient:

`web_services/soap/account_checker.rb`

```
Line 1    require 'soap/rpc/standaloneServer'

          class AccountCheckerServer < SOAP::RPC::StandaloneServer
            def initialize(*args)
      5       super
              @log.level = Logger::Severity::DEBUG
              add_servant(AccountChecker.new)
            end
          end
```

That's the whole server! We have to derive our server class from SOAP::RPC::StandaloneServer, and in the initialize() method we pass all arguments to the superclass. Then we set the log level of our server to DEBUG so we can see which documents are exchanged during development.

The real magic happens in line 7, because here we make all public methods of our AccountChecker class available as SOAP endpoints by calling add_servant() and passing it an AccountChecker instance. Let's start the server:

`web_services/soap/account_checker.rb`

```
server = AccountCheckerServer.new(
  'Account Checker',      # Application Name
  'urn:AccountChecker',   # Default Namespace
  '0.0.0.0',              # Host
  2000                    # Port
)
trap(:INT) { server.shutdown }
server.start
```

When you run the program, it listens for incoming requests on port 2000, and it can be stopped by sending it an INT signal. With the following client, we can test whether everything works as expected:

`web_services/soap/account_checker_client.rb`

```
Line 1    require 'soap/rpc/driver'

          account_checker = SOAP::RPC::Driver.new(
            'http://localhost:2000',
      5     'urn:AccountChecker'
          )
          account_checker.add_method('check_account', 'bic', 'iban')
```

```
     bic, iban = ARGV
10   name, status = account_checker.check_account(bic, iban)
     if status
       puts "Account is OK and belongs to #{name}."
     else
       puts 'Account is not OK.'
15   end
```

In line 3, we create a proxy for our SOAP server that is running on localhost and that is listening on port 2000. Then, in line 7, we tell the proxy that the server has a method named check_account() that expects two parameters named bic and iban. Now we can use the server as if it were a regular object in our local process. Run the client, and it outputs the following:

```
mschmidt> ruby account_checker_client.rb  123456 987654
Account is OK and belongs to National Bank.
```

Everything is fine, and if you take a look at the server's log file, you can see which documents have been exchanged between the server and the client. Although this way of creating a SOAP client seems easy, it gets a bit tedious to add every single method manually if your target service has many methods. In Recipe 35, *Use SOAP Services with WSDL*, on the facing page, you can learn about an alternative approach.

A final note about performance: *soap4r* uses *WEBrick* by default, which is absolutely fine for small applications. If you need more power, you should take a look at *mongrel-soap4r.*[10]

Also See

- See Recipe 35, *Use SOAP Services with WSDL*, on the next page to learn about an alternative approach to building SOAP clients.

---

10. http://mongrel-soap4r.rubyforge.org/

Use SOAP Services with WSDL

Problem

You want to use a SOAP service described by a WSDL file from your Ruby application.

Ingredients

- See the ingredients in Recipe 34, *Build Your Own SOAP Services*, on page 215.

Solution

In Recipe 34, *Build Your Own SOAP Services*, on page 215, we have built a SOAP service for checking bank accounts, and we have written a Ruby client manually. Depending on the complexity of a service's interface, this can become pretty tedious, so it's often advantageous to describe a SOAP service's interface in a higher-level language and generate the client code automatically. The Web Service Description Language (WSDL) has been invented for exactly this purpose, and a description of our service reads like this (I've created it manually, because generating it automatically is a difficult problem in dynamic languages):

web_services/soap/account_checker.wsdl

```
Line 1   <?xml version="1.0"?>
    -    <definitions name="AccountCheckerInterfaceDescription"
    -      targetNamespace="http://www.example.com/wsdl/AccountChecker.wsdl"
    -      xmlns="http://schemas.xmlsoap.org/wsdl/"
    5      xmlns:soap="http://schemas.xmlsoap.org/wsdl/soap/"
    -      xmlns:tns="http://www.example.com/wsdl/AccountChecker.wsdl"
    -      xmlns:xsd="http://www.w3.org/2001/XMLSchema">
    -
    -      <message name="check_account_in">
    10       <part name="bic"  type="xsd:string"/>
    -        <part name="iban" type="xsd:string"/>
    -      </message>
    -
    -      <message name="check_account_out">
    15       <part name="status" type="xsd:integer"/>
    -        <part name="name"    type="xsd:boolean"/>
    -      </message>
```

```
       <portType name="AccountCheckerInterface">
20       <operation name="check_account">
           <input message="tns:check_account_in"/>
           <output message="tns:check_account_out"/>
         </operation>
       </portType>
25

       <binding name="AccountCheckerBinding"
                type="tns:AccountCheckerInterface">
         <soap:binding style="rpc"
                       transport="http://schemas.xmlsoap.org/soap/http"/>
30       <operation name="check_account">
           <soap:operation soapAction="check_account"/>
           <input>
             <soap:body
                 encodingStyle="http://schemas.xmlsoap.org/soap/encoding/"
35               namespace="urn:AccountChecker"
                 use="encoded"/>
           </input>
           <output>
             <soap:body
40               encodingStyle="http://schemas.xmlsoap.org/soap/encoding/"
                 namespace="urn:AccountChecker"
                 use="encoded"/>
           </output>
         </operation>
45       </binding>

       <service name="AccountCheckerService">
         <documentation>
           A service for checking bank accounts.
50       </documentation>
         <port binding="tns:AccountCheckerBinding"
               name="AccountCheckerPort">
           <soap:address location="http://localhost:2000"/>
         </port>
55     </service>
     </definitions>
```

That's a lot of stuff, but most of it is boilerplate.

If you ignore all namespace declarations and everything related to encoding, you can see that this WSDL file defines a single method named check_account(bic,iban) that returns the name of a bank and a verification status. If the status is false, the name of the bank is empty (that's an interesting detail that cannot be expressed easily using WSDL). The service can be used via HTTP, and it's listening on port 2000 on localhost.

Let's create a client automatically:

web_services/soap/wsdl_client.rb

```ruby
require 'soap/wsdlDriver'

wsdl = "file://#{File.expand_path('account_checker.wsdl')}"
account_checker = SOAP::WSDLDriverFactory.new(wsdl).create_rpc_driver
bic, iban = ARGV
name, status = account_checker.check_account(bic, iban)
if status
  puts "Account is OK and belongs to #{name}."
else
  puts 'Account is not OK.'
end
```

With a single statement in line 4, we create a proxy for the account checker service described in the WSDL file. Then we can use it as if it were a regular Ruby object. We only have to convert the filename of the WSDL file into a file URL, because the WSDLDriverFactory expects a URL. This makes sense, because often you get the interface descriptions of a service from the same host the service is running on and not from a local file system.

## Chapter 8

Talk to Message Brokers

Historically, software applications were built as large monolithic creations, the result of linking together hundreds of individual object files produced by a compiler. Over the years, common functions have been separated into libraries that could be shared by several programs, but still the applications were completely self-contained.

As network technologies became more popular, the design of software started to change. Long before the advent of Web, developers created their first mashups. They weren't the fancy kind of mashups where you can see your friends' current positions on a colorful map, but they were able to separate pieces of business logic and reuse them from several applications. For example, in the insurance and banking industry, developers created client/server architectures where services performed complex calculations needed by many applications. For the first time, we had a real separation of concerns and code reuse on a larger scale.

But every approach has its downsides, and building distributed applications using clients and servers still led to tight coupling. It was not as tight as in the monolithic applications approach, but it remained a problem. Whenever an important server was unavailable, the whole system stopped. In addition to this lack of robustness, scalability and performance became issues.

The biggest problem was that clients and servers had to talk directly to each other; in other words, they had to communicate in a synchronous manner. Message brokers changed the situation completely and solved a lot of the existing problems. Instead of communicating directly, processes now can send messages to the message broker, which is responsible for delivering it to its destination. If the target application is unavailable, it will wait until it is up and running again. Asynchronous communication has a lot of advantages:

- When applied correctly, your applications become *more robust*, because in an asynchronous architecture, it usually doesn't matter whether the receiver of a message is currently available. The message will be delivered when the receiver is up again.

- It makes your application *more responsive*, because you can run time-consuming tasks in a background process, so your users do not have to wait for it to complete.

- It's *more scalable*, because you can break your tasks into small pieces that can be queued and processed by independent servers.

- You can share not only pieces of business logic but even complete business processes.

In the past, it was difficult to integrate Ruby processes with modern message brokers, but in the past few years the situation has changed dramatically. Finally we have the tools and technologies to talk to nearly every message broker in the market; in this chapter, you'll learn how to do it.

Before we start to work with complex message-oriented middleware, we take a look at a much simpler way of message distribution in Recipe 36, *Transfer Messages with Files*, on the facing page. Then we'll build a complete asynchronous messaging architecture based on ActiveMQ in Recipe 37, *Create a Messaging Infrastructure*, on page 233. It will allow for arbitrary combinations of Ruby and Java processes.

Most message brokers today support the Java Message Service (JMS) API, but Ruby does not speak JMS by default. In Recipe 38, *Integrate with JMS*, on page 243, you'll learn how to overcome this shortcoming and connect Ruby to any of your JMS-compliant services.

Your Rails projects will certainly benefit from *ActiveMessaging*, a library that makes integrating your fancy new web application with a messaging architecture a breeze. Learn more about it in Recipe 39, *Connect to Message Queues with ActiveMessaging*, on page 249.

Transfer Messages with Files

Problem

You have several processes that gather orders from various sources. Some come from your own web application, and others are produced automatically by the software systems of your business partners. The orders are encoded as XML documents, they are stored in text files, and they all have a unique ID that is part of the filename.

You'd like to treat these orders as messages that get processed individually and asynchronously, but you do not want to set up a messaging infrastructure to process them. You are looking for something more pragmatic.

Ingredients

- Install all gems related to secure network protocols:[1]

  ```
  $ gem install net-ssh
  $ gem install net-sftp
  $ gem install net-scp
  ```

Solution

For many distributed applications, sending messages using files is still an appropriate solution (we use files and messages interchangeably in this recipe, and a file may contain several messages), especially if your messages are very big or if you have to transfer large amounts of them. In this recipe, you'll see how to create a server that watches for new files and processes them individually. Additionally, you'll learn how to distribute files using various file transfer mechanisms.

---

1. http://net-ssh.rubyforge.org/

We start with a message consumer, that is, with a server that observes a certain local directory and waits for new XML files:

`messaging/files/consumer.rb`

```ruby
Line 1  require 'ftools'
        require 'logger'

        class MessageConsumer
     5    attr_accessor :input_dir, :done_dir, :error_dir
          attr_accessor :sleep_interval, :filename_pattern

          def initialize
            @sleep_interval = 2
    10      @filename_pattern = '*.xml'
            @logger = Logger.new(STDOUT)
          end

          def start
    15      while true do
              files = Dir[File.join(@input_dir, @filename_pattern)]
              files.each do |filename|
                begin
                  new_filename = filename.sub(/\.xml$/, "-#{$$}.xml")
    20            if File.move(filename, new_filename)
                    filename = new_filename
                    if process(filename)
                      File.move(filename, @done_dir)
                    else
    25                File.move(filename, @error_dir)
                    end
                  end
                rescue Errno::ENOENT
                  @logger.info "Another process handles #{filename}."
    30          rescue => ex
                  @logger.error "Error processing #{filename}: #{ex}"
                  File.move(filename, @error_dir) if File.exist?(filename)
                end
              end
    35        sleep @sleep_interval
            end
          end

          def process(filename)
    40      message_id = File.basename(filename, '.xml')
            @logger.info "Processing #{message_id}."
            true
          end
        end
```

Although the server is really simple, it actually does a lot: every two seconds it reads all new files with an .xml extension from a configurable input directory and passes their names to the process() method. process() can do whatever it wants with the file, but it has to return a processing status. If it returns true, the input file will be moved to a directory for files that have been processed successfully (done); otherwise, it will be moved to an error directory. Our sample implementation logs only the message ID, which is the filename without its extension, and always returns true.

The core of our server is file handling, so we use a lot of Ruby's goodies. For example, in line 16, we use the DIR class' []() operator to find all files that have a certain extension in our input directory. In the same line, File's join() method creates the right path to a particular file no matter which platform the consumer is running on.

In lines 19 and 20, we handle an important aspect of every message consumer: concurrency. To handle more workload, we make sure right from the beginning that it's possible to start more than one consumer process observing the same input directory. We have to synchronize these processes so that no incoming message gets processed twice. To achieve this, we rename the input file and add the consumer's process ID (PID) to the filename. If the file can be renamed (moved) successfully, it is processed regularly. Otherwise, another consumer process has grabbed it already. In this case, we raise an exception and log an info message in line 28.

There are some alternatives to support concurrency. For example, we could start several processes with different input directories, but such solutions quickly turn into a configuration management nightmare. We also could use the operating system's file locking mechanisms, but they are often complicated, they are rarely portable, and they do not work on every file system.

At the end of the start() method, we put the program to sleep for a while, so other processes get a chance to do their work. You can start a consumer as follows:

`messaging/files/consumer.rb`

```
receiver = MessageConsumer.new
receiver.input_dir = 'data/in'
receiver.done_dir = 'data/done'
receiver.error_dir = 'data/err'
receiver.start
```

Now we need a client to send a new message to the consumer.

Let's begin with a solution that communicates with our consumer using a local file system:

messaging/files/fs_sender.rb

```ruby
class LocalFileMessageSender
  def initialize(target_dir)
    @target_dir = target_dir
  end

  def send(message_id, content)
    filename = "#{message_id}.xml"
    File.open(File.join(@target_dir, filename), 'w') do |file|
      file.write(content)
    end
  end
end
```

The core of our LocalFileMessageSender class is the send() method. It expects a message's ID and its content and sends it to a message consumer by writing it to the right directory.

Let's send a first XML document to the consumer:

messaging/files/fs_sender.rb

```ruby
sender = LocalFileMessageSender.new('data/in')
message = "<?xml version='1.0'?>\n<order id='0815'/>\n"
sender.send('order-0815', message)
```

The consumer's output looks as follows:

```
I, [2008-07-23T09:58:04.227777 #4892]  INFO -- : Processing order-0815.
```

That might not look like much, but we actually have two processes communicating with each other using the file system. We have effectively set up a messaging infrastructure! Before you go now and ask your boss for a pay rise, we'd better enhance it a bit.

The biggest problem of our current solution is that the communicating processes have to be on the same machine. At the least they have to share the same file system, which might well be a network file system. To make the distribution of our processes more flexible, we'll add support for FTP to the client:

messaging/files/ftp_sender.rb

```ruby
require 'net/ftp'
require 'tempfile'

class FileTransferMessageSender
  attr_accessor :host, :username, :password, :target_dir
```

```
     def initialize
       @host = 'localhost'
       @username = 'anonymous'
10     @target_dir = '.'
     end

     def send(message_id, content)
       tmp_file = Tempfile.new(message_id)
15     tmp_file.write(content)
       tmp_file.flush
       filename = "#{message_id}.xml"
       Net::FTP.open(@host) do |ftp|
         ftp.login(@username, @password)
20       ftp.chdir(@target_dir)
         ftp.puttextfile(tmp_file.path, filename)
       end
     end
   end
```

send( ) has still the same signature, but its implementation became a bit more complex. First we have to write the message's content to be sent into a temporary file, because to transfer files using FTP we actually need a file to be transferred (sounds reasonable, doesn't it?).

Ruby has a dedicated class for this purpose named Tempfile. We create an instance in line 14, fill it with the message's content, and flush it to make sure it's available immediately.

Caution: By default Tempfile creates files in your operating system's directory for temporary files, which potentially can be accessed by a lot of users. If your messages contain sensitive information, it's better to create them in a directory that can be read only by the process owner. You can pass a directory name explicitly to the constructor: Tempfile.new(message_id, 'path/to/dir')).

Now that we have a local file containing our message, we send it to the remote consumer using Net::FTP. We create a connection to the remote host in line 18. Then we send our credentials, change to the directory the message consumer is observing, and finally transfer the file.

We just need to set some more attributes to use the new client while the rest stays the same (of course, the message consumer has to observe the directory the client writes to):

`messaging/files/ftp_sender.rb`

```
sender = FileTransferMessageSender.new
sender.host = 'localhost'
sender.username = 'maik'
```

```
sender.password = 'tOp$ecret'
sender.target_dir = 'data/in'
message = "<?xml version='1.0'?>\n<order id='0815'/>\n"
sender.send('order-0815', message)
```

For internal systems we have a nice solution now, but what if you're communicating with an external customer? For that you should use a more secure protocol such as Secure Shell File Transfer Protocol (SFTP).[2] By using Net::SFTP, that's easy:

`messaging/files/sftp_sender.rb`

```
Line 1   require 'net/sftp'

         class SecureFileTransferMessageSender
           def send(message_id, content)
     5       filename = File.join(@target_dir, "#{message_id}.xml")
             Net::SFTP.start(@host, @username, :password => @password) do |sftp|
               sftp.file.open(filename, 'w') do |f|
                 f.write(content)
               end
    10        end
           end
         end
```

For brevity we show only the new implementation of the send() method, because the rest of the class is the same as in the FTP variant. In line 6 we create an SFTP connection calling start(). The connection is passed to a code block, and there we open a file for writing on the remote host. Afterward, we write our message to the file, and we're done. (Net::SFTP has lots of convenient methods such as upload() and download() that are well worth a look at its excellent API documentation.)

Instead of writing the message data directly to the remote host, we could have used the temporary file approach as we did in our FTP implementation, but this way our client is more secure. By the way, when you run the client, you'll be probably asked to enter your password for a file named ~/.ssh/id_rsa. That's because SFTP is based on the Secure Shell (SSH) protocol[3] and its public key infrastructure.[4]

Another popular file transfer protocol based on SSH is Secure Copy (SCP),[5] and it can be used similarly to SFTP.

---

2. http://en.wikipedia.org/wiki/SSH_file_transfer_protocol
3. http://en.wikipedia.org/wiki/Ssh
4. Read http://kimmo.suominen.com/docs/ssh/ to learn how to circumvent this.
5. http://en.wikipedia.org/wiki/Secure_copy

messaging/files/scp_sender.rb

```
Line 1    require 'net/scp'

          class SecureCopyMessageSender
            def send(message_id, content)
    5         filename = File.join(@target_dir, "#{message_id}.xml")
              Net::SCP.start(@host, @username, :password => @password) do |scp|
                scp.upload! StringIO.new(content), filename
              end
            end
   10     end
```

This time we have used the upload!() method in line 7, and we have passed it a StringIO object, so we do not have to create a temporary file.

Discussion

You might say that our first approach to building a messaging system is a bit primitive and has some disadvantages. For instance, right now it works in only one direction, and it does not support any acknowledge mechanisms. Its performance is suboptimal if you have to send many small messages, and it does not scale well across different hosts. Finally, it does not support a way to address the target consumer in a fine-grained manner.

But it also has some invaluable advantages. You can implement it easily in a short amount of time. It allows for large amounts of data to be transferred, and you can write clients in nearly every programming language in the world. You can even use a simple cp command to send a message.

Create a Messaging Infrastructure

For a new customer project, your company has to create a large distributed application. It should be fast, robust, and highly scalable, and its components should not depend on a single programming language. You came to the conclusion that only an asynchronous messaging system can fulfill all the customer's requirements.

You decided to set up a full-blown messaging infrastructure based on a mature message broker. It should have persistence mechanisms, and it should support clients in various programming languages. At the least, it has to support Ruby and Java processes acting as both senders and consumers.

- Download and unpack Apache's ActiveMQ[6] for your platform. It runs out of the box, and you do not have to perform any additional installation steps (a Java virtual machine has to be installed, too).

- Install the *STOMP* library for Ruby:[7]

  ```
  $ gem install stomp
  ```

Although our problem sounds like a really big one, it can be easily solved when we break it down into smaller pieces. In this recipe, you'll first learn how to write message consumers and producers in Ruby. After we have them working, we'll start to add Java processes, so at the end we'll have Java and Ruby programs interchanging messages in all directions.

The first problem to be solved is choosing the right message broker. Various products are available, but most of them come with bindings

---

6. http://www.activemq.org/
7. http://stomp.rubyforge.org/

only for Java and C++. ActiveMQ is one of the best open source message brokers, and it has excellent support for dynamic languages like Ruby, because it implements the Streaming Text Orientated Messaging Protocol (STOMP).[8] STOMP has been developed to make it easier for dynamic languages to integrate with message brokers.

When starting ActiveMQ, you typically find the following messages in the console output:

```
mschmidt> bin/activemq
ACTIVEMQ_HOME: /Users/mschmidt/activemq
ACTIVEMQ_BASE: /Users/mschmidt/activemq
Loading message broker from: xbean:activemq.xml
...
Listening for connections at: tcp://localhost:61616
TransportConnector          - Connector openwire Started
Listening for connections at: ssl://localhost:61617
TransportConnector          - Connector ssl Started
Listening for connections at: stomp://localhost:61613
TransportConnector          - Connector stomp Started
Listening for connections at: xmpp://localhost:61222
TransportConnector          - Connector xmpp Started
```

A message broker's job is to manage the communication between processes, and ActiveMQ allows these processes to connect in various ways. It starts several listeners that all deal with different protocols. Java programs will usually use OpenWire, while Ruby programs use STOMP. Although the processes use different protocols, they access the same message queues and topics.

Now that the broker is running, we will create a first Ruby consumer:

messaging/activemq/consumer.rb

```
Line 1   require 'stomp'
   -
   -     user, password = '', ''
   -     host, port = 'localhost', 61613
   5     connection = Stomp::Connection.open(user, password, host, port)
   -     destination = ARGV[0]
   -     connection.subscribe destination, { :ack => 'auto' }
   -     puts "Waiting for messages in #{destination}."
   -     while true
   10      message = connection.receive
   -       message_id = message.headers['message-id']
   -       puts "Got a message: #{message.body} (#{message_id})"
   -     end
   -     connection.disconnect
```

---

8. http://stomp.codehaus.org/

\\\// Joe Asks...
ᴖᴗᴖ
 ͜   **Queues? Topics? What's the Difference?**

Nearly all message brokers support two different communication models:

- Message queues are used for *point-to-point* communication where each message can be consumed by only one client.

- The *publish/subscribe* model is represented by *topics*, and it is used if a message can be consumed by more than one client.

In messaging APIs such as JMS, you often find a class hierarchy that is split into two parts: one deals with queues, and the other one deals with topics. STOMP uses a more simplistic approach; you have to use special name prefixes to identify the correct destination: /queue/ or /topic/. If, for example, you want to address a message queue named orders.input in your message-oriented middleware (MOM), you have to call it /queue/orders.input in your STOMP configuration. For a topic named news.of.today, you'd use /topic/news.of.today.

We create a new Stomp::Connection object using the host and port information we found in ActiveMQ's console log (Ruby's STOMP library has a more convenient class named Stomp::Client, but for demonstration purposes Stomp::Connection is better). Because we did not set up any explicit ActiveMQ users, we leave the user and password arguments blank. We could also have left out all arguments, because open() uses the same defaults as ActiveMQ.

In line 7, we subscribe to a particular destination, which can be a queue or a topic that is provided on the command line. By setting the ack option to auto, we make sure that every message we receive gets acknowledged immediately, so the sender knows we got it. Alternatively, we could set this option to client. In this case we'd have to call ack() on the connection using the message's ID. Otherwise, it would get delivered again by the message broker.

You can subscribe to as many destinations as you like by calling subscribe() for every destination. Whenever you receive a new message, you can find the name of its destination in the destination header (message. headers['destination'] in our case).

In line 9, we start the inevitable event loop waiting for new messages to arrive. Whenever we get one, we output its body and its message-id header (that's the one you'd use for an explicit acknowledge) and continue to wait for new stuff using receive().

We have written a complete message consumer in only a dozen lines of code. That's certainly impressive, but without a corresponding sender it's only half the fun:

`messaging/activemq/sender.rb`

```ruby
Line 1   require 'stomp'
    -
    -    user, password = '', ''
    -    host, port = 'localhost', 61613
    5    connection = Stomp::Connection.open(user, password, host, port)
    -    destination, message = ARGV[0..1]
    -    options = { 'persistent' => 'false' }
    -    connection.send destination, message, options
    -    connection.disconnect
```

As you might have expected, it looks similar to the consumer, because before we do anything else we have to connect to ActiveMQ first. We take the destination queue and the message to be sent from the command line and initialize the options we'd like to use when sending a message. Right now we declare only that we do not want our messages to be stored by the message broker, so we set persistent to false. In line 8, we send our message and close the connection to the message broker afterward.

Now we will benefit from a messaging architecture for the first time: without starting the consumer process first, run the sender twice to send two messages to the queue named orders.input:

```
mschmidt> ruby sender.rb /queue/orders.input Foo
mschmidt> ruby sender.rb /queue/orders.input Bar
```

Unsurprisingly, nothing special happened. In both cases the client connected to ActiveMQ, delivered its message, and quit. See what happens when we start the consumer now:

```
mschmidt> ruby consumer.rb /queue/orders.input
Waiting for messages in /queue/orders.input.
Got a message: Foo (ID:localhost-51542-1206098404495-5:40:-1:1:1)
Got a message: Bar (ID:localhost-51542-1206098404495-5:41:-1:1:1)
```

Alternative Messaging Protocols

There are alternatives to STOMP, such as the Advanced Message Queuing Protocol (AMQP)[*] and ActiveMQ's REST interface.[†] Both of them are not as mature as STOMP at the moment, but they might become alternatives in the future, and Apache's Qpid project[‡] already comes with a Ruby client.

---

*. http://amqp.org/
†. http://activemq.apache.org/rest.html
‡. http://cwiki.apache.org/qpid/

That should give you a good understanding of asynchronous messaging. Although the message consumer wasn't running when we sent our messages, they still arrived when we started it. If we had set the persistent option to true in the sender, we even could have shut down ActiveMQ for a while before starting the consumer. This behavior makes asynchronous messaging a perfect choice for building robust systems.

Now that our consumer is running anyway, why not use a Java program to give it something to do?

messaging/activemq/src/com/example/messaging/MessageSender.java

```
Line 1  package com.example.messaging;

        import org.springframework.context.ApplicationContext;
        import org.springframework.context.support.*;
     5  import org.springframework.jms.core.JmsTemplate;

        public class MessageSender {
            public void setDestination(JmsTemplate destination) {
                this.destination = destination;
    10      }

            public void sendMessage(String message) throws Exception {
                this.destination.convertAndSend(message);
            }
    15
            public static void main(String[] args) throws Exception {
                final String configFile = args[0];
                final String message = args[1];
                final ApplicationContext factory =
    20              new FileSystemXmlApplicationContext(configFile);
```

```
          final MessageSender sender =
              (MessageSender)factory.getBean("messageSender");
          sender.sendMessage(message);
25    }

      private JmsTemplate destination;
}
```

It might surprise you that the Java client does not need a lot of code either. Our secret ingredient is the Spring framework,[9] an application framework based on dependency injection. Basically, it allows you to design applications in a way that makes it very easy to configure them from the outside, and it comes with a lot of useful classes such as JmsTemplate. JmsTemplate hides a lot of the mechanics needed for typical JMS tasks, and we use it in sendMessage() to send a message to a certain message queue.

An instance of JmsTemplate is also the only member variable of the MessageSender class, and it can be set using setDestination(). You certainly have noticed that this method is not called anywhere in the whole source file, so who calls it? It's the FileSystemXmlApplicationContext class belonging to the Spring framework. Its constructor takes a list of XML configuration files and automatically creates and combines objects according to the declarations in these files. We need only one, and its important part looks like this:

`messaging/activemq/etc/sender.xml`

```
<bean id="messageSender" class="com.example.messaging.MessageSender">
  <property name="destination" ref="orderQueue"/>
</bean>

<bean id="connectionFactory"
      class="org.apache.activemq.ActiveMQConnectionFactory">
  <property name="brokerURL" value="tcp://localhost:61616" />
</bean>

<bean id="orderQueue"
      class="org.springframework.jms.core.JmsTemplate">
  <property name="connectionFactory" ref="connectionFactory"/>
  <property name="defaultDestinationName" value="orders.input"/>
</bean>
```

Spring calls objects it instantiates *beans*, and we configure three of them: messageSender, connectionFactory, and orderQueue.

---

9. http://springframework.org/

Each bean is associated with a certain class that is specified with the class= attribute, and they all have properties that can be defined with the <*property*> element. When Spring creates a bean, it sets its properties by calling the appropriate setter method. For example, to set the destination property of the messageSender bean, it calls setDestination() and passes the orderQueue bean, which has to be instantiated before. Note that we set the default destination name (that is, the queue name) to orders.input and not to /queue/orders.input as we did in the Ruby programs (see the sidebar the *Joe Asks...* on page 235 for details).

Now you can see how the destination queue is set in our MessageSender class: in line 19, we initialize all Spring beans, and in line 22, we get a reference to our fully initialized MessageSender instance (our sample configuration is for demonstration purposes only, and if you actually use Spring and JMS, you'd better study the official documentation carefully).[10]

To start the Java program, use the following shell script:

`messaging/activemq/start_sender.sh`

```
export CLASSPATH=bin:lib/spring.jar
export CLASSPATH=$CLASSPATH:lib/activemq-all-5.0.0.jar
export CLASSPATH=$CLASSPATH:lib/commons-logging-1.1.jar
javac -d bin src/com/example/messaging/MessageSender.java
java com.example.messaging.MessageSender etc/sender.xml "$1"
```

We make sure that the class path contains all necessary Java archives and our own classes. Then we compile the MessageSender class, and finally we start it, passing the Spring configuration file and the message to be sent as command-line arguments. When we run it as follows:

```
mschmidt> ./start_sender.sh 'Hello, Java!'
```

our Ruby consumer will output this:

```
Waiting for messages in /queue/orders.input.
Got a message: Hello, Java! (ID:localhost-53210-1206130854111-0:0:1:1:1)
```

Wow! We have set up an architecture that passes asynchronous messages seamlessly from Java processes to Ruby processes. And vice versa?

---

10. http://activemq.apache.org/jmstemplate-gotchas.html

Here we go:

messaging/activemq/src/com/example/messaging/MessageReceiver.java

```
Line 1   package com.example.messaging;

         import javax.jms.Message;
         import javax.jms.MessageListener;
    5    import javax.jms.TextMessage;
         import javax.jms.BytesMessage;

         import org.springframework.context.support.*;

   10    public class MessageReceiver implements MessageListener {
             public void onMessage(final Message message) {
                 try {
                     String content = null;
                     if (message instanceof BytesMessage) {
   15                    BytesMessage bytesMessage = (BytesMessage)message;
                         long messageLength = bytesMessage.getBodyLength();
                         byte[] buffer = new byte[(int)messageLength];
                         bytesMessage.readBytes(buffer);
                         content = new String(buffer);
   20                } else if (message instanceof TextMessage) {
                         content = ((TextMessage)message).getText();
                     }
                     System.out.println("We've got a message: " + content);
                 }
   25            catch (Exception e) {
                     System.err.println(e.getMessage());
                 }
             }

   30        public static void main(final String[] args) {
                 new FileSystemXmlApplicationContext(args);
             }
         }
```

Again, we use the Spring framework, so our main() method does nothing but set up the application context. The actual message handling happens in onMessage(). It gets called whenever we receive a new message and first checks the message's type in line 14. If we have received a binary message, we convert it into a String; otherwise, we read the content directly.

In most messaging APIs, messages have a type; they can be text messages, or they can be binary messages. STOMP does not support such types by default, but some brokers have ways to simulate them by setting various headers. ActiveMQ, for example, treats messages as text messages if their content-length header is 0. Ruby's *STOMP* library always sets this header to the correct length, so all messages sent using the library are treated as binary messages. You're better off if you check the type of an incoming message.

The important part of our Spring configuration looks as follows:

`messaging/activemq/etc/receiver.xml`

```
<bean id="messageReceiver"
      class="com.example.messaging.MessageReceiver"/>

<bean id="orderQueue"
  class="
  org.springframework.jms.listener.DefaultMessageListenerContainer">
    <property name="connectionFactory"   ref="connectionFactory" />
    <property name="messageListener"     ref="messageReceiver" />
    <property name="destinationName"     value="orders.input" />
    <property name="concurrentConsumers" value="1" />
    <property name="sessionTransacted"   value="true"/>
</bean>
```

We can start the MessageReceiver with a shell script similar to the one we used for the sender and send it some messages with our Ruby sender. We are done!

If you have used message-oriented middleware from Java or C++ in the past, you might ask yourself whether STOMP is too simple to fulfill your needs. Be assured that it isn't, because its inventors added all the important features. For example, STOMP even has support for transactions.[11]

With only a few lines of code and configuration, we have implemented an asynchronous messaging system that supports arbitrary combinations of senders and consumers no matter if they've been written in Java or Ruby. The only important prerequisite is support for STOMP. That is, if your message broker supports STOMP natively, you can connect with your Ruby clients immediately. If it doesn't, read Recipe 38, *Integrate with JMS*, on page 243 to learn how to turn every message broker into a STOMP broker.

---

11. See http://svn.codehaus.org/stomp/ruby/trunk/test/test_client.rb to learn how to use them.

Integrate with JMS

You are surrounded by services that are based on the Java Message Service API (JMS), and you want to know how to connect to a JMS message broker with Ruby.

- Perform all installation steps described in Recipe 37, *Create a Messaging Infrastructure*, on page 233.

- Download the latest *StompConnect*[12] release (at the time of this writing it's a single .jar file named stompconnect-1.0.jar).

Put simply, JMS is to message brokers what JDBC is to database management systems, and every message broker vendor today adds a JMS binding to its product. That's good news for all the Java programmers out there, but the poor Ruby people cannot benefit from it. They could use JRuby and actually use a native JMS binding, but that's not an appropriate solution in all cases.

The messaging protocol that is supported best by Ruby is STOMP (see Recipe 37, *Create a Messaging Infrastructure*, on page 233), but at the moment only a few message brokers support it. Wouldn't it be nice if we could turn every JMS broker into a STOMP broker automatically? In this recipe, you'll learn how to do this.

Let's say you have to work with an ActiveMQ installation whose STOMP connector has been disabled, as is often the case in companies using Java exclusively. You'd like to talk to a service waiting for new messages in a message queue named testqueue using a Ruby client.

StompConnect is the tool that we need now. It is a protocol adapter (academics probably call it a *message mediator*) that turns STOMP requests into JMS messages, and vice versa. The architecture we'll build now

---

12. http://stomp.codehaus.org/StompConnect

looks like Figure 8.1, on the facing page; in other words, *StompConnect* will run as a separate process communicating with the JMS client of the process we'd like to address. Here's how to start *StompConnect*:

messaging/jms/stomp_connector.sh

```
export CLASSPATH=lib/commons-logging-1.1.jar
export CLASSPATH=$CLASSPATH:lib/activemq-all-5.0.0.jar
export CLASSPATH=$CLASSPATH:lib/stompconnect-1.0.jar
export properties=-Djava.naming.factory.initial=\
org.apache.activemq.jndi.ActiveMQInitialContextFactory
export properties="$properties \
-Djava.naming.provider.url=tcp://localhost:61616"
java $properties org.codehaus.stomp.jms.Main \
tcp://localhost:62222 ConnectionFactory
```

As usual, we build up the class path, which contains the Java archives for *StompConnect* and for the message broker we'd like to use. In addition, *StompConnect* needs *Commons-Logging*.[13] Then we define two Java properties telling *StompConnect* where to get JMS connections from (java.naming.factory.initial) and which message broker should be used (java.naming.provider.url). Finally, we start *StompConnect*, passing it the URL of the STOMP connector to be created. Here's the output of our script:

```
mschmidt> ./stomp_connector.sh
Mar 25, 2008 6:12:35 PM org.codehaus.stomp.jms.StompConnect\
   createConnectionFactory
INFO: Looking up name: ConnectionFactory in JNDI InitialContext for JMS\
   ConnectionFactory
Mar 25, 2008 6:12:35 PM org.codehaus.stomp.tcp.TcpTransportServer\
   doStart
INFO: Listening for connections at: tcp://localhost:62222
```

As expected, a new STOMP connector is listening on port 62222, and it will delegate requests to the ActiveMQ broker waiting for OpenWire requests on port 61616. We can try it with a little Ruby sender:

messaging/jms/sender.rb

```
require 'stomp'

user, password = '', ''
host, port = 'localhost', 62222
connection = Stomp::Connection.open(user, password, host, port)
destination = '/queue/testqueue'
options = { 'persistent' => 'false' }
message = "Hello, world!\n"
connection.send destination, message, options
connection.disconnect
```

---

13. http://commons.apache.org/logging/

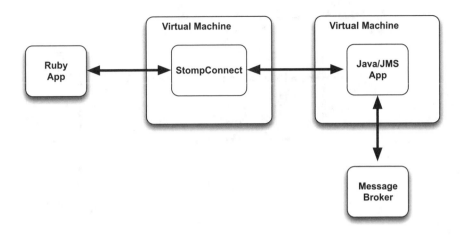

Figure 8.1: *StompConnect* USING SEVERAL VIRTUAL MACHINES

It's a perfectly normal Ruby STOMP client (see Recipe 37, *Create a Messaging Infrastructure*, on page 233 to learn more about Ruby and STOMP), and the only thing worth mentioning is the queue name. To address the queue named testqueue, we have to use /queue/testqueue in our STOMP client (see the *Joe Asks...* on page 235).

That's already a nice solution for bringing STOMP support to a JMS broker, but it comes at a price: all messages have to be passed from one Java virtual machine (JVM) to another. It would be much more efficient if *StompConnect* were running in the same JVM as the service to which it connects. See the resulting architecture in Figure 8.2, on the next page.

To achieve this, we need to take a closer look at the service we are using. Let's say it is a really simple Java JMS service that looks like this:

messaging/jms/src/com/example/messaging/MessageReceiver.java

```
package com.example.messaging;

import javax.jms.Message;
import javax.jms.MessageListener;
import javax.jms.TextMessage;
import javax.jms.BytesMessage;

import org.springframework.context.support.*;
```

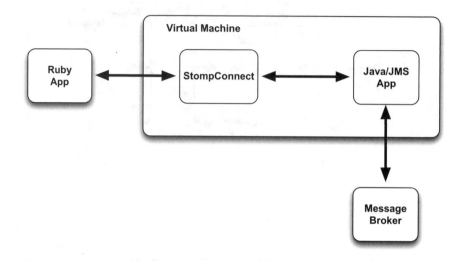

Figure 8.2: *StompConnect* USING A SINGLE VIRTUAL MACHINE

```java
public class MessageReceiver implements MessageListener {
    public void onMessage(final Message message) {
        try {
            String content = null;
            if (message instanceof BytesMessage) {
                System.out.println("Bytes");
                BytesMessage bytesMessage = (BytesMessage)message;
                long messageLength = bytesMessage.getBodyLength();
                byte[] buffer = new byte[(int)messageLength];
                bytesMessage.readBytes(buffer);
                content = new String(buffer);
            } else if (message instanceof TextMessage) {
                System.out.println("Text");
                content = ((TextMessage)message).getText();
            }
            System.out.println("We've got a message: " + content);
        }
        catch (Exception e) {
            System.err.println(e.getMessage());
        }
    }

    public static void main(final String[] args) throws Exception {
        new FileSystemXmlApplicationContext(args);
    }
}
```

This service waits for new messages, and whenever a new message arrives, it prints its content to the console. It doesn't matter whether it has been a textual or a binary message. The service has to be configured using the Spring framework,[14] and to actually run it, we need its Spring configuration:

`messaging/jms/etc/receiver_activemq.xml`

```
<bean id="messageReceiver"
  class="com.example.messaging.MessageReceiver"/>

<bean id="connectionFactory"
      class="org.apache.activemq.ActiveMQConnectionFactory">
  <property name="brokerURL" value="tcp://localhost:61616" />
</bean>

<bean id="testQueue"
  class="
  org.springframework.jms.listener.DefaultMessageListenerContainer">
  <property name="connectionFactory"   ref="connectionFactory" />
  <property name="messageListener"     ref="messageReceiver" />
  <property name="destinationName"     value="testqueue" />
  <property name="concurrentConsumers" value="5" />
  <property name="sessionTransacted"   value="false"/>
</bean>
```

There's nothing special about it: we configure the message receiver, wrap it in a bean named testQueue, and declare a bean for the message broker connection. We could instantiate a *StompConnect* object directly now in our service if we did not use Spring. In that case, we'd need access to the source code, and we'd have to recompile and to deploy the service. But by adding one more bean, we can turn this service into a STOMP service without all the hassle:

`messaging/jms/etc/stomp_connect.xml`

```
<bean id="stompConnect"
      class="org.codehaus.stomp.jms.StompConnect"
      init-method="start">
  <property name="connectionFactory" ref="connectionFactory" />
  <property name="uri"               value="tcp://localhost:62222"/>
</bean>
```

We inject the message broker's connection factory and the URL to be used for the STOMP connector into the stompConnect bean. When you restart the service, it will behave as before, but it will expose its messaging endpoints via STOMP, too. This service can be used by Ruby

---

14. http://springframework.org/

clients with ease now! We needed access only to the service's configuration, but often this is much easier than configuring the message broker (to be concise, we also have to add *StompConnect*'s Java archive to the service's class path).

StompConnect is a powerful tool and works with every JMS-compliant message broker in the market. It brings Ruby support to every message broker available. It works seamlessly with *ActiveMessaging*, so it brings full JMS support to your Rails applications, too.

Connect to Message Queues with ActiveMessaging

Most of your company's infrastructure is based on asynchronous messaging; in other words, vital components can be used only by exchanging messages with them. One of them is a central order handler.

It's your task to build a Rails application for placing orders by sending messages to the company's central order handler. Orders will be stored in a local database, and the application will listen for order status messages emitted by the order handler. This way, the front end can provide a nice and responsive user experience while it can still keep track of the current status of the orders.

Ingredients

- Perform all installation steps described in Recipe 37, *Create a Messaging Infrastructure*, on page 233.

- From your Rails application's root directory, install the *ActiveMessaging*[15] plug-in:

```
mschmidt> script/plugin install \
> http://activemessaging.googlecode.com/svn/trunk/plugins/\
> activemessaging
```

Solution

This scenario is pretty common: a time-consuming task is handed to a back-end service that sends back a result asynchronously when it has finished the task (see a simplified view of our architecture in Figure 8.3, on page 251).

In Recipe 37, *Create a Messaging Infrastructure*, on page 233, you can see how to integrate ordinary Ruby code with message-oriented middleware. This time Rails gets added to the game, and it does not support

---

15. http://code.google.com/p/activemessaging/

access to messaging architectures natively. But *ActiveMessaging* is a plug-in that makes messaging with Rails a piece of cake.

Before we send and receive messages, we'll build a model for orders in the database:

`messaging/activemessaging/msgdemo/db/migrate/001_create_orders.rb`

```
create_table :orders do |t|
  t.column :customer, :string
  t.column :product,  :string
  t.column :quantity, :int
  t.column :status,   :string, :default => 'OPEN'
  t.timestamps
end
```

Admittedly, this is a rather lightweight order model, but for our purposes it's sufficient. It stores the customer's name, the order's status, and the name and quantity of the product that has been ordered (for an order entry form, see Figure 8.4, on page 252). We could already implement a controller for manipulating it, but our controller does not need to store only orders; it also has to send them to a message queue. We have to edit some configuration files first that have been installed together with the *ActiveMessaging* plug-in.

One of them, broker.yml, defines all connection parameters for the message broker. We'll use ActiveMQ with the STOMP protocol, so our configuration looks as follows (*ActiveMessaging* supports more message brokers, but for the rest of the recipe I assume you're running ActiveMQ in its standard configuration):

`messaging/activemessaging/msgdemo/config/broker.yml`

```
development:
    adapter: stomp
    login: ""
    passcode: ""
    host: localhost
    port: 61613
    reliable: true
    reconnectDelay: 5
```

The next configuration file is messaging.rb. It defines symbolic names for all message queues that we are going to use:

`messaging/activemessaging/msgdemo/config/messaging.rb`

```
ActiveMessaging::Gateway.define do |s|
  s.destination :order,        '/queue/orders.input'
  s.destination :order_status, '/queue/orders.status'
end
```

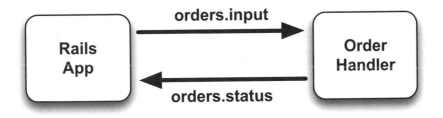

Figure 8.3: HIGH-LEVEL ARCHITECTURE

In our application we need two messages queues: one for sending orders (:order) and one for receiving order status messages (:order_status). The symbolic :order queue is mapped to a physical message queue named /queue/orders.input. It's used in the OrderController class to send incoming orders to the central order handler where they get processed asynchronously:

`messaging/activemessaging/msgdemo/app/controllers/order_controller.rb`

```ruby
Line 1  require 'activemessaging/processor'

        class OrderController < ApplicationController
          include ActiveMessaging::MessageSender
     5
          publishes_to :order

          def add
            order = Order.new(params[:order])
    10      if request.post? and order.save
              flash.now[:notice] = 'Order has been submitted.'
              publish :order, order.to_xml
              redirect_to :action => 'show_status', :id => order.id
            end
    15    end

          def show_status
            @order = Order.find(params[:id])
          end
    20  end
```

Our first Rails controller with *ActiveMessaging* support does not differ much from an ordinary controller.

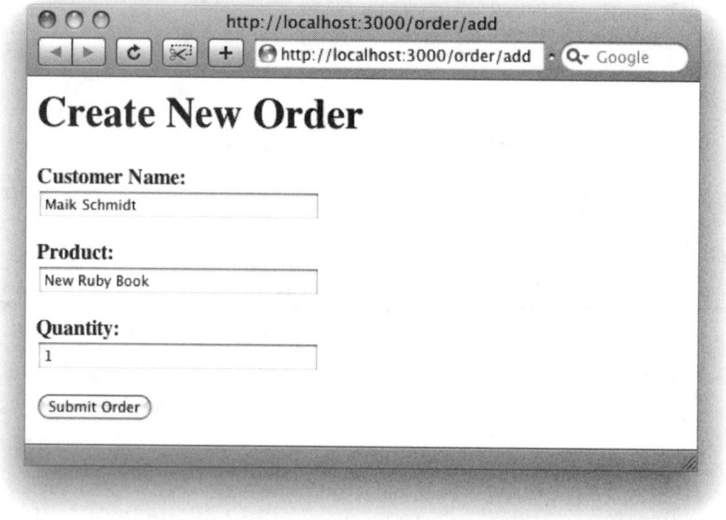

Figure 8.4: CREATE A NEW ORDER.

We mix in ActiveMessaging::MessageSender, and in line 6, we tell Rails that this controller will send messages to the order queue we defined earlier in messaging.rb.

The add() method works like an ordinary Rails action; it takes the form parameters from a view, creates a new Order instance, and stores it in the database. Then, in line 12, we use the publish() method to send an XML representation of the newly created order to the order handler.

After the order has been placed, it will have the default status OPEN, as you can see in Figure 8.5, on page 254. This status will not change no matter how often you click the refresh button, because at the moment we do not process the status messages published by the order handler. To change this, we have to add a *processor* to our Rails application. The corresponding generator is part of the *ActiveMessaging* plug-in, and you can run it like this:

```
mschmidt> ruby script/generate processor OrderStatus
```

This creates a skeleton file named order_status_processor.rb that looks as follows after we have added all functionality we need:

`messaging/activemessaging/msgdemo/app/processors/order_status_processor.rb`

```
Line 1   require 'rexml/document'

         class OrderStatusProcessor < ApplicationProcessor
           subscribes_to :order_status
5
           def on_message(message)
             doc = REXML::Document.new(message)
             order_id = doc.root.attributes['id']
             order_status = doc.root.text
10           order = Order.find(order_id)
             order.status = order_status
             order.save
             logger.debug "Status of order #{order_id} is #{order_status}."
           end
15       end
```

Similar to the OrderController, we have to declare that we are using messaging facilities. In line 4, we tell Rails that our OrderStatusProcessor listens for new messages in the :order_status queue. That's all we have to do, because the rest of the messaging mechanism is more or less passive: whenever a new message arrives in the order status queue, the on_message() action gets invoked automatically by *ActiveMessaging*. In the action, we parse the XML document contained in the message, extract its order ID and the order status, and store it in the database. The incoming XML documents are very simple and typically look like this:

```
<order-status id="47110815">SHIPPED</order-status>
```

To be concise, on_message() is not invoked completely automatically, because that would mean the listener is running within the Rails framework itself. To circumvent this, the *ActiveMessaging* developers have created a *poller daemon* that waits for messages and invokes the appropriate Rails actions whenever it receives something new. The poller script is part of the *ActiveMessaging* plug-in, and when you start it like this:

```
mschmidt> ruby script/poller run
```

you'll see the following in your application's log file:

```
ActiveMessaging: Loading ... app/processors/application.rb
ActiveMessaging: Loading ... app/processors/order_status_processor.rb
=> Subscribing to /queue/orders.status (processed by \
   OrderStatusProcessor)
```

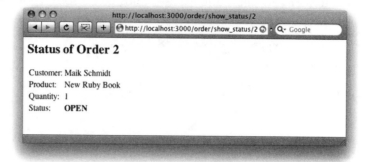

Figure 8.5: THE ORDER HAS BEEN SUBMITTED.

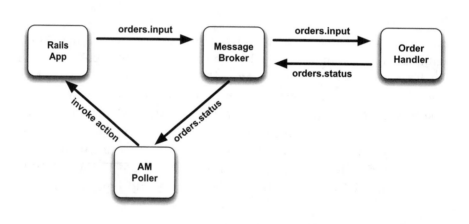

Figure 8.6: SYSTEM DESIGN

For a more detailed view of the architecture we have developed in this recipe so far, see Figure 8.6. The Rails application puts messages into a queue named orders.input, which is managed by the ActiveMQ message broker. The broker passes the message to the order handler, which actually processes the order. When the order has been processed, the order handler sends the result to another message queue named orders. status, which is also managed by ActiveMQ. Afterward, the status message is transmitted to the poller daemon, and the daemon turns it into a call to the right on_message() action.

Only one component of the overall architecture is missing in our test environment: the order handler. Perhaps we could use a copy of the production system, but for testing purposes it's always better to have your own simulator at hand:

`messaging/activemessaging/order_handler.rb`

```ruby
require 'stomp'
require 'rexml/document'

class OrderHandler
  attr_accessor :user, :password, :host, :port

  def initialize
    @user, @password = '', ''
    @host, @port = 'localhost', 61613
  end

  def handle_orders(in_queue, out_queue)
    connection = Stomp::Connection.open @user, @password, @host, @port
    connection.subscribe in_queue, { :ack => 'client' }
    puts "Waiting for messages in #{in_queue}."
    while true
      message = connection.receive
      body = message.body
      message_id = message.headers['message-id']
      puts "Got a message: #{body} (#{message_id})"
      order_status = get_order_status(body)
      options = { 'persistent' => 'false' }
      connection.send out_queue, order_status, options
      connection.ack message_id
    end
    connection.disconnect
  end

  private

  def get_order_status(body)
    doc = REXML::Document.new(body)
    order_id = doc.root.attributes['id']
    "<order-status id='#{order_id}'>SHIPPED</order-status>"
  end
end
```

Our OrderHandler's complete business logic can be found in the handle_orders() method. Basically, it takes order documents from an input queue, parses them, and creates output documents that have the same order ID and a constant status (SHIPPED). That might not be very sophisticated, but for testing the other components it's good not to have too many variable parts.

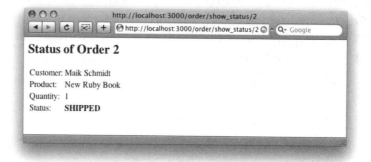

Figure 8.7: THE ORDER HAS BEEN SHIPPED.

As usual, we start a STOMP connection, subscribe to a destination, and start an event loop. This time we chose to use the client acknowledge mechanism in line 14; in other words, we have to explicitly acknowledge incoming messages in line 24. Otherwise, the message would be delivered again by the message broker.

After you have started the order handler like this:

`messaging/activemessaging/order_handler.rb`

```
order_handler = OrderHandler.new
order_handler.handle_orders(
  '/queue/orders.input',
  '/queue/orders.status'
)
```

you can refresh your browser window a few times and eventually see a picture similar to Figure 8.7.

We already knew that messaging with Ruby is easy, but *ActiveMessaging* makes it even more comfortable. Using only a minimal set of configuration parameters and three methods (publishes_to(), subscribes_to(), and publish()), we've been able to combine an existing messaging architecture and a Rails application in record time.

Part IV

Integration & Administration Recipes

Chapter 9

Speak Foreign Languages

Ruby is a great programming language, and perhaps it's the most beautiful and most productive language available today. But Ruby isn't perfect, and there never will be a perfect programming language. C and assembly language will always be the fastest in execution speed, while Java and C# will probably always have bigger standard libraries. But Ruby is an open and liberal language and plays nicely with others.

For many people, one of the most critical issues when working with dynamic languages is performance. Admittedly, Ruby certainly isn't the fastest language in the world, but in Recipe 40, *Embed C and C++*, on page 261, you'll learn how to beef it up with the raw power of good ol' C and C++ code.

Although Ruby's standard library is getting bigger with every release, it still lacks some significant classes and algorithms that every Java programmer takes for granted. Don't worry, because in Recipe 41, *Mix Java and Ruby Code*, on page 269 you'll learn how to integrate Java code into your Ruby programs.

Some language integration tasks are more common than others. For example, there are countless Java legacy applications using Remote Method Invocation (RMI) on the planet. Consequently, we have devoted a whole recipe to this topic (Recipe 42, *Use RMI Services*, on page 275).

With the advent of IronRuby, the entire world of .NET and all of its libraries became available to Ruby programmers. In Recipe 43, *Mix Ruby and .NET with IronRuby*, on page 279, you will learn how to mix Ruby with all the other .NET languages.

Embed C and C++

Your company has gone through a typical IT evolution. Although in the last years most software has been developed in Java, you still have a lot of legacy C or C++ code floating around. This code often has to be integrated even into new programs, and in addition you are afraid that Ruby sometimes might not meet all your performance needs.

In this recipe, you'll learn how to embed C/C++ code directly into your Ruby programs so you can add the power of C on the fly whenever it's needed.

Ingredients

- Install the *ruby-inline* gem:[1]

  ```
  $ gem install RubyInline
  ```

  Unfortunately, *ruby-inline* does not work very well on Microsoft Windows systems.

Solution

The techniques you will learn in this recipe should be used only if you have to increase the performance of a certain method or if you urgently need a particular function that is available only in a C library. Whenever you need a complete binding for a library, you should create a regular Ruby extension (Dave Thomas, Chad Fowler, and Andy Hunt have written a whole chapter about this in *Programming Ruby* [TFH08]).

To keep things clear, we start with the inevitable factorial example, which looks as follows in pure Ruby:

`foreign_languages/c/factorial_test.rb`

```ruby
class FactorialTest
  def factorial(n)
    result = 1
    n.downto(2) { |x| result *= x }
    result
  end
end
```

---

1. http://rubyinline.rubyforge.org/

There's really nothing special about it: we have defined a method calculating the factorial of a given number with only a few lines of Ruby
code. Now we replace it with a C solution:

```
foreign_languages/c/factorial_test.rb
require 'inline'
class FactorialTest
  inline(:C) do |builder|
    builder.c <<-CSOURCE
    long factorial_c(const int n) {
      long result = 1, i = n;
      while (i >= 2)
        result *= i--;
      return result;
    }
    CSOURCE
  end
end
```

The previous code actually defines a new method named factorial_c()
in the FactoryTest class. It is compiled on the fly by the *Ruby Inline*
library. Its most important method is named inline(), which gets a symbol determining the programming language to be inlined. We pass it
the symbol C (the default) to indicate we'd like to embed some C code.
inline() expects a code block and passes it a builder instance for the
programming language chosen.

On the builder instance, we invoke the c() method. It expects a string
containing C code, compiles it, and automatically converts basic data
types from C to Ruby, and vice versa. For example, it turns integer
values into Fixnum instances, and String objects become char*. Here we
have a little benchmark test comparing the performance of our two
methods:

```
foreign_languages/c/factorial_test.rb
require 'benchmark'
label_width = 6
test = FactorialTest.new
Benchmark.bm(label_width) do |x|
  x.report('ruby: ') { 1.upto(10_000_000) { test.factorial(12) } }
  x.report('C: ')    { 1.upto(10_000_000) { test.factorial_c(12) } }
end
```

And here are the results (measured on an Apple MacBook Pro):

```
mschmidt> ruby factorial_test.rb
              user      system     total        real
ruby:    44.490000    0.150000   44.640000 ( 44.665101)
C:        2.570000    0.010000    2.580000 (  2.577188)
```

Unsurprisingly, the C function is about twenty times faster than its Ruby equivalent. But before you get too enthusiastic and start to write your software in C again, we'd better take a look at the downsides of our approach. The following program:

foreign_languages/c/factorial_test.rb

```
test = FactorialTest.new
puts "factorial(15)   = #{test.factorial(15)}"
puts "factorial_c(15) = #{test.factorial_c(15)}"
```

produces this:

```
factorial(15)   = 1307674368000
factorial_c(15) = 2004310016
```

What happened? Is there a logical bug in one of these trivial methods? Not really, but we forgot that Ruby automatically turns Fixnum objects into Bignum objects if necessary. The Ruby factorial method returns correct results even for bigger numbers, while the C version suffers from the usual overflow errors. The factorial of 15 is too big to fit into 32 bits, and instead of indicating an error, the C runtime system silently cuts off some bits and returns a wrong result.

Despite these shortcomings, *Ruby Inline* is very nice, because we can write time-critical algorithms in C now while the library handles typical data conversions automatically. It's even possible to add new converters using the add_type_converter() method.

But what if we need a tighter integration with Ruby? Let's take a look at a more complex example; in Recipe 20, *Master Binary Data*, on page 127, we have implemented a method for decoding multibyte integer values, that is, for integer values that are encoded with a flexible amount of bytes. If the most significant bit (MSB) of a byte is set, we add its lower seven bits to our integer and read the next byte. If the MSB is zero, we have found the last seven bits of our integer value. For example, the two bytes 0x81 and 0x06 result in the decimal integer value 134, because the bytes are encoded in binary as follows:

```
1000 0001  0000 0110
```

The MSB of the first byte is set, while the MSB of the second is not. Hence, our integer value consists of the lower seven bits of the two bytes:

```
00 0000 1000 0110
```

Our Ruby implementation for converting such values looked like this:

foreign_languages/c/multi_byte_int.rb

```ruby
class MultiByteIntegerReader
  def self.get_multibyte_integer(raw_data)
    multi_int = 0
    while raw_data[0][7] == 1
      multi_int = (multi_int << 7) | (raw_data.shift & 0x7f)
    end
    (multi_int << 7) | raw_data.shift
  end
end
```

raw_data is an array of unsigned integer values that gets modified in the get_multibyte_integer() method, because whenever we need a new byte, we call shift() on the array. If we want to rewrite this method in C, we actually have to pass it a Ruby Array object, and we have to modify it, too. Sound complicated? Here we go:

foreign_languages/c/multi_byte_int.rb

```ruby
require 'inline'
class MultiByteIntegerReader
  inline do |builder|
    builder.c_singleton <<-CSOURCE
    VALUE get_multibyte_integer_c(VALUE raw_data) {
      unsigned int multi_int     = 0;
      unsigned int current_value = FIX2INT(rb_ary_shift(raw_data));
      while ((current_value & 0x80)) {
        multi_int = (multi_int << 7) | (current_value & 0x7f);
        current_value = FIX2INT(rb_ary_shift(raw_data));
      }
      return INT2FIX((multi_int << 7) | current_value);
    }
    CSOURCE
  end
end
```

This time we call c_singleton() to create a Ruby class method, and again we pass it the source code of the C function we'd like to add to the MultiByteIntegerReader class. Right in the first line of our C code we get in contact with Ruby's most important internal structure: VALUE. The Ruby interpreter uses this structure to represent all objects, and whenever you need a concrete instance of an object, you have to con-

vert the VALUE object first using a macro. Our builder does this automatically and converts a Ruby array we pass to get_multibyte_integer_c()
using RARRAY() behind the scenes. You have to keep that in mind: our
raw_data variable is now a Ruby array in the same way as the Ruby
interpreter usually sees them.

After initializing multi_int, we call rb_ary_shift(), passing it our Ruby array.
This is what happens whenever you invoke shift() on an Array in your
Ruby programs. rb_ary_shift() is Ruby's internal C function for shifting a
value from an Array. Because our array contains Fixnum objects, we have
to convert them with the FIX2INT() macro into regular integer values.
current_value now contains the integer representation of the first value
stored in the raw_data array.

The rest of the function looks like the Ruby version, because the binary
operators are the same in C and Ruby. We only have to use INT2FIX() to
convert our integer result to a Fixnum object before returning it to the
Ruby world (note that the return value of our function is of type VALUE).

Now that we have both alternatives available, let's run a little benchmark to see which one is faster:

foreign_languages/c/multi_byte_int.rb
```ruby
require 'benchmark'
label_width = 6
runs = 10_000_000
Benchmark.bm(label_width) do |x|
  x.report('ruby: ') do
    1.upto(runs) do
      MultiByteIntegerReader.get_multibyte_integer([0x81, 0x06])
    end
  end
  x.report('C: ') do
    1.upto(runs) do
      MultiByteIntegerReader.get_multibyte_integer_c([0x81, 0x06])
    end
  end
end
```

The result looks as follows:

```
mschmidt> ruby multi_byte_int.rb
             user     system      total        real
ruby:   27.990000   0.060000   28.050000 ( 28.059626)
C:       6.490000   0.000000    6.490000 (  6.494582)
```

As expected, the C version is faster than Ruby, but all in all it's still
a surprising result. The C code absolutely mirrors the Ruby code and

even uses internal Ruby functions to emulate the original Ruby version. Despite all this, the Ruby code is about four times slower. That's the price you have to pay when working with an interpreted language, but these figures might change in upcoming Ruby versions. Ruby 1.9 compiles programs to byte code, for example, to improve performance.

C and C++ are similar in many respects, so you can use *Ruby Inline* for embedding C++ code, too:

foreign_languages/c/cpp_message_printer.rb

```ruby
require 'inline'

class MessagePrinter
  inline(:C) do |builder|
    builder.include '<iostream>'
    builder.include '<string>'
    builder.add_compile_flags '-x c++', '-lstdc++'
    builder.c <<-CSOURCE
    void shout_message(int i, char* message) {
      std::string upperCase = std::string(message);
      std::transform(
        upperCase.begin(), upperCase.end(),
        upperCase.begin(), ::toupper
      );
      while (i-- > 0)
        std::cout << upperCase << std::endl;
    }
    CSOURCE
  end
end
```

This code defines a simple MessagePrinter class and a single method named shout_message() that prints a particular message in uppercase several times. In lines 5 and 6, we include the C++ *iostream* and *string* libraries. Then we add some compile flags to make sure our embedded function is treated as C++ code and to link the *stdc++* library to our program.

The rest of the code is simple: we convert the message argument into a std::string object and turn it into uppercase (look at the code, and you'll certainly remember why you switched to Ruby). Then we'll start a loop and print the upperCase variable i times using the C++ I/O facilities. We can use the MessagePrinter class as follows:

foreign_languages/c/cpp_message_printer.rb

```ruby
MessagePrinter.new.shout_message 3, 'Hello, world!'
```

And here's what you get when you run the sample program on the command line:

```
mschmidt> ruby cpp_message_printer.rb
HELLO, WORLD!
HELLO, WORLD!
HELLO, WORLD!
```

Although our example program looks nice and clean, things get complicated rather quickly when combining Ruby and C++ using *Ruby Inline*. For example, there are no specific type conversions for C++, not even for basic types such as std::string. If you need a tighter integration between Ruby and C++, you should take a look at *Rice*.[2] Rice is a C++ wrapper around the Ruby's C API and makes it very easy to combine C++ code with Ruby's internals.

---

2. http://rice.rubyforge.org/

Mix Java and Ruby Code

Java has become one of the most widespread programming languages not only in modern enterprise environments but also in the open source world. Consequently, countless Java libraries are available solving almost every programming task you can imagine.

Although Ruby has been gaining popularity rather quickly, it still lacks a lot of even basic functionality that's mature in Java. Wouldn't it be great if you could embed Java solutions into your Ruby programs? In this recipe, you'll learn how to do that.

Ingredients

- Install the Ruby Java Bridge (RJB):[3]

  ```
  $ gem install rjb
  ```

- Download and unpack the Apache Xerces[4] XML parser.

- Download and unpack JDOM.[5]

Solution

One of the things that is missing most when using Ruby in enterprises is the validation of XML documents. Whenever you receive XML documents from an external source, you should check whether they adhere to the structure you are expecting before you actually process them. Many validation techniques are available, such as Document Type Definition (DTD),[6] XML Schema,[7] and RELAX NG[8] or *Schematron*.[9]

For Java, many excellent validating XML parsers are available that support these standards. In Ruby, a validating XML parser is still missing

---

3. http://rjb.rubyforge.org/
4. http://xerces.apache.org/xerces2-j/
5. http://jdom.org/
6. http://en.wikipedia.org/wiki/Document_Type_Definition
7. http://www.w3.org/XML/Schema
8. http://relaxng.org/
9. http://xml.ascc.net/resource/schematron/schematron.html

and is urgently needed (although the latest version of *LibXML* looks promising). But we can use a Java parser until someone builds a Ruby solution.

Let's say you have implemented a web service for sending short messages in cellular networks. Clients send an XML document describing a short message, and your service is responsible for transmitting it to its receiver. An XML schema representing a short message document looks as follows:

foreign_languages/java/sms.xsd

```
<xs:schema xmlns:xs="http://www.w3.org/2001/XMLSchema">
  <xs:element name="sms">
    <xs:complexType>
      <xs:sequence>
        <xs:element name='sender'   type='xs:token'/>
        <xs:element name='receiver' type='xs:token'/>
        <xs:element name='content'  type='xs:string'/>
      </xs:sequence>

      <xs:attribute name="created-at" type="xs:dateTime"/>
    </xs:complexType>
  </xs:element>
</xs:schema>
```

Our schema is pretty trivial and describes <*sms*> elements that have a single, optional attribute named created-at= and three child elements named <*sender*>, <*receiver*>, and <*content*>. Here is an instance of our XML schema:

foreign_languages/java/sms.xml

```
<sms created-at='2008-10-18T13:40:00'>
  <sender>12345678</sender>
  <receiver>987654321</receiver>
  <content>Hello, world!</content>
</sms>
```

In Java we can use the Apache Xerces XML parser to validate the previous document against our schema:

foreign_languages/java/src/SchemaValidator.java

```
Line 1  import java.io.StringReader;
     -  import java.io.File;
     -  import org.jdom.Document;
     -  import org.jdom.input.SAXBuilder;
     5
     -  public class SchemaValidator {
     -    public static Document isValid(
     -      String xmlFileName,
     -      String xmlSchemaFileName)
```

```
10   {
       try {
         final SAXBuilder builder =
           new SAXBuilder("org.apache.xerces.parsers.SAXParser", true);
         builder.setFeature(
15         "http://apache.org/xml/features/validation/schema",
           true
         );
         builder.setFeature(
           "http://apache.org/xml/features/validation/" +
20           "schema-full-checking",
           true
         );
         builder.setFeature(
           "http://xml.org/sax/features/validation",
25         true
         );
         builder.setFeature(
           "http://xml.org/sax/features/namespaces",
           false
30       );
         builder.setProperty(
           "http://apache.org/xml/properties/schema/" +
             "external-noNamespaceSchemaLocation",
           new File(xmlSchemaFileName).toURL().toString()
35       );
         return builder.build(xmlFileName);
       }
       catch (Exception e) {
         System.err.println("Document is invalid: " + e.getMessage());
40       return null;
       }
     }
   }
```

Admittedly, this code looks horrible, but it's not difficult to understand. Instead of working with DOM documents and elements directly, we use JDOM to represent the documents we are interested in. Under the hood, JDOM uses the Xerces parser to handle all the XML parsing, but the JDOM classes make it much easier to navigate in the resulting tree.

In line 12, we create a SAXBuilder instance that we'll use to parse XML documents. SAXBuilder is a JDOM convenience class and needs a real XML parser. As announced before, we use the Xerces parser. Then we set a lot of features and properties describing how we'd like to validate our documents. You do not have to understand them in detail. Just believe me that you need them all to validate a document against an XML schema.

After the builder has been configured properly, we actually parse a document in line 36. If the document can be parsed without problems, we return its JDOM representation. Otherwise, an exception is raised, and we return null in line 40.

In Java that's all we need, and we could use the following sample program to validate an XML document against an XML schema on the command line:

foreign_languages/java/src/SchemaValidator.java

```java
public static void main(String[] args) {
  String xmlFile = args[0];
  String schemaFile = args[1];
  if (isValid(xmlFile, schemaFile) != null) {
    System.out.println(xmlFile + " is valid.");
  } else {
    System.out.println(xmlFile + " is invalid.");
  }
}
```

But that's not exactly what we want. We want to use the SchemaValidator class in a Ruby program. Fortunately, Ruby programmers are in a very privileged situation regarding the integration of Java code, because they can choose from two mature solutions:

- The *Ruby Java Bridge* (RJB) uses the Java Native Interface (JNI) to combine Ruby and Java.

- *JRuby* is a Java implementation of the Ruby language; it actually is a Ruby interpreter written in Java.

Both of them have pros and cons, and in this recipe we take a look at alternative solutions of our original problem. Let's see how to integrate the SchemaValidator class using Rjb:

foreign_languages/java/rjb_validator.rb

```ruby
require 'rjb'
classpath = '.:lib/jdom.jar:lib/xercesImpl.jar'
Rjb::load(classpath)
SchemaValidator = Rjb::import('SchemaValidator')
xml_file, xml_schema_file = ARGV[0 .. 1]
doc = SchemaValidator.isValid(xml_file, xml_schema_file)
if doc.nil?
  puts "#{xml_file} is invalid."
else
  puts "#{xml_file} is valid."
  puts "Receiver: " + doc.getRootElement.getChild('receiver').getText
end
```

That's a real textbook example, isn't it? First we define the classpath that has to be used. It points to the current directory, to the JDOM library, and to the Xerces parser. In line 4, we import the SchemaValidator class into the Ruby namespace, and at this point SchemaValidator is indistinguishable from a regular Ruby class. Then we read the name of the file to be validated and the name of the XML Schema file to be used for validation from the command line.

In line 6, we call the isValid() method to check whether our XML document actually contains a valid short message. If the result is nil, we print an error message. Otherwise, we print the receiver's phone number by calling some JDOM methods. Yes, getRootElement(), and so on, are all methods that have been imported from Java libraries automatically. Run the program, and it prints the following to the console:

```
mschmidt> ruby rjb_validator.rb sms.xml sms.xsd
sms.xml is valid.
Receiver: 987654321
```

That's all great, but as promised, I'll show you an alternative: JRuby. As explained earlier, JRuby is a complete rewrite of the original Ruby interpreter in Java. That means it is a Java program that has to be installed separately.

You might ask why somebody would do that, but actually the JRuby interpreter has a lot of advantages over the C version: it's portable, it's fast, it supports real threads, and it has access to all the byte code that has been created for the Java Virtual Machine (JVM). Yes, with JRuby you can use all code that runs on a JVM, and JRuby makes it a breeze to integrate this code with Ruby:

foreign_languages/java/jruby_validator.rb

```
Line 1  require 'java'
   -    include_class 'SchemaValidator'
   -
   -    xml_file, xml_schema_file = ARGV[0 .. 1]
   5    doc = SchemaValidator.is_valid(xml_file, xml_schema_file)
   -    if doc.nil?
   -      puts "#{xml_file} is invalid."
   -    else
   -      puts "#{xml_file} is valid."
   10     puts "Sender: " + doc.get_root_element.get_child('sender').get_text
   -    end
```

That's a JRuby program that integrates our SchemaValidator class. We have to require the *java* library, and we have to explicitly include the classes we'd like to use by calling include_class() (in Rjb we had to use import()). From this point, the Java classes and the Ruby code become indistinguishable again. In line 5, we call SchemaValidator's is_valid() method. But wait—the method was named isValid(), wasn't it? That's one of JRuby's services: you can use the Java naming style, but you can also use the Ruby conventions. Nice, eh?

We use this feature again in line 10: all JDOM method calls use the Ruby naming style, and they are automatically converted to the right Java methods. We could have also used the following version:

```
puts "Receiver: " + doc.getRootElement.getChild('sender').getText
```

Then our program would have looked exactly like its Rjb counterpart. Here's the output of a test run:

```
mschmidt> jruby jruby_validator.rb sms.xml sms.xsd
sms.xml is valid.
Sender: 12345678
```

As you see, combining Java and Ruby code is seamless, and such hybrid approaches may well be the future of programming. You can write critical system code that has to be executed fast in a static language like Java, but your application code and your domain-specific languages can be written in a dynamic language like Ruby.

Discussion

Now that you know two excellent Java integration technologies, you might ask yourself which one you should use. As often, the answer is that it depends.

Rjb comes as a RubyGem and can be integrated into your project within a minute. If you are in the middle of a Ruby project and urgently need some functionality that you can find only in Java, Rjb is an excellent choice (see Recipe 42, *Use RMI Services*, on the facing page for an example). But it has some serious shortcomings and does not support multithreading, for example. Hence, you cannot integrate all Java code such as the Swing library.

If you know up front that an essential part of your application will consist of Java code, you should take a look at JRuby. JRuby actually is a good candidate for becoming Ruby's most popular platform, because it is actively supported by Sun Microsystems and provides a lot of convenient goodies. For example, it supports Ruby method name conventions in Java classes, turns Java iterators automatically into each() methods, and is an excellent platform for Rails projects.

Use RMI Services

During the late 90s many companies created a lot of Java services using Java Remote Method Invocation (RMI). Today there are better alternatives, but at that time it was a reasonable choice. Most of the services have been replaced already by REST and SOAP servers, but some critical components still can be used only by RMI clients, which usually have to be written in Java.

There is no native RMI binding for Ruby, but in this recipe you'll learn how to overcome this shortcoming so you can use RMI services from your Ruby and Rails applications.

- Install the Ruby Java Bridge (RJB):[10]

  ```
  $ gem install rjb
  ```

The service we're going to use is the company's central user account manager. Its interface looks as follows:

foreign_languages/rmi/src/com/example/AccountManager.java

```java
package com.example;

import java.rmi.Remote;
import java.rmi.RemoteException;

public interface AccountManager extends Remote {
    User authenticate(
        String username,
        String password) throws RemoteException;
}
```

It's a simple interface that consists of a single method named authenticate(). It expects a username and a password, and it returns a User object if a user could be authenticated successfully. Otherwise, it returns null.

---

10. http://rjb.rubyforge.org/

The User class looks like this:

foreign_languages/rmi/src/com/example/User.java

```java
package com.example;

public class User implements java.io.Serializable {
    public User(String forename, String surname) {
        this.forename = forename;
        this.surname = surname;
    }

    public String getForename() {
        return this.forename;
    }

    public String getSurname() {
        return this.surname;
    }

    public String toString() {
        return this.forename + " " + this.surname;
    }

    private String forename;
    private String surname;
}
```

A real User class would have a lot more attributes, but for demonstration purposes the forename and surname are sufficient. Because we'd like to transfer User objects using RMI, we have to implement the java.io.Serializable interface. Let's create an account management server:

foreign_languages/rmi/src/com/example/Server.java

```java
package com.example;

import java.rmi.registry.Registry;
import java.rmi.registry.LocateRegistry;
import java.rmi.RemoteException;
import java.rmi.server.UnicastRemoteObject;

public class Server implements AccountManager {
    public User authenticate(String username, String password) {
        User user = null;
        if (username != null && username.equals("maik"))
            if (password != null && password.equals("tOp$ecret"))
                user = new User("Maik", "Schmidt");
        return user;
    }

    public static void main(String args[]) throws Exception {
        AccountManager manager =
```

```
        (AccountManager)UnicastRemoteObject.exportObject(
            new Server(), 0
        );
    Registry registry = LocateRegistry.getRegistry();
    registry.bind("AccountManager", manager);
    System.out.println("Started Account Manager.");
    }
}
```

Our current implementation of the authenticate() method is pretty simple, but we do not need anything more sophisticated at the moment. In the main() method we only create a new Server object and bind it to the local RMI registry so clients can find it by its name (AccountManager) We compile the server and all the other classes we need as follows:

```
mschmidt> mkdir classes
mschmidt> javac -d classes src/com/example/*.java
```

Then we start the RMI registry and the server:

```
mschmidt> cd classes
mschmidt> rmiregistry &
mschmidt> java com.example.Server
Started Account Manager.
```

It's important to change to the classes directory first, because otherwise the RMI registry would not find our classes. Now that we have the server up and running, we need a client:

foreign_languages/rmi/src/com/example/Client.java

```
package com.example;

import java.rmi.registry.LocateRegistry;
import java.rmi.registry.Registry;

public class Client {
    public Client() throws Exception {
        Registry registry = LocateRegistry.getRegistry();
        this.accountManager =
            (AccountManager)registry.lookup("AccountManager");
    }

    public User authenticate(
        String username,
        String password) throws Exception
    {
        return this.accountManager.authenticate(username, password);
    }

    private AccountManager accountManager;
}
```

The Java client looks up the AccountManager object in the local RMI registry and delegates all requests to it. We'll integrate it into a small Ruby program now using Rjb:

foreign_languages/rmi/authenticate.rb

```
Line 1    require 'rjb'
    -     classpath = 'classes'
    -     Rjb::load(classpath)
    -     Client = Rjb::import('com.example.Client')
    5     client = Client.new
    -     username, password = ARGV[0 .. 1]
    -     user = client.authenticate(username, password)
    -     puts user ? user.toString : "Could not authenticate #{username}."
```

Rjb provides access to Java code via the Java Native Interface (JNI). In line 3, we load the Java Virtual Machine, passing it our class path. Then we obtain a reference to the Client class in the com.example package. Rjb automatically maps it to a Ruby class, so we can instantiate an object and invoke its authenticate() method. The resulting User object gets mapped, too, and we check the result in the last line. A sample run looks as follows:

```
mschmidt> ruby authenticate.rb maik t0p\$ecret
Maik Schmidt
mschmidt> ruby authenticate.rb maik wrong_password
Could not authenticate maik.
```

Works like a charm, doesn't it? Rjb maps Java code to Ruby, and vice versa, quite naturally, and it's a perfect solution if you have to reuse existing Java code of reasonable complexity. Because of Ruby's threading model, though, it's not possible to use Java code that uses Java's native threads.

Mix Ruby and .NET with IronRuby

Problem

You've developed a lot of software on the Microsoft .NET platform, and you'd like to use Ruby for a new application. The application has to use some of the libraries you've created over the years, and it will depend on some of the .NET core classes. In this recipe, you'll learn it all.

Ingredients

- On RubyForge[11] you'll find a binary distribution of IronRuby[12] that you can unzip and copy to your Programs folder. Don't forget to add ironruby/bin to your path.

- Download and install Microsoft Visual C# Express Edition.[13]

- Download and install an Oracle database server or at least an Oracle client[14] for Microsoft Windows.

Solution

.NET is a flexible platform when it comes to new languages. While Java is a platform-independent language, .NET is a language-independent platform, meaning code from different languages can be combined arbitrarily. At least that is true for all programming languages that can be compiled to Common Language Runtime (CLR) byte code. In principle, the CLR is a virtual machine similar to the JVM.

IronRuby is an implementation of a Ruby interpreter written in C#, and it targets the CLR. It allows you to mix Ruby code with any .NET code, no matter whether it has been written in C#, VB .NET, or any other CLR language. At the time of this writing, IronRuby is in an early stage of development, so it is not feature-complete and still has bugs and

---

11. http://ironruby.rubyforge.org/
12. http://ironruby.net/
13. http://www.microsoft.com/Express/
14. http://www.oracle.com/technology/software/products/database/

quirks. But it's mature enough to start some experiments, and it will certainly become more stable within a short period of time.

In this recipe, we'll use IronRuby to implement a small report generator that reads some statistical information from an Oracle database (it will work similarly on other database systems such as Microsoft SQL Server, for example) and outputs them in a real Microsoft Windows window (see Figure 9.1, on page 286).

The database table we create a report for contains orders and is defined as follows:

foreign_languages/net/orders.sql

```sql
CREATE TABLE orders (
   id          NUMBER(10) NOT NULL PRIMARY KEY,
   product     VARCHAR2(100),
   state       VARCHAR2(30),
   created_at DATE
);
```

Orders have an ID, the name of the product that has been ordered, a state, and a creation timestamp. The state can be open or closed. To create the report, we use some C# code:

foreign_languages/net/Report/StandardReport.cs

```csharp
Line 1  using System;
        using System.Data.OracleClient;

        namespace Report {
5         public class ReportData {
            public int totalOrders;
            public int closedOrders;
          }

10        public class StandardReport {
            public StandardReport(string user, string password) {
              connection = new OracleConnection();
              connection.ConnectionString = GetConnectionString(user, password);
              connection.Open();
15          }

            public ReportData Create() {
              ReportData reportData = new ReportData();
              OracleCommand command = connection.CreateCommand();
20            command.CommandText = "select count(*) from orders";
              OracleDataReader reader = command.ExecuteReader();
              reader.Read();
              reportData.totalOrders = reader.GetInt32(0);
```

```
        command.CommandText =
 25       "select count(*) from orders where state='closed'";
        reader = command.ExecuteReader();
        reader.Read();
        reportData.closedOrders = reader.GetInt32(0);
        command.Dispose();
 30     return reportData;
      }

      private string GetConnectionString(string user, string password) {
        return "User ID=" + user + ";Password=" + password +
 35       ";Unicode=True";
      }

      private OracleConnection connection;
    }
 40 }
```

If you know C++ or Java, you should be able to understand the program. First it imports the System and System.Data.OracleClient namespaces. Then it defines two classes (named ReportData and StandardReport) in the Report namespace. ReportData is a simple storage class that contains all the statistical information we need, which includes the total number of orders and the number of orders that have been closed already.

In line 11, we define the constructor for StandardReport objects. It takes the username and the password that are needed for connecting to the database, and it also establishes a connection using the OracleConnection class.

The Create() method beginning in line 17 contains the main business logic of our report generator. It executes two SQL statements to determine the total number of orders and the number of closed orders and stores them in a ReportData object. The GetConnectionString() method at the end of the program generates a connection string as needed by the OracleClient.

We did not care much about resource management, and we did not close the resources we used to make the program shorter, but all in all this code should look familiar if you've ever written database code in Java, C++, or C#.

To make the code available to other programs on the .NET platform, it has to be converted to a *.NET assembly* (DLL). Doing so on the command line is pretty tedious, so I recommend using Microsoft Visual

Studio Edition for C# for this task. Create a new class library project (call it Report), add the previous code, and add a reference to System.Data.OracleClient. In the project properties, go to the Signing tab, and choose the "Sign the assembly" option. Afterward, build the project, and you'll find a file named Report.dll in the bin\Release directory belonging to the project.

Let's use the DLL in our first IronRuby program:

foreign_languages/net/sample.rb

```
require 'Report.dll'
sr = Report::StandardReport.new('maik', 'tOp$ecret')
report_data = sr.create
puts "Total orders: #{report_data.totalOrders}"
```

The most important feature in this short program is that we can directly import the .dll file with a require() statement. Afterward, we can treat the imported C# classes as if they were regular Ruby classes.

Run the program, and its output will look like this (ir is a shortcut for the IronRuby interpreter):

```
c:\mschmidt> ir sample.rb
Total orders: 27
```

Easy, isn't? But before we try more complicated things, we need to take another look at the DLL import, because there are several alternatives for embedding a DLL into an IronRuby program. If the .dll file is in IronRuby's library path, you can require it directly as we've done it here. But, usually, library assemblies are installed globally, and then you have to specify it in more detail. In our case, the require() statement would look like this:

```
require 'Report, Version=1.0.0.0,
        Culture=neutral, PublicKeyToken=44371d941e7ae83f'
```

You have to pass the following attributes:

- The assembly's name (without a file extension).

- The assembly's version.

- A *culture*, that is, the locale of the assembly. It should be neutral if possible.

- A 64-bit hash value of the public key belonging to the private key that has been used to sign the assembly.

To determine the public key token of a DLL, use the sn (*strong name*) tool:

```
c:\mschmidt> sn -T Report.dll

Microsoft (R) .NET Framework Strong Name Utility  Version 3.5.21022.8
Copyright (c) Microsoft Corporation.  All rights reserved.

Public key token is 44371d941e7ae83f
```

If you want to install the DLL in the global assembly cache, use gacutil:

```
c:\mschmidt> gacutil /i Report.dll
```

Uninstalling it works similarly (do not use the .dll in this case):

```
c:\mschmidt> gacutil /u Report
```

Now we'll concentrate on our original problem and build a small application on top of our C# library. First we put the username and the password needed to log in to the database into an XML configuration file that looks as follows:

foreign_languages/net/config.xml

```xml
<?xml version='1.0' encoding='utf-8'?>
<config>
  <database>
    <user>maik</user>
    <password>t0p$ecret</password>
  </database>
</config>
```

The following statements parse and process the XML file:

foreign_languages/net/report.rb

```ruby
Line 1  require 'mscorlib'
   -    require 'System, Version=2.0.0.0,
              Culture=neutral, PublicKeyToken=b77a5c561934e089'
   -    require 'System.Xml, Version=2.0.0.0,
   5          Culture=neutral,PublicKeyToken=b77a5c561934e089'
   -
   -    Xml = System::Xml
   -    doc = Xml::XmlDocument.new
   -    doc.load('config.xml')
  10
   -    def doc.get_first_element(name)
   -      get_elements_by_tag_name(name).item(0).inner_text
   -    end
   -
  15    user = doc.get_first_element('user')
   -    password = doc.get_first_element('password')
```

We load all assemblies we need, and in line 7 we define an abbreviation for the System::Xml namespace (that is a trick that we will use often). Then we create an XmlDocument instance and call its load() method to load and parse the config.xml file. Experienced .NET developers will notice that the method should be called Load() instead (method names start with an uppercase letter by convention on the .NET platform), but IronRuby supports both the .NET and Ruby naming conventions for classes and methods.

Then, in line 11, we do something really interesting and define a singleton method named get_first_element() on the doc object. We know that we have to extract two text elements from the configuration file (*<user>* and *<password>*), and we know that XmlDocument has only a GetElementsByTagName() method that always returns a whole list of elements, which is not what we want. We define our own method that does exactly what we want: it searches for elements that have a certain name, takes the first one (we know there's only one), and extracts its text content. Please note that get_first_element() is a Ruby method that has been added to a class written in C#!

Extracting the username and password is easy now, so we can use them to create the report data:

foreign_languages/net/report.rb

```
require 'Report.dll'

StandardReport = Report::StandardReport
ReportData = Report::ReportData

class ReportData
  def to_s
    "total: #{totalOrders}/closed: #{closedOrders}"
  end
end

sr = StandardReport.new(user, password)
report_data = sr.create
puts report_data
```

That's similar to our first sample, but this time we have reopened the ReportData to add a better to_s() method and to show off a bit.

As promised, we'll show the report data not only on the console but in a fancy and colorful window.

Here's the code:

`foreign_languages/net/report.rb`

```ruby
require 'PresentationFramework, Version=3.0.0.0,
         Culture=neutral, PublicKeyToken=31bf3856ad364e35'
require 'PresentationCore, Version=3.0.0.0,
         Culture=neutral, PublicKeyToken=31bf3856ad364e35'

Window = System::Windows::Window
Application = System::Windows::Application
Button = System::Windows::Controls::Button
StackPanel = System::Windows::Controls::StackPanel
Label = System::Windows::Controls::Label
Thickness = System::Windows::Thickness

window = Window.new
window.title = 'Fancy .NET Report'
stack = StackPanel.new
stack.margin = Thickness.new 15
window.content = stack

[
  "Here's our Report:",
  "Total orders: #{report_data.totalOrders}",
  "Closed orders: #{report_data.closedOrders}"
].each do |message|
  label = Label.new
  label.font_size = 24
  label.content = message
  stack.children.add label
end

button = Button.new
button.content = 'Close'
button.font_size = 24
button.click { |sender, args| Application.exit }
stack.children.add button
app = Application.new
app.run window
```

Line numbers: 1, 5, 10, 15, 20, 25, 30, 35.

Admittedly, the first lines look a bit scary, but we load only the assemblies from the Windows Presentation Foundation (WPF) framework that
we need, and we define abbreviations for all classes that we'll use.

The fun stuff begins in line 13 where we create a new window that has
a stack layout (using this layout, all GUI elements that are added to
the window pile up to a stack). Then we print three lines of text by
creating a new Label object for each of them. In line 27, the labels are

Figure 9.1: AN IRONRUBY .NET APPLICATION

added to the stack layout. A close button is defined beginning in line 30, and its event handler is specified in line 33. Event handlers get a reference to the event sender and several arguments describing the event in more detail, but we ignore them and stop the application. The button gets added to the stack, too, and at the end we create and start the application shown in Figure 9.1.

Despite the ugly require statements and namespace abbreviations, this is pretty nice and expressive code. Although IronRuby is at an early stage of development, it's already a useful tool and will certainly become an interesting alternative for Ruby developers who work on the Windows platform anyway.

Discussion

If you want to write Ruby programs only on the Windows platform, you can use the One-Click Installer for Windows,[15] but this means you do not have access to the wonderful world of the whole .NET API in your Ruby programs.

The biggest problem with IronRuby at the moment of this writing is that it is not complete yet. Important libraries are missing (Rails makes good progress but is far from being mature enough to use it in production), and it will have to catch up with Ruby 1.9. But IronRuby has

---

15. http://rubyinstaller.rubyforge.org/

great momentum, and chances are good that it will become another
full-blown Ruby platform.

Also See

- See *Rails for .NET Developers* [CE08] to learn more about Ruby
  and Rails on .NET.

## Chapter 10

Maintain and Administer Your Applications

Developing software in and for enterprise environments is different from most other approaches. Usually, enterprise developers work in big teams, they often have to reuse proprietary libraries and applications, and they have to work closely together with the operations and QA departments.

There are even more differences: in contrast to desktop applications, for example, many enterprise applications don't have a user interface and run in the background as daemons or services. Depending on the operating system, it can be tricky to implement such background processes yourself, so in Recipe 44, *Turn Your Code into Daemons and Services*, on page 291, you'll learn to automate this task.

Another big challenge when creating enterprise software solutions is not only to write programs but also to operate them. In contrast to ordinary desktop applications, enterprise software often has to run 24/7, and outages usually cost a lot of money. It's inevitable that you have to monitor critical components and act appropriately if something goes wrong. In Recipe 45, *Monitor Your Applications with Monit*, on page 301 and in Recipe 46, *Let god Take Care of Your System*, on page 307, you'll learn how to monitor your Ruby applications, how to restart them automatically when they crash, and how to send notifications in case of problems.

Many companies have lots of standards for all kinds of things: developers have to name objects according to a certain scheme, web applications have to follow a particular style guide, and so on. To make your life simpler, it's a good idea to encapsulate as many of these standards in reusable components, so in Recipe 47, *Create Plug-ins for Common Tasks*, on page 313, you'll learn how to create your own Rails plug-ins, and Recipe 48, *Avoid Code Duplication with Generators*, on page 319 shows you how to create your own generators.

Turn Your Code into Daemons and Services

In an enterprise environment you often have to create *daemon processes*,[1] which are processes running without a controlling terminal in the background (HTTP servers are a good example of this class of processes). Although it's not rocket science to turn a process into a daemon manually, it's still complicated enough that it's better to let it be done automatically by a library.

In this recipe, you'll learn how to turn a Ruby application into a daemon on Unix-like operating systems or into a *service* on the Microsoft Windows platform (that's what daemons are called on Windows).

Ingredients

- If you want to run daemons on a Unix-like operating system, install the *daemons* gem:[2]

  ```
  $ gem install daemons
  ```

- In a Microsoft Windows environment, install the *win32-service* gem:[3]

  ```
  $ gem install win32-service
  ```

Solution

Before we turn a process into a daemon process, we need a small test application. The following server observes a directory for new files; it waits for new orders encoded in XML. The input filenames must start with the prefix order, and they must have the extension .xml.

---

1. http://en.wikipedia.org/wiki/Daemon_%28computer_software%29
2. http://daemons.rubyforge.org/
3. http://win32utils.rubyforge.org/

```
                   administration/daemons/order_import.rb

Line 1   require 'logger'

   -     working_dir = ARGV[0] || '/tmp/orders'
   -     interval = (ARGV[1] || 10).to_i
   5     logger = Logger.new File.join(working_dir, 'order_import.log')
   -     logger.info 'Started order import...'
   -
   -     loop do
   -       orders = Dir["#{working_dir}/order*.xml"]
   10      orders.each do |filename|
   -         logger.info "Processing #{filename}."
   -
   -         # Do something with order file...
   -
   15        File.delete(filename)
   -       end
   -       sleep interval
   -     end
```

At the beginning of the program, we define a couple of variables: working_dir points to the directory where we expect new orders to arrive, interval defines how often we check the working directory for new files (the default is ten seconds), and logger references a Logger object that we use to log the program's activity to a file. Log files are an inevitable tool for daemons, because without them it's nearly impossible to check whether the daemon actually does what it should do.

Then we start an endless loop, and in line 9, we read a list of all new order input files from the working directory. We iterate over the files, process them (actually we do nothing with them, because that's not important for what we want to achieve), and at the end the files are deleted so they don't get processed twice. All important events are written to the log file, and in line 17, the program sleeps for the amount of seconds defined.

So far, so good. We can start the program and feed it with new orders by copying .xml files to its input directory. But it would run in the foreground, and our goal is to turn it into a daemon running in the background. Here's where the *Daemons* library comes into play, because it has some convenient mechanisms for creating and controlling daemon processes. Add the following lines at the beginning of the current program:

```
                   administration/daemons/instant_daemon.rb

require 'daemons'
Daemons.daemonize :backtrace => true
```

That's all. If you start the program, it will automatically detach itself from the current terminal and will run in the background. The method that makes all this possible is daemonize(). It accepts an options hash and currently supports two optional options. We use the backtrace option, because it makes debugging a daemon a lot easier. When the backtrace option is set, the daemon writes a backtrace of the last exceptions to pid/(app_name).log. If ontop is set to true, the program is not daemonized, which is also useful when debugging.

You should call daemonize() as early as possible; otherwise, you'd probably get some surprising results. If you daemonize the current program after the Logger instance has been initialized, for example, the logger can be invalid, because its I/O stream would have been closed (daemons usually close all streams that are not needed on startup). In any case, you have to make sure that all file paths you're using are absolute paths, because a daemon process usually changes its current working directory to /.

Creating a daemon process with the *Daemons* library is trivial, but usually the creation is only a small step. After the daemon has been created, you need some tools to stop and restart it. Nearly all popular daemons use the same trick: when the process starts, it writes its process ID (PID) to a file with the extension .pid. An external script uses this file to control the daemon. For example, it could pass the file's content to the kill command to stop the daemon.

The *Daemons* library has excellent support for these mechanisms, and the only thing you have to do is create a simple control script:

`administration/daemons/order_import_control.rb`

```
require 'daemons'
Daemons.run(File.join(File.dirname(__FILE__), 'order_import.rb'))
```

Now you can control the order import process with the following commands (while the daemon is running, you find its PID in a file named order_import.rb.pid):

```
$# Start the process in the background:
$ ruby order_import_control.rb start
$# Restart the process:
$ ruby order_import_control.rb restart
$# Stop the process:
$ ruby order_import_control.rb stop
$# Start the process in the foreground:
$ ruby order_import_control.rb run
```

> ### Process.daemon on Ruby 1.9
>
> In Ruby 1.9 the Process class has a new class method named daemon(stay_in_dir=false,keep_stdio_open=false). It "daemonizes" the current process and puts it into the background. Like a good daemon, it sets the current working directory to / unless stay_in_dir is true. In this case, it stays in the current directory. Standard input, output, and error are redirected to /dev/null. If you do not want this, set keep_stdio_open to true.
>
> This method is really convenient, but it is not available on all platforms, so you should use it only if your platform is supported and you do not want to migrate your application to other platforms.

The run option is useful when debugging a daemon process. You can pass command-line arguments to the original script after a double hyphen. The following statement starts the order import process with the /tmp working directory and a sleep interval of five seconds:

```
$ ruby order_import_control.rb start -- /tmp 5
```

That's all fine when you're working on some kind of Unix, but it doesn't help you much on a Microsoft Windows box. Here we need completely different mechanisms that are provided by the *win32-service* library.

Microsoft Windows offers a life-cycle API for services and controls them using a special management console. This is a graphical tool that can be used to start, stop, and pause services, for example. This is completely different from Unix where every developer has to create their own script to control new daemon processes.

win32-service brings Window's service API to Ruby, so here's the order import process implemented as a Windows service:

administration/daemons/win/order_import.rb

```
Line 1   require 'logger'
    -    require 'win32/daemon'
    -    include Win32
    -
    5    class OrderImportService < Daemon
    -      def initialize(opts = {})
    -        super()
    -        @opts = opts
    -      end
   10
```

```ruby
  def service_init
    @interval = @opts[:interval] || 10
    @working_dir = @opts[:working_dir] || 'c:/orders'
    @logger = Logger.new(@opts[:logfile] || 'c:/order_import.log')
    @logger.info 'Starting order import...'
  end

  def service_main
    @logger.info 'Order import has been started.'
    while running?
      orders = Dir["#{@working_dir}/order*.xml"]
      orders.each do |filename|
        @logger.info "Processing #{filename}."

        # Do something with order file...

        File.delete(filename)
      end
      sleep(@interval)
    end
    @logger.info 'Order import has been stopped.'
  end
end

if __FILE__ == $0
  order_import_service = OrderImportService.new
  order_import_service.mainloop
end
```

The service does not differ much from the Unix version, but we had to define a class named OrderImportService that is derived from Daemon. Daemon handles all Windows specifics behind the scenes, so we only have to provide the life-cycle management methods our service needs. In our case, we have two of them: service_init() and service_main().

service_init() is called when the service is started and can be used to initialize data and files that are needed by the service. We define some member variables including the log file, which is just as important on Windows as it is on Unix.

service_main() implements the service's main logic and contains the code that will be running constantly after the service has been started. It looks nearly exactly like the former version; there are only two differences: we use member variables now instead of regular variables, because we are in a class now. More important, we use Daemon's running?() method in line 20 to check whether the service is still running.

At the end of the program, we actually start the service, and in line 37, we call another Daemon method named mainloop() that registers the service so it can wait for new events.

Before a service can be started, it has to be installed. Service management unsurprisingly is done by the Service class, and we use it to write a method for installing Ruby services more or less automatically:

administration/daemons/win/install_service.rb

```ruby
require 'win32/service'
include Win32

def install_service(name, display_name, executable)
  Service.create(
    name,
    nil,
    :display_name => display_name,
    :binary_path_name => 'ruby ' + File.expand_path(executable)
  )
  puts "Service #{name} has been installed."
end
```

We need only the class method create(), which expects a service's logical name, the name of the host it should run on, and an options hash containing the service's properties. We set the host to nil (it defaults to localhost), and we set only two properties (there are many more). With display_name, we specify the string that will be displayed in the system's service management console, and binary_path_name points to the service's executable. Because our service is written in Ruby, we build a string that executes the Ruby interpreter and passes it the absolute path of the script we want to turn into a service. The following statement installs the OrderImportService:

administration/daemons/win/install_service.rb

```ruby
install_service(
  'order_import',
  'Order Import',
  'order_import.rb'
)
```

After you have installed the service, it can be managed like any other Windows service with the management console you can see in Figure 10.1, on the facing page. Click Start, and you will find a log file at c:\order_import.log.

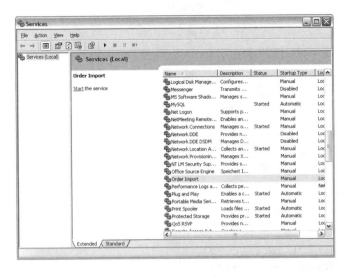

Figure 10.1: MICROSOFT WINDOWS SERVICE CONSOLE

Sometimes you might want to manage your services yourself, and the Service class lets you do whatever you want with a service. In the following program, we play a bit with our order import service:

administration/daemons/win/service_management.rb

```
Line 1  require 'win32/service'
     -  include Win32
     -
     -  def wait_for_state(state)
     5    print "Waiting for state '#{state}'"
     -    i = 0
     -    while Service.status('order_import').current_state != state
     -      i += 1
     -      print '.' if i % 1000 == 0
    10    end
     -    puts
     -  end
     -
     -  puts "Display name: #{Service.get_display_name('order_import')}"
    15
     -  Service.configure(
     -    'order_import',
     -    nil,
     -    :display_name => 'Order Import 2008'
    20  )
```

```
  -     Service.start('order_import')
  -     wait_for_state('running')
  -     puts 'Service has been started.'
  -
 25     Service.pause('order_import')
  -     wait_for_state('paused')
  -     puts 'Service has been paused.'
  -
  -     Service.resume('order_import')
 30     puts 'Service has been resumed.'
  -     wait_for_state('running')
  -
  -     Service.stop('order_import')
  -     wait_for_state('stopped')
 35     puts 'Service has been stopped.'
  -
  -     Service.delete('order_import')
  -     puts 'Service has been uninstalled.'
```

All methods do exactly what their names promise, and nearly all expect the service's name as the first argument with only one exception: the configure() method gets the same arguments as create(). In line 14, we demonstrate how to read a service's display name, and in the wait_for_ state() method you can see how to wait for a certain service state. The program's output looks like this:

```
C:\tmp> ruby service_management.rb
Display name: Order Import
Waiting for state 'running'
Service has been started.
Waiting for state 'paused'
Service has been paused.
Service has been resumed.
Waiting for state 'running'
Waiting for state 'stopped'....................
Service has been stopped.
Service has been uninstalled.
```

As you can see, it can take a long time to stop a service.

All in all, Ruby's support for daemons and services is excellent. No matter which platform you're working on, you will always find a convenient solution quickly if you need to put some code into the background. The biggest problem still is that it's pretty hard to write portable services that will work on any platform, but that's not specific to Ruby.

Also See

- After you have put a process into the background, it's easy to forget about it. That's OK as long as the process does what it's supposed to do and as long as it starts automatically after a system reboot. But when working with daemons, you shouldn't be too confident (read some of Edgar Allan Poe's books if you don't believe me), so take a look at Recipe 45, *Monitor Your Applications with Monit*, on page 301 or Recipe 46, *Let god Take Care of Your System*, on page 307 to learn how to check whether your processes are working properly.

Monitor Your Applications with Monit

Problem

You've written a lot of Ruby programs that have become vital parts of your company's infrastructure. Although you gave your best, sometimes one of them crashes and has to be restarted. As a pragmatic programmer, you decided to monitor them so they get restarted automatically when they crash. In this recipe, you'll learn about *monit*, a monitoring tool that will do all the heavy lifting for you.

Ingredients

- Install *monit*,[4] (if there's a more recent version, use that instead of 4.10.1):

```
$ wget http://www.tildeslash.com/monit/dist/monit-4.10.1.tar.gz
$ tar xzvf monit-4.10.1.tar.gz
$ cd monit-4.10.1
$ ./configure && make && sudo make install
```

Solution

Monitoring processes on a Unix-like system usually can be reduced to the same techniques:

- The process to be monitored can be started and stopped using different command-line options or different scripts, and it writes its process ID (PID) to the file system.

- A process monitor reads the PID files and looks up the current status of the processes to be monitored at fixed intervals from the process list.

In this recipe, we take a look at a tool that follows these principles and that can be used to monitor arbitrary processes: *monit*. We'll use it to observe the order import daemon we wrote in Recipe 44, *Turn Your Code into Daemons and Services*, on page 291, because it fulfills the

---

4. http://www.tildeslash.com/monit/

prerequisites we defined earlier: the order import daemon is controlled by a script named order_import_control.rb that accepts a *start* option and a *stop* option. It also writes the PID of the current order import daemon to the file system.

monit is a popular, all-purpose process monitor that is written in C and that has a powerful configuration language. Here's the configuration file that monitors nearly every important aspect of our system and of the order import daemon:

administration/monitoring/monitrc.conf

```
Line 1   set daemon 60
    -    set logfile '/tmp/monitoring.log'
    -    set mailserver smtp.example.com username "sysadm" password "t0p$ecret"
    -    set alert admin@example.com { nonexist, timeout } with mail-format {
    5      from: monit@example.com
    -    }
    -    set alert boss@example.com only on { timeout }
    -    set httpd port 2812 and
    -      use address localhost
   10      allow localhost
    -      allow admin:monit
    -
    -    # Check the system's status:
    -    check system localhost
   15      if loadavg(1min) > 4 then alert
    -      if loadavg(5min) > 2 then alert
    -      if memory usage > 75% then alert
    -      if cpu usage(user) > 70% then alert
    -      if cpu usage(system) > 30% then alert
   20      if cpu usage(wait) > 20% then alert
    -
    -    # Check status of order import daemon:
    -    check process order_import with pidfile /tmp/order_import.rb.pid
    -      start program = "/tmp/order_import_control.rb start"
   25      stop program  = "/tmp/order_import_control.rb stop"
    -      if cpu > 60% for 2 cycles then alert
    -      if cpu > 80% for 5 cycles then restart
    -      if totalmem > 100.0 MB for 5 cycles then restart
    -      if loadavg(5min) greater than 8 for 6 cycles then stop
   30      if 3 restarts within 5 cycles then timeout
    -      group server
```

Let's dissect it line by line:

- Line 1 tells *monit* to start as a daemon and to check all monitored processes every 60 seconds (this monitoring interval is called a *cycle*).

- In line 2, we configure a log file *monit* uses to log important events. Instead of writing to a log file, you can also send events to the *syslog* daemon.

- *monit* is able to send emails in case of important events, so in line 3 we configure the mail server to be used.

- For every monitoring system it's vital to specify who gets notified when certain errors occur. *monit* is no exception, so we define two email recipients in lines 4 and 7. The first recipient gets an email whenever a service crashes or does not respond any longer. The second recipient gets an email only in the case of timeouts. *monit* emails always have the same layout, but you can configure them in nearly any way you like. For example, we set the from header to monit@example.com.

- To give you a quick and comprehensive overview of your processes' status, *monit* comes with an integrated HTTP server. Its configuration starts in line 8, and we want it to start on port 2812. In addition, we specify that it should accept connections only from localhost and that access to the web server is protected by a username (*admin*) and password (*monit*).

- Beginning in line 14, we specify critical system conditions that are independent of a particular application. The configuration should not need much explanation, because it reads like plain English, doesn't it? For example, we tell *monit* to send an alert whenever more than 75 percent of the system's memory is used or whenever more than 70 percent CPU time is spent in the user space.

- The configuration of the order import process starts in line 23 and looks similar to the earlier configuration of the system's monitoring. In addition, we specify the commands for starting and stopping the order import process, and we tell *monit* what to do if the process cannot be restarted three times within five cycles (five minutes in our case). All checks in this section (CPU, memory, and so on) refer to the process' usage and not to the overall system's usage.

- *monit* supports process groups, and in line 31 we put the order import process into the "server" group.

Now that we have a configuration file, let's use it to actually monitor the order import daemon:

```
mschmidt> monit -c monitrc.conf
Starting monit daemon with http interface at [localhost:2812]
```

The previous command starts a *monit* process in the background. Its log file should look like this:

```
[Jul 15 21:21:25] info  : Starting monit daemon with http interface at \
   [localhost:2812]
[Jul 15 21:21:25] info  : Starting monit HTTP server at [localhost:2812]
[Jul 15 21:21:25] info  : monit HTTP server started
[Jul 15 21:21:25] info  : Monit started
[Jul 15 21:21:25] error : 'order_import' process is not running
[Jul 15 21:21:25] info  : 'order_import' trying to restart
[Jul 15 21:21:25] info  : 'order_import' start: \
   /tmp/order_import_control.rb
[Jul 15 21:22:25] info  : Monit has not changed
[Jul 15 21:22:25] info  : 'order_import' process is running with pid 759
```

monit started its HTTP interface, immediately noticed that the order import process wasn't working, and restarted it. In addition, it sent an email that you can see in Figure 10.2, on the facing page. *monit* starts all processes immediately if you invoke it like this:

```
mschmidt> monit -c monitrc.conf start all
```

It's also possible to start, stop, or restart process groups that have been defined using the group declaration in the configuration file:

```
mschmidt> monit -c monitrc.conf -g server restart all
```

If you no longer need *monit*, you can terminate it with a single command as well:

```
mschmidt> monit -c monitrc.conf quit
monit daemon with pid [7636] killed
```

Now that the order import process is running, *monit* checks periodically whether it's doing fine. If it crashes or if you stop it deliberately, you'll find the following in *monit*'s log file within a minute:

```
[Jul 15 21:30:26] error : 'order_import' process is not running
[Jul 15 21:30:26] info  : 'order_import' trying to restart
[Jul 15 21:30:26] info  : 'order_import' start: \
   /tmp/order_import_control.rb
[Jul 15 21:31:26] info  : 'order_import' process is running with pid 779
```

Observing the log file is certainly not the most convenient way to check your system's overall status, so it's time to remember that we have configured *monit*'s web server. Point your web browser to http://localhost: 2812, click the "order_import" link. and you'll see something like Figure 10.3, on page 306.

That's what a sysadmin's dreams are made of! *monit*'s web front end reports nearly every little aspect of a process's status. Despite this,

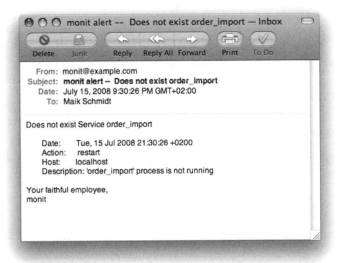

Figure 10.2: EMAIL SENT BY *monit*

always use as many and as specific tests as possible in your configuration. Even if a process is running, it doesn't mean that it does what it's expected to do (monitoring processes is a bit like watching your office mates: some of them only pretend to be working).

Also See

- See Recipe 46, *Let god Take Care of Your System*, on page 307 to learn about another monitoring tool that can be completely configured with Ruby.

- If you want to learn how to turn your programs into daemons, take a look at Recipe 44, *Turn Your Code into Daemons and Services*, on page 291.

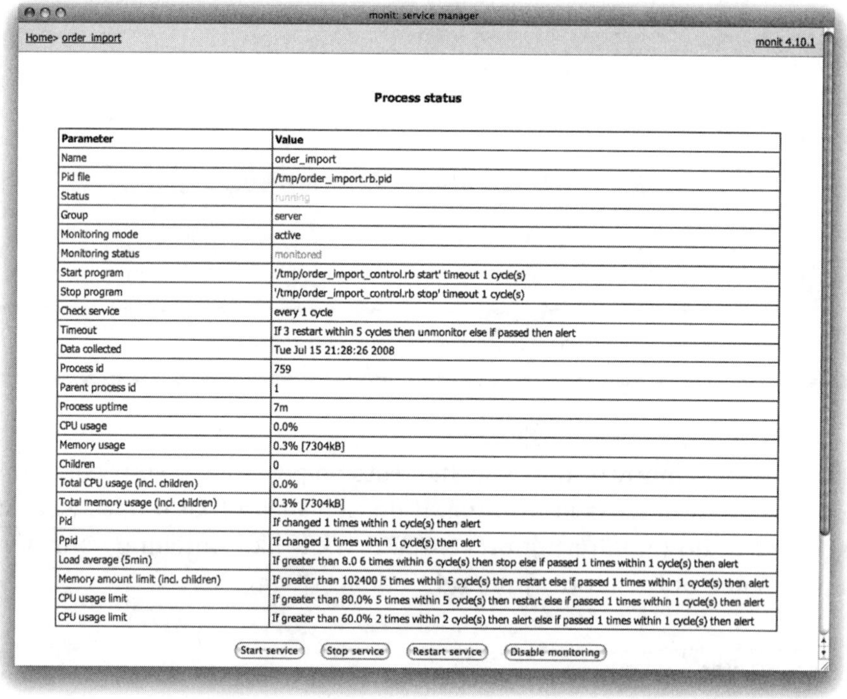

Process status

Parameter	Value
Name	order_import
Pid file	/tmp/order_import.rb.pid
Status	running
Group	server
Monitoring mode	active
Monitoring status	monitored
Start program	'/tmp/order_import_control.rb start' timeout 1 cycle(s)
Stop program	'/tmp/order_import_control.rb stop' timeout 1 cycle(s)
Check service	every 1 cycle
Timeout	If 3 restart within 5 cycles then unmonitor else if passed then alert
Data collected	Tue Jul 15 21:28:26 2008
Process id	759
Parent process id	1
Process uptime	7m
CPU usage	0.0%
Memory usage	0.3% [7304kB]
Children	0
Total CPU usage (incl. children)	0.0%
Total memory usage (incl. children)	0.3% [7304kB]
Pid	If changed 1 times within 1 cycle(s) then alert
Ppid	If changed 1 times within 1 cycle(s) then alert
Load average (5min)	If greater than 8.0 6 times within 6 cycle(s) then stop else if passed 1 times within 1 cycle(s) then alert
Memory amount limit (incl. children)	If greater than 102400 5 times within 5 cycle(s) then restart else if passed 1 times within 1 cycle(s) then alert
CPU usage limit	If greater than 80.0% 5 times within 5 cycle(s) then restart else if passed 1 times within 1 cycle(s) then alert
CPU usage limit	If greater than 60.0% 2 times within 2 cycle(s) then alert else if passed 1 times within 1 cycle(s) then alert

Figure 10.3: *monit* PROCESS STATUS

Let god Take Care of Your System

You'd like to monitor all your applications automatically, but some of them are difficult to monitor, because you have to check a lot of things to make sure they're actually doing what they are supposed to do. You need a monitoring tool that can be configured with a full-grown programming language, and in this recipe you'll learn about one: *god*.

Ingredients

- Install *god*,[5] a monitoring tool written completely in Ruby:

  ```
  $ gem install god
  ```

Solution

In this recipe, we'll take a look at a monitoring tool named *god* that was written in Ruby and—even better—can be configured using Ruby. We'll use it to observe the order import daemon we wrote in Recipe 44, *Turn Your Code into Daemons and Services*, on page 291, and here's a *god* configuration file that monitors it:

administration/monitoring/god_conf.rb

```
Line 1   God.load File.join(File.dirname(__FILE__), 'email_conf.rb')

   -     control_script = '/tmp/order_import_control.rb'
   -     God.watch do |w|
   5       w.name = 'order_import'
   -       w.interval = 60.seconds
   -       w.start = "#{control_script} start"
   -       w.stop = "#{control_script} stop"
   -       w.restart = "#{control_script} restart"
  10       w.start_grace = 10.seconds
   -       w.restart_grace = 10.seconds
   -       w.pid_file = '/tmp/order_import.rb.pid'
   -       w.group = 'server'
   -
```

---

5. http://god.rubyforge.org/

```
15      w.behavior(:clean_pid_file)

        w.start_if do |start|
          start.condition(:process_running) do |c|
            c.interval = 20.seconds
20          c.running = false
            c.notify = 'admin'
          end
        end

25      w.restart_if do |restart|
          restart.condition(:memory_usage) do |c|
            c.above = 100.megabytes
            c.times = [3, 5]
            c.notify = 'admin'
30        end

          restart.condition(:cpu_usage) do |c|
            c.above = 60.percent
            c.times = 5
35          c.notify = %w(admin boss)
          end
        end
      end
```

Admittedly, it's much longer than the *monit* configuration file you saw in Recipe 45, *Monitor Your Applications with Monit*, on page 301, but it's plain Ruby. We start by loading the email configuration (we'll look at it later) and by setting control_script to the name of the order import process's control script. This way we do not have to repeat it in the rest of the configuration file (that's the advantage when you use a full-blown programming language). In line 4, the real configuration starts, and every process that should be monitored by *god* has to have its own code block passed to *god*'s watch() method.

In lines 5 to 13, we define some global parameters like the process's logical name, the interval *god* should use to watch the process, the names of the start/stop/restart commands, and the name of the process's PID file. Interestingly, you do not have to specify the pid_file parameter. In this case, *god* daemonizes your program automatically.

god allows for special commands to be applied before a process is started or stopped. For example, it's often useful to delete the PID file of a process that has crashed before restarting it. That's what we specify in line 15.

The monitoring rules for the order import process start in line 17. Here we use the start_if() method to define when the process has to be started.

start_if() contains at least one condition that is defined using the condition() method. If any of the condition blocks return true, the *start* action gets executed. We check the running status, so the order import process gets started if it is not running (sounds reasonable, doesn't it?). In addition, we set interval to twenty seconds, so *god* checks every twenty seconds whether the process is running. Such local interval definitions overwrite the global one, so you can check important conditions more often, for example. Finally, the notify attribute specifies who gets notified if the process gets started. You'll see how the *admin* recipient is defined in a minute.

A restart is triggered when any of the conditions defined in the code block beginning in line 25 is met. We check whether the process's memory usage has been greater than 100 megabytes in three of five checks. If yes, the *admin* recipient is notified, and the process is restarted. Nearly the same happens if the CPU consumption has been more than 60 percent for five checks. In that case, the boss gets notified, too.

We have specified all email recipients and settings in a separate file that gets included in the main configuration:

administration/monitoring/email_conf.rb

```
God::Contacts::Email.message_settings = {
  :from => 'god@example.com'
}

God::Contacts::Email.server_settings = {
  :address => 'smtp.example.com',
  :port => 25,
  :domain => 'example.com',
  :authentication => :plain,
  :user_name => 'sysadm',
  :password => 't0p$ecret'
}

God.contact(:email) do |c|
  c.name = 'admin'
  c.email = 'admin@example.com'
end

God.contact(:email) do |c|
  c.name = 'boss'
  c.email = 'boss@example.com'
end
```

god uses a default layout for notification emails and their subjects. You can freely redefine all components of this layout, and we set the from header to god@example.com in line 2 (it will probably help to improve your software quality if you get an email from *god* in case of any failures). Then we configure our mail server's settings.

At the end, we define all possible contacts—all those people who might potentially get notifications from *god*. At the moment we declare those contacts who get notified via email, but *god* has an extensible notification framework, so you can implement more notification channels yourself. For example, you can easily notify contacts using short messages on a cell phone.

When you start *god* with the current configuration, it will print something like this (timestamps have been removed for brevity):

```
mschmidt> god -D -c god_conf.rb
INFO: Using pid file directory: /Users/mschmidt/.god/pids
INFO: Started on drbunix:///tmp/god.17165.sock
INFO: order_import move 'unmonitored' to 'up'
INFO: order_import moved 'unmonitored' to 'up'
INFO: order_import [trigger] process is not running (ProcessRunning)
INFO: order_import move 'up' to 'start'
INFO: order_import before_start: no pid file to delete (CleanPidFile)
INFO: order_import start: /tmp/order_import_control.rb start
INFO: order_import moved 'up' to 'up'
INFO: order_import [ok] process is running (ProcessRunning)
INFO: order_import [ok] memory within bounds [7156kb] (MemoryUsage)
INFO: order_import [ok] cpu within bounds [0.0%] (CpuUsage)
INFO: order_import [ok] process is running (ProcessRunning)
```

The -D option tells *god* not to turn itself into a daemon, so we can watch its log output on the console. As expected, *god* notices that the order import process isn't running and starts it immediately. In the next lines, you can see that *god* permanently checks the process's CPU and memory usage. Everything works fine!

god supports many of the same commands as *monit*. You can quit *god* with the quit command (terminate quits not only *god* but also all processes it is monitoring), for example, and you can also apply commands to groups of processes. One of the most useful commands is log that prints the last 1,000 log messages belonging to a process to the console and updates every second:

```
mschmidt> god log order_import
INFO: order_import [ok] process is running (ProcessRunning)
INFO: order_import [ok] memory within bounds [7152kb] (MemoryUsage)
INFO: order_import [ok] cpu within bounds [0.0%] (CpuUsage)
INFO: order_import [ok] process is running (ProcessRunning)
```

⌣ Joe Asks...
monit or god?

You shouldn't ask yourself whether monitoring your processes is a good thing (it definitely is!), but you might ask which tool you should use. Both *monit* and *god* are excellent monitoring tools, so in principle you can choose either of them. Unfortunately, both tools share a common disadvantage: they do not support Microsoft Windows, and they probably never will.

god's biggest advantage is that it can be configured using Ruby, so if you have processes that are tricky to manage, *god* might be the better choice. It can also monitor nondaemonizing scripts. On the other hand, *monit* is more mature, has a bigger community, has commercial support (which is a strong argument for many big companies), and—at the moment—has many more features like the web front end you've seen before.

You can monitor not only Ruby applications with *god* but also *Mongrel* processes, database servers, files, directories, network services, and so on. In this recipe, we have barely scratched the surface of all its features.

Also See

- See Recipe 45, *Monitor Your Applications with Monit*, on page 301 to learn about another popular monitoring tool.

- If you want to learn how to turn your programs into daemons, take a look at Recipe 44, *Turn Your Code into Daemons and Services*, on page 291.

Create Plug-ins for Common Tasks

You have written several Ruby on Rails applications in the past, and quite naturally you've gathered a lot of code that you reuse in new applications. Although this is quite a good thing, it does not feel very convenient, because you often copy files from various locations, and you often have to adjust a few lines here and there manually. These times are gone now, because in this recipe you'll learn to create your own plug-ins and generators for Rails applications, so you'll never have to copy and manually adjust code again.

Rails has great support for plug-ins and generators, and you've probably already used some of them such as *open_id_authentication* in Recipe 8, *Implement a Single Sign-on System with OpenID*, on page 37, for example. In this recipe, we'll create a plug-in named *acts_as_proprietary* that adds some functionality to your Rails applications that we'll imagine is needed in the company you're working for. It adds a dump() method to your database models that creates a textual representation of a model's content. We'll assume that your operations department insists on this format in log files.

Creating plug-ins is easy, because Rails comes with a plug-in generator. To create the *acts_as_proprietary* plug-in, run the following command:

```
mschmidt> script/generate plugin acts_as_proprietary
```

After the command runs successfully, you'll find a new subdirectory named acts_as_proprietary in the vendor/plugins directory that contains:

```
README
MIT-LICENSE
Rakefile
init.rb
install.rb
uninstall.rb
lib/acts_as_proprietary.rb
tasks/acts_as_proprietary_tasks.rake
test/acts_as_proprietary_test.rb
```

All plug-ins are stored in vendor/plugins and share the same directory layout. Some of the files are self-explanatory: the README file contains information about the plug-in (you have to fill this file, of course), and MIT-LICENSE contains a copy of the MIT license that plug-ins usually use. When a plug-in is installed, install.rb is run, so it can create configuration files and so on. uninstall.rb is executed when it is uninstalled.

I'll explain the meaning of the other files in the following paragraphs. We start with lib/acts_as_proprietary.rb. Right after the plug-in skeleton code has been generated, the file is empty, and it is supposed to be used for the plug-in's main code (if you need more than one file to implement your plug-in's logic, add them all to the lib directory). The code that adds a dump() method to an ActiveRecord model looks as follows:

administration/plugins/plugin_demo/vendor/plugins/acts_as_proprietary/lib/acts_as_proprietary.rb

```
Line 1  module EnterprisePlugin
   -      module Acts
   -        module Proprietary
   -          def self.included(base)
   5            base.extend ClassMethods
   -          end
   -

   -          module ClassMethods
   -            def acts_as_proprietary(options = {})
   10             cattr_accessor :sort_attributes
   -              self.sort_attributes = options[:sort_attributes] || false
   -              include InstanceMethods
   -              extend SingletonMethods
   -            end
   15           end
   -

   -          # This module contains instance methods.
   -          module InstanceMethods
   -            def dump
   20             result = "Model:#{self.class.name}\n"
   -              keys = attributes.keys
   -              keys.sort! if self.sort_attributes
   -              keys.each { |key| result << "#{key}:#{attributes[key]}\n" }
   -              result
   25           end
   -          end
   -

   -          # This module contains class methods.
   -          module SingletonMethods
   30           end
   -        end
   -      end
   -    end
```

This is a wonderful piece of Ruby code, isn't it? It makes use of some fairly advanced features that we'll dissect now. The file starts with three nested module declarations that aren't absolutely necessary, but it's good style to choose an unambiguous namespace for all the code belonging to your plug-ins. Usually the code will be used in an unknown environment, and choosing good names prevents namespace clashing.

In line 4, we define the included() method for our module that is invoked whenever our module is included in another module or class. When included() is called, it adds the methods of the ClassMethods module to the including module or class.

Right now the ClassMethods module contains only one method named acts_as_proprietary(), which is the method we'd like to call later in a database model to add a dump() method to it. acts_as_proprietary() gets an options hash that can be used to vary the plug-in's behavior. At the moment, only the sort_attributes option is supported. It controls whether a model's attributes get sorted before they are dumped. To store the option, we define and initialize a class variable using cattr_accessor(). Then we turn all members of the InstanceMethods module into instance methods of the including class, and we turn all members of the SingletonMethods module into class methods of the including class.

Finally, we define the dump() method in the InstanceMethods module. It turns the name of the current class and all entries of the attributes hash into a nicely formatted text. Depending on the value of sort_attributes, the entries get sorted up front. Please note that attributes is a member of the ActiveRecord::Base class; you'll see in a minute how we connect our code to ActiveRecord.

Actually, Rails does not have an explicit plug-in API, so our library does not contain any special plug-in code. When a Rails application starts, it initializes all plug-ins in the vendor/plugins directory; in other words, it runs the init.rb file of every plug-in. To make our *acts_as_proprietary* plug-in available, we have to add the following to init.rb:

`administration/plugins/plugin_demo/vendor/plugins/acts_as_proprietary/init.rb`

```
require 'acts_as_proprietary'
ActiveRecord::Base.send(
  :include,
  EnterprisePlugin::Acts::Proprietary
)
```

This loads the *acts_as_proprietary* library and adds the new functionality to the ActiveRecord::Base class so it is available in all model classes.

Let's try it with a Customer model that has been created with the following migration:

administration/plugins/plugin_demo/db/migrate/20080712165043_create_customers.rb

```
create_table :customers do |t|
  t.string :forename
  t.string :surname
  t.date    :date_of_birth
  t.timestamps
end

Customer.create(
  :forename      => 'John',
  :surname       => 'Doe',
  :date_of_birth => Date.new(1968, 7, 22)
)
```

The model class looks like this:

administration/plugins/plugin_demo/app/models/customer.rb

```
class Customer < ActiveRecord::Base
  acts_as_proprietary :sort_attributes => true
end
```

It's a normal model class, but it uses our new *acts_as_proprietary* plug-in. Every Customer instance should have a dump() method now:

```
mschmidt> ruby script/console
Loading development environment (Rails 2.1.0)
>> puts Customer.find(1).dump
Model:Customer
created_at:Sat Jul 12 16:57:07 UTC 2008
date_of_birth:1968-07-22
forename:John
id:1
surname:Doe
updated_at:Sat Jul 12 16:57:07 UTC 2008
=> nil
```

Works like a charm, doesn't it? The *acts_as_proprietary* example shows a common pattern that is used by many popular plug-ins. Keep in mind that although our plug-in enhanced the ActiveRecord::Base class, plug-ins are free to enhance any part of Rails, add new classes, or do anything else that you want to do. In principle, you can do whatever you want in your plug-in code. The only trick is that your plug-in's init.rb automatically runs at startup.

Also See

- To learn about another way to reuse code across applications, see Recipe 48, *Avoid Code Duplication with Generators*, on page 319.

Avoid Code Duplication with Generators

Many enterprise applications share common functionality that is often replicated by copying code. In this recipe, you'll learn how to prevent this and how to write a generator that creates Rails code automatically.

Solution

Let's assume that all your company's web applications must have a special controller named InfoController that reports the application's current state. We'll create a generator for an InfoController that has a predefined status() method returning status information for the current application. The following command creates all the necessary stubs and skeletons:

```
mschmidt> script/generate plugin acme_monitoring --with-generator
```

A plug-in does not necessarily need a generator, so we've added the --with-generator option to create one. The command has created a subdirectory named vendor/plugins/acme_monitoring/generators, and for each new generator a directory with the generator's name has to be created in this directory. Our generator is named *info_controller*, so we create a subdirectory named info_controller. This way we can invoke the generator with script/generate info_controller when we're done. Here's the generator's code:

administration/plugins/generator_demo/vendor/plugins/acme_monitoring/generators/info_controller/info_controller_generator.rb

```
Line 1   class InfoControllerGenerator < Rails::Generator::Base
           def initialize(runtime_args, runtime_options = {})
             super
             @application_name = args.shift || 'UnknownApplication'
     5       @custom_methods = args || []
           end

           def manifest
             record do |m|
    10         m.template(
                 'info_controller.rb',
                 'app/controllers/info_controller.rb',
                 :collision => :skip,
```

```
15          :assigns => {
              :application_name => @application_name,
              :custom_methods    => @custom_methods
            }
          )

20        m.directory 'app/views/info'
          @custom_methods.each do |method|
            m.template(
              'view.html.erb',
              "app/views/info/#{method}.html.erb",
25            :collision => :skip,
              :assigns => { :method_name => method }
            )
          end
        end
30    end
    end
```

Rails comes with several base classes for all kinds of generators, and we have derived InfoControllerGenerator from Rails::Generator::Base, which is the most general one. There are more specific base classes (for model generators, for example), so before you start to write a new generator, choose your base class carefully.

In the initialize() method, we read the arguments that have been passed to the generator on the command line from the args variable. The first argument is the name of the application to create the InfoController for, and the rest of the arguments contain a list of methods to create method stubs for.

Every generator has to define a manifest() method that returns a Rails:: Generator::Manifest object. In principle, the manifest describes which files and directories will be created, and it describes how they will be created, too. record() is a convenience method that makes creating a new manifest a piece of cake. It expects a code block that gets passed the Manifest to be finalized. The Manifest class has some useful methods, and in line 10 we use its template() method.

Our generator generates a file named app/controllers/info_controller.rb, and it creates .html.erb files in the app/views directory for every method that has been passed to the generator on the command line. For both the controller and for the view files, we need ERb templates stored in the templates directory.

template() expects the name of the template file to be copied, the name of the destination, and some options. Before the file is copied, it is run through the ERb engine, so the template may contain arbitrary Ruby code. With template()'s assigns option, you can define parameters that are available as variables in the template. By setting collision to skip, we make sure that the generator does not override an existing file.

In line 20, the app/views/info directory is created if it does not exist already, and in the following line we create an .html.erb file for every method of the InfoController class using the template() method.

The rest of the generator logic can be found in the template files, and the template for the InfoController class looks as follows:

administration/plugins/generator_demo/vendor/plugins/acme_monitoring/generators/info_controller/templates/info_controller.rb

```
Line 1   class InfoController < ApplicationController
  -        def status
  -          application_name = '<%= application_name %>'
  -          status = "Everything's OK with #{application_name}."
  5          render :text => status
  -        end
  -        <% for method in custom_methods %>
  -        <% next if method == 'status' %>
  -        def <%= method %>
 10          # Your code here.
  -        end
  -        <% end %>
  -      end
```

Most of the template is regular text, but we create a customized status message in line 4, and we iterate over all custom method names that have been passed to generate a method stub for each of them in line 7. The template for the views is much simpler and contains only a placeholder:

administration/plugins/generator_demo/vendor/plugins/acme_monitoring/generators/info_controller/templates/view.html.erb

```
<%= method_name %>: Your view code here.
```

Let's test the *info_controller* generator:

```
mschmidt> script/generate info_controller --svn FancyApplication init
      create  app/controllers/info_controller.rb
A          app/controllers/info_controller.rb
A          app/views/info
A          app/views/info/init.html.erb
```

As expected, two files have been created. Although we did not define what to do with the --svn switch, our generator added the generated files to the current Subversion repository exactly like all the other Rails generators.

All standard options are supported by default, and if you'd like to improve the usage message that is printed when the --help option is passed, add a file named USAGE to the info_controller directory so it gets included automatically.

The generated controller looks like this:

administration/plugins/generator_demo/app/controllers/info_controller.rb

```ruby
class InfoController < ApplicationController
  def status
    application_name = 'FancyApplication'
    status = "Everything's OK with #{application_name}."
    render :text => status
  end

  def init
    # Your code here.
  end

end
```

That's it! The only thing left to do is make the new plug-in available to your colleagues. This is easy, because Rails' plugin command supports all important network protocols available. For example, you could upload the whole *acme_monitoring* directory code to an HTTP server, to a Subversion repository, or to a Git repository. If you have uploaded the code to svn://example.com/acme_monitoring, for example, you could install the plug-in with the following command from your application's root directory (Git has been supported since Rails 2.1, and for a Git repository, pass the Git URL, respectively):

mschmidt> **./script/plugin install svn://example.com/acme_monitoring**

All in all, writing plug-ins and generators surely is not a trivial task, but it's not rocket science either. The next time you think about copying and modifying some files, ask yourself whether it's time for a new plug-in—maybe even a plug-in the whole Rails community might benefit from.

Also See

- See Recipe 47, *Create Plug-ins for Common Tasks*, on page 313 to learn about another way to reuse code across applications.

## Chapter 11

Test the Easy Way

For software developers, there's nothing as great as writing code, but professional software developers need other skills, too: testing, for example. That's especially true when writing enterprise software, because many big companies have strict quality and documentation standards.

Nearly all Ruby developers use Test::Unit, because it's part of every Ruby distribution and works nicely with Rails. It's certainly one of the most convenient unit testing frameworks available, but unit testing is not the only way to make sure your software works as it is supposed to work. There's a new kid on the block named *behavior-driven development*, and you can learn more about it in Recipe 49, *Improve Your Testing with RSpec*, on page 325 and Recipe 50, *Integrate RSpec with Rails*, on page 333.

When you think of testing, you almost certainly think of mock objects, too. Even trivial enterprise applications often depend on external components that are difficult to integrate into your tests. In Recipe 51, *Create Mock Objects with RSpec*, on page 337, you'll learn how to simulate them using *RSpec*'s mock features.

Unit testing is not the only important testing discipline; integration tests, for example, are important too, especially when you are working with distributed applications consisting of many components. Whenever new components have to be written, it's advantageous if you can quickly build an interface prototype that other applications can integrate with as soon as possible. Recipe 52, *Prototype Services with Sinatra*, on page 345 shows you how this can be done.

Improve Your Testing with RSpec

As a modern software developer you are writing unit tests for every new piece of code, and they have increased the quality of your applications tremendously. Despite this, you might not feel comfortable when writing tests, because you might think you are describing how your application should not behave instead of specifying how it should.

You are not alone, and in this recipe you will learn what behavior-driven development (BDD) is and how to benefit from it in your Ruby and Rails applications.

Ingredients

- If you do not want to use *RSpec* in a Rails application, it's sufficient to install the *rspec* gem:[1]

```
$ gem install rspec
```

Solution

In this recipe, you'll learn how to work with *RSpec*, a tool supporting BDD.[2] BDD is quite similar to good old unit testing, but it uses a completely different vocabulary. Instead of focusing on the technical details, BDD focuses on the purpose of a piece of software. This makes it easier to translate specifications into user stories and test cases. In addition, it allows technical and businesspeople to use the same language.

As an example, in this recipe we'll use two small classes:

`testing/rspec/stock.rb`

```ruby
Product = Struct.new(:name)

class Stock
  attr_reader :products
```

---

1. http://rspec.info/
2. http://en.wikipedia.org/wiki/Behavior_driven_development

```ruby
  def initialize
    @products = []
  end

  def empty?
    @products.empty?
  end

  def add_product(product)
    raise ArgumentError if product.nil? or product.name.nil?
    @products << product
  end

  def products_by_name(name)
    @products.select { |p| p.name == name }
  end

  def count
    @products.size
  end
end
```

Product represents a product identified only by its name, and Stock implements a stock containing several products. We can check whether the stock is empty, we can add new products to the stock, and we can look up products by their names. In addition, we have a reader named products that returns all products currently in stock.

Back in the old days of unit testing, you probably wrote test cases similar to the following:

testing/rspec/unit_test_stock.rb

```ruby
require 'test/unit'
require 'stock'

class StockTest < Test::Unit::TestCase
  def setup
    @stock = Stock.new
  end

  def test_new_stock_is_empty
    assert @stock.empty?
  end

  def test_empty_stock_should_not_contain_a_product_having_a_name
    assert_equal 0, @stock.products_by_name('foo').size
  end
end
```

That's a perfectly normal unit test suite. The setup() method gets called before each test method and initializes a new Stock instance. All test methods start with the prefix test_, and we use the assertions of the Test::Unit framework such as assert_equal() to make sure certain conditions are met. When we run it, we get the following result:

```
mschmidt> ruby unit_test_stock.rb
Loaded suite unit_test_stock
Started
..
Finished in 0.000513 seconds.

2 tests, 2 assertions, 0 failures, 0 errors
```

You might think that this is a good way to test your code, and from a technical point of view you are absolutely right. There's no redundancy because we have used the setup() method and because every test case has its own method with a meaningful name. Still, it's not satisfying from a psychological point of view, because it reads like a test specification and not like a specification of the Stock class' behavior. Also, the names of the test cases are a bit awkward because of their prefixes, and you have to know a bit about Test::Unit to know what the setup() method is all about.

Here's an alternative version using *RSpec*:

testing/rspec/stock_simple_spec.rb

```
Line 1    describe Stock, '(newly created)' do
    -       before(:each) do
    -         @stock = Stock.new
    -       end
    5
    -       it { @stock.should be_empty }
    -
    -       it 'should not contain products having a certain name' do
    -         @stock.should have(0).products_by_name('foo')
   10       end
    -    end
```

Although it does the same as the unit testing variant, it reads much better, doesn't it? It starts with a describe() declaration that takes the name of the class whose behavior we'd like to specify. Optionally, it takes a string describing the circumstances under which we're testing the class in more detail. We are going to test the behavior of a newly created Stock object, so we pass it the string "(new one)" (you'll see why we've put it in parentheses in a minute).

Instead of defining a setup() method that gets magically called by the Test::Unit framework, we use a more expressive method named before(), which gets a code block that will be called before each test (you probably guessed it already: yes, there is an after() method, too).

Then we specify two aspects of our Stock class' behavior by calling the it() method. it() accepts a string describing the test case and a block of test code (if you don't pass it a string, it derives one from the test code, as we'll see in a minute). Before we dissect the code that actually tests the Stock class, let's run it for the first time:

```
mschmidt> spec stock_simple_spec.rb --format specdoc

Stock (newly created)
- should be empty
- should not contain products having a certain name

Finished in 0.008053 seconds

2 examples, 0 failures
```

With the *rspec* framework comes a command-line tool named spec for executing *RSpec* specifications. We pass it the specification's filename and the format option (by default, spec produces the same output as Test::Unit). In the output you find all the strings we have used in our specification, and *RSpec* has generated a "should be empty" message for the it() declaration that did not declare one explicitly. It actually reads like a specification for the behavior of an empty stock, doesn't it?

But let's take a closer look at the test code. In both cases we have called a method named should() that has been added by *RSpec* to every object (there's also a should_not() method). In line 6, we use it to make sure that the empty?() method returns true for an empty stock. empty?() is a predicate—a method returning either true or false. For these predicates, *RSpec* has a mechanism that allows us to put a be_ prefix in front of the predicate's name and pass it to should(). So, @stock.should be_empty does exactly what it says and makes sure that the empty?() method of the Stock object that has been created in the before() block returns true.

In line 9, we invoke have() to check whether a collection (an array, for example) contains a particular number of items. Alternatively, we could have written @stock.products_by_name('foo').should have(0).items, and instead of *items* at the end of the method chain, we could have even used any other name such as *elements*, for example. It's just added for better readability.

Although the statement does the same as assert_equal 0, @stock.products_ by_name('foo').size in the corresponding unit test, it reads much better, and that's what BDD is about: naming things. That's really the main idea: you'll think differently about testing your code if you use a different vocabulary. Instead of "test," say "should," and your test cases will read and feel better.

To explore more of *RSpec*'s features, we will specify our Stock class in a more detailed manner. First we extract behavior that is needed in more than one situation. *RSpec* calls this *shared examples*, and they are defined as follows:

testing/rspec/stock_spec.rb

```ruby
shared_examples_for 'non-empty stock' do
  it { @stock.should_not be_empty }
  it { @stock.should have_at_least(1).products }
end
```

A shared example defines test cases that can be imported (like Ruby mixins) by describe() blocks, and you can define as many shared examples as you need. We include the "nonempty stock" example in the following specification:

testing/rspec/stock_spec.rb

```ruby
Line 1  describe Stock do
   -      before(:each) do
   -        @stock = Stock.new
   -      end
   5
   -      it 'should not accept empty products' do
   -        lambda { @stock.add_product(nil) }.should raise_error(ArgumentError)
   -      end
   -
  10      describe '(empty)' do
   -        it { @stock.should be_empty }
   -
   -        it 'should not contain products having a certain name' do
   -          @stock.should have(0).products_by_name('foo')
  15        end
   -
   -        it 'should add a product' do
   -          lambda {
   -            @stock.add_product Product.new('foo')
  20          }.should change(@stock, :count).by(1)
   -        end
   -      end
   -
```

```
     describe 'with a single foo product' do
25     before(:each) do
         @stock.add_product Product.new('foo')
       end

       it_should_behave_like 'non-empty stock'
30
       it 'should find a product named "foo"' do
         @stock.should have(1).products
         @stock.should have(1).products_by_name('foo')
         @stock.products.first.name.should be_eql('foo')
35     end
     end
   end
```

In this specification, you'll find many things I've already explained, but there are also some new features. First you'll recognize that a describe( ) block may contain describe( ) blocks itself. Then, in line 7, you can see how to make sure a certain method raises an exception. We cannot use should( ) directly on the method that should raise an exception for obvious reasons, so we have to turn it into a Proc object using the lambda( ) method.

Line 20 demonstrates another nice function of the *RSpec* framework, namely, the change( ) method. We add a new product to the current stock and use change( ) to make sure that the number of items in stock has changed by one exactly.

Do you remember the shared examples we defined some paragraphs earlier? In line 29, we use them to declare that a stock containing a single item should behave like an nonempty stock by calling it_should_ behave_like( ). That's a really useful feature, and it not only reads nicely, but it also supports the DRY principle. Whenever you define new test cases dealing with nonempty Stock instances, you can run the standard cases by adding a single line of code.

Finally, in line 34, we use be_eql( ) to check two strings for equality. be_eql( ) checks whether two objects have the same value, while be_equal( ) would check whether two objects are the same. There are more variants such as be_true( ), be_false( ), or be_nil( ), for example, and you should check *RSpec*'s excellent documentation for details.

If we feed the earlier program to the spec command, it prints the following (tested) specification:

```
mschmidt> spec stock_spec.rb --format specdoc

Stock
- should not accept empty products

Stock (empty)
- should be empty
- should not contain products having a certain name
- should add a product

Stock with a single foo product
- should not be empty
- should have at least 1 products
- should find a product named "foo"

Finished in 0.096581 seconds

7 examples, 0 failures
```

Discussion

If you have written lots of unit tests for your current applications, there's no urgent need to migrate them to *RSpec*, but in your next project you definitely should give BDD a chance, especially because in this recipe we have covered *RSpec*'s specification features only. It also has a framework for describing and executing user stories, and it comes with a great library for mocking objects.

In the beginning, it's a bit difficult to think in specifications and not in tests, but after you get used to it, it will make your tests more expressive, more readable, and more fun.

Also See

- If you'd like to test your Rails applications with *RSpec*, too, take a look at Recipe 50, *Integrate RSpec with Rails*, on page 333.

Integrate RSpec with Rails

You've used *RSpec* to test your regular application code for a while, and now you'd like to use it in your Rails applications, too.

- When using *RSpec* in a Rails application, it's good practice to install both the *rspec* module and the *rspec_on_rails* plug-in locally. This makes sure they fit together:

```
$ script/plugin install git://github.com/dchelimsky/rspec.git
$ script/plugin install git://github.com/dchelimsky/rspec-rails.git
```

  Then generate all files needed by *RSpec* and its documentation:

```
$ script/generate rspec
$ rake doc:plugins
```

  The documentation then can be found in doc/plugins/rspec_on_rails/index.html.

In Recipe 49, *Improve Your Testing with RSpec*, on page 325, you can see how to create an executable specification for an ordinary Ruby class. Wouldn't it be great if we could use *RSpec* for testing Rails components such as models and controllers, too? That's where *rspec-rails* comes into play. It adds full support for *RSpec* to Ruby on Rails applications, and we'll use it to test and specify a Product model that has been created with the following database migration:

`testing/rspec/rspecsample/db/migrate/20080708191641_create_products.rb`

```ruby
create_table :products do |t|
  t.string :name
  t.timestamps
end
```

And here's the model class:

`testing/rspec/rspecsample/app/models/product.rb`

```ruby
class Product < ActiveRecord::Base
  validates_presence_of :name
end
```

As you certainly know (because you are writing tests for every new piece of code!), Rails comes with excellent support for automatic tests based on the Test::Unit framework. All tests (functional, integration, and unit tests) can be found in the test directory and its subdirectories. *rspec-rails* is similar but expects all files in the spec directory. Model tests go to the models subdirectory, controller tests can be found in controllers, and so on. Here is a minimum specification for the Product model:

testing/rspec/rspecsample/spec/models/product_spec.rb

```
require File.dirname(__FILE__) + '/../spec_helper'

describe Product do
  it 'should not accept empty names' do
    product = Product.new
    product.should have(1).errors_on(:name)
  end
end
```

Along with the *rspec-rails* framework, a lot of rake tasks get installed (run rake -T to see all tasks available). One of them is the *spec* task that runs all specifications in the spec directory:

```
mschmidt> rake spec
.


Finished in 0.226938 seconds

1 example, 0 failures
```

If you want to run certain specifications, use rake spec:models to test only models, rake spec:controllers to test only controllers, and so on. To change the output format, you have to edit spec/spec.opts and adjust the format option accordingly. To print all specifications without running the tests, use the *spec:doc* task:

```
mschmidt> rake spec:doc

Product
- should not accept empty names
```

Finally, we will create a ProductsController and a specification that makes sure the show() action works properly. When the *rspec-rails* plug-in is installed, we can create a controller and its according specification stubs with the *rspec_controller* generator:

```
mschmidt> script/generate rspec_controller Products
```

This command generates a regular controller but instead of the normal Rails test cases in the test directory, it creates test stubs in spec (there's

a rspec_model command, too). After we have added a minimal show()
action, the controller looks like this:

testing/rspec/rspecsample/app/controllers/products_controller.rb

```
class ProductsController < ApplicationController
  def show
    @product = Product.find(params[:id])
  end
end
```

And here's a small specification that checks whether the show() action
works correctly:

testing/rspec/rspecsample/spec/controllers/products_controller_spec.rb

```
require File.dirname(__FILE__) + '/../spec_helper'

describe ProductsController do
  before(:each) do
    Product.create(:id => 1, :name => 'Ruby Book')
  end

  it 'should show single product' do
    get :show, :id => 1
    response.should be_success
    assigns[:product].should == Product.find(1)
  end
end
```

It looks like yet another *RSpec* specification, and there are no surprising
new features. First we create a new Product instance before every new
test case (you can use fixtures to initialize the database, too). Then we
send a GET request to the show() action to look up the product with the
ID 1. We check whether the request has been successful and whether
the right product has been assigned to the controller variable @product.

rspec-rails defines many functions that make testing Rails applications
much easier, and you'll find more details in the online documentation.
But our example should be sufficient to show you how *RSpec* integrates
with Rails.

Also See

- See Recipe 49, *Improve Your Testing with RSpec*, on page 325 to
  learn the basics of *RSpec*.

Create Mock Objects with RSpec

You're testing your application with *RSpec*, but your tests need too much time, because a lot of them access the database frequently. In addition, some tests depend on external services, which makes testing quite difficult:

- You cannot rely on the service to be available all the time; some test cases will not run properly if the service isn't available.

- You cannot ask the service provider to switch off a service to test your application's behavior in case of network failures. Also, you cannot ask the provider to return specific error conditions so you can test how your application deals with them.

- Perhaps you have to pay for each service request even if it's a test request. This could make your test suite very expensive.

- Some services do not have a testing interface, and you do not want to test with real-world data.

The solution is to use mock objects for these components, and in this recipe you'll learn how to mock objects with *RSpec*.

- See the extra ingredients in Recipe 50, *Integrate RSpec with Rails*, on page 333.

Mock objects are often used in unit tests, and simply put, they are crash-test dummies for real objects. That is, instead of testing your application with a real database, for example, you test it with mock objects that behave as if they would access a real database. They offer the same API, but their behavior can be fully controlled by the programmer. That way, unit tests can test how your software behaves under extreme conditions that could hardly be simulated otherwise.

For example, mock objects can raise database exceptions that cannot be provoked in reality without pulling some plugs.

In this recipe, we'll assume that we've built a web shop shipping products. Because of customer demand, we'll add a tracking function so customers can see the current state of their shipments. The logistics service we're working with has a RESTful web service for tracking packages. Its URL scheme is /package-history/:tracking_number; in other words, it expects a tracking number and returns XML documents that look as follows:

testing/rspec/tracking_service.xml

```
<?xml version="1.0" encoding="UTF-8"?>
<package-history id="42-xyz-4711">
  <steps>
    <step ts="2008-10-09 00:45">Received package</step>
    <step ts="2008-10-10 08:23">First delivery attempt</step>
    <step ts="2008-10-10 08:24">Receiver not at home</step>
    <step ts="2008-10-11 09:51">Second delivery attempt</step>
    <step ts="2008-10-11 09:53">Delivered</step>
  </steps>
  <state>delivered</state>
</package-history>
```

The document is easy to understand: at the first delivery attempt the customer was not at home, so the logistics company tried it a second time and succeeded. The package's overall state is "delivered," and writing a client for this service is a piece of cake with Ruby:

testing/rspec/rspecmocks/lib/tracking_service.rb

```ruby
require 'open-uri'
require 'rexml/document'

class TrackingService
  def initialize(url = 'http://localhost:4567')
    @url = url
  end

  def track(tracking_number)
    request_uri = "#{@url}/package-history/#{tracking_number}"
    doc = REXML::Document.new(open(request_uri).read)
    doc.elements['/package-history/state'].text
  end
end
```

The track() method builds the URL for the history of the package and requests it with *open-uri*. REXML parses the resulting XML document and extracts the package's current state (see Recipe 29, *Find Solutions Quickly with open-uri*, on page 183 to learn more about *open-uri* and

Recipe 22, *Use XML Files as Models*, on page 139 to get familiar with REXML).

Next we'll create a ShipmentController and an Order model:

```
mschmidt> ./script/generate rspec_controller Shipment
mschmidt> ./script/generate rspec_model Order
```

We've used the *RSpec* generators that create not only the controller and the model but also stubs for the appropriate *RSpec* specifications. In the database, orders are defined as follows:

testing/rspec/rspecmocks/db/migrate/20080727090427_create_orders.rb
```
create_table :orders do |t|
  t.string  :product, :tracking_number
  t.integer :quantity
  t.timestamps
end
```

An order contains the name of the product that was ordered, the quantity the customer ordered, and the tracking number we have from the logistics partner when the order shipped. Here's the code of the ShipmentController we need for tracking an order:

testing/rspec/rspecmocks/app/controllers/shipment_controller.rb
```
class ShipmentController < ApplicationController
  def track
    @order = Order.find(params[:id])
    @state = begin
      TrackingService.new.track(@order.tracking_number)
    rescue
      :unavailable
    end
  end
end
```

We read the order from the database and pass its tracking number to the tracking service client to determine the order's current state. If the track() method raises an exception, @state will be set to :unavailable.

Before writing a first test, we create a fixture that makes sure we always have at least one order in the database:

testing/rspec/rspecmocks/spec/fixtures/orders.yml
```
beer:
  id: 1
  product: Beer
  quantity: 6
  tracking_number: 42-xyz-4711
```

And here's our first specification for the ShipmentController:

testing/rspec/rspecmocks/spec/controllers/shipment_controller_spec.rb

```
Line 1  describe ShipmentController, 'track' do
     -    fixtures :orders
     -
     -    it 'should track package correctly' do
     5      get :track, :id => orders(:beer)
     -      assigns[:state].should eql('delivered')
     -    end
     -  end
```

First we load our fixtures file, and in the it() call we invoke the track() action, passing it the order we've defined in the fixtures file. In line 6, we check whether the controller has set the @state variable to "delivered." Let's run the test:

```
mschmidt> rake spec
(in ./testing/rspec/rspecmocks)
F


1)
'ShipmentController track should track package correctly' FAILED
expected "delivered", got :unavailable (using .eql?)
./spec/controllers/shipment_controller_spec.rb:9:

Finished in 0.214836 seconds

1 example, 1 failure
```

Oops! That didn't work as expected, did it? Obviously, the tracking service did not return delivered but :unavailable. It's even worse: there is no tracking service at all, so our client tried to open a connection but got an error instead. Even if we had access to a tracking service, how'd it know about our test order and the tracking number that we made up?

To test our controller's behavior, we need to simulate a real tracking service; that is, we have to create a *mock object* that acts like a tracking service but returns constant results:

testing/rspec/rspecmocks/spec/controllers/shipment_controller_spec.rb

```
Line 1  describe ShipmentController, 'track with mock service' do
     -    fixtures :orders
     -
     -    before :each do
     5      tracking_service = mock('tracking service')
     -      tracking_service.stub!(:track).and_return('delivered')
     -      TrackingService.stub!(:new).and_return(tracking_service)
     -    end
     -
```

```
10    it 'should track package correctly' do
 -      get :track, :id => orders(:beer)
 -      assigns[:state].should eql('delivered')
 -    end
 -  end
```

That's the same specification as earlier, but it contains an additional before() call where we define our tracking service simulation. In line 5, we call *RSpec*'s mock() method to create a general mock object (an instance of Spec::Mocks:Mock to be concise). Then we use stub!() and and_return() to teach this mock object to return "delivered" whenever its track() method is invoked. We use stub!() again to change the behavior of TrackingService's new() method. It will no longer return a new instance of the TrackingService service class but our mock object instead. That's the whole trick: create mock objects that return only constant results, and redefine methods of the classes you'd like to test. Let's see whether it works:

```
mschmidt> rake spec
(in ./testing/rspec/rspecmocks)
.


Finished in 0.267375 seconds

1 example, 0 failures
```

We can simulate every single aspect of the tracking service, so let's make the tracking service unavailable for the next specification:

testing/rspec/rspecmocks/spec/controllers/shipment_controller_spec.rb

```
Line 1  describe ShipmentController, 'tracking service unavailable' do
 -        fixtures :orders
 -
 -        before :each do
 5          tracking_service = mock('unavailable tracking service')
 -          tracking_service.stub!(:track).and_raise(IOError)
 -          TrackingService.stub!(:new).and_return(tracking_service)
 -        end
 -
10       it 'should not be able to track package' do
 -          get :track, :id => orders(:beer)
 -          assigns[:state].should eql(:unavailable)
 -        end
 -      end
```

Instead of returning a constant state, we let the tracking service raise an IOError exception in line 6. To make the test pass, we have to check whether @state was set to :unavailable in line 12.

We have completely decoupled our test specification from any real-world tracking service, so the only external component the specification relies on is the database. It is used when loading the fixtures file, and the controller needs it to find the order to be tracked. Wouldn't it be great if we could get rid of it, too? You guessed it: *RSpec* allows us to mock up models:

testing/rspec/rspecmocks/spec/controllers/shipment_controller_spec.rb

```
Line 1  describe ShipmentController, 'track with mock model' do
    -     before :each do
    -       order = mock_model(Order, :tracking_number => '42')
    -       Order.stub!(:find).and_return(order)
    5       tracking_service = mock('tracking service')
    -       tracking_service.stub!(:track).and_return('delivered')
    -       TrackingService.stub!(:new).and_return(tracking_service)
    -     end
    -
    10    it 'should track package correctly without database access' do
    -       get :track, :id => 42
    -       assigns[:state].should eql('delivered')
    -     end
    -   end
```

With mock_model() in line 3, we create a mock object for the Order model that has a constant tracking number. In the following line, we replace Order's original find() method, so it now always returns our mock object. No matter which ID you pass when invoking the ShipmentController's track() action, it will always find our test order and pass it to the tracking service mock object.

At the end of this recipe we'll cover another important feature of *RSpec* that will help you make sure your mock objects are used correctly. Usually, you do not use mock objects directly, but they are used by the software you are testing. For example, the mock object representing our tracking service is used in the ShipmentController class. In our case it's used in only one place, but sometimes mock objects are used in more complex environments, so it's helpful if you can check in your specification what exactly has happened to the mock object:

testing/rspec/rspecmocks/spec/controllers/shipment_controller_spec.rb

```
Line 1  describe ShipmentController, 'track with expectation' do
    -     fixtures :orders
    -
    -     before :each do
    5       @tracking_service = mock('tracking service')
    -       @tracking_service.stub!(:track).and_return('delivered')
    -       TrackingService.stub!(:new).and_return(@tracking_service)
    -     end
    -
```

```
10    it 'should track package correctly' do
        @tracking_service.should_receive(:track).with('42-xyz-4711').
          once.and_return('delivered')
        get :track, :id => orders(:beer)
        assigns[:state].should eql('delivered')
15    end
    end
```

This time we've assigned the mock object to a member variable so we can use it in the specification. The magic happens in line 11 (it's a fairly long line, so we had to split it into two) where we tell *RSpec* what we expect: the ShipmentController should call the track() method exactly once, passing it the "42-xyz-4711" argument. track() should return the "delivered" string. If any of these conditions isn't met (for example, if track() is called twice), the *RSpec* specification will fail.

RSpec has a lot of methods for checking what happened to a mock object. Here are a few of them:[3]

`testing/rspec/mock_sample.rb`

```
mock.should_receive(:method).with(no_args())
mock.should_receive(:method).with(any_args())
mock.should_receive(:method).with(/foo/)
mock.should_receive(:method).with('foo', anything(), true)
mock.should_receive(:method).with(duck_type(:walk, :talk))
mock.should_receive(:method).twice
mock.should_receive(:method).exactly(3).times
mock.should_receive(:method).at_least(:once)
mock.should_receive(:method).at_most(:twice)
mock.should_receive(:method).any_number_of_times
```

Thanks to Ruby's expressiveness, this shouldn't need much explanation. With no_args() and any_args(), you specify that a method should receive no arguments or an arbitrary amount of arguments, respectively. anything() is a placeholder that stands for any type of argument, and with duck_type() we make sure that the argument understands the walk() and talk() messages. As you've seen in our last specification, you can freely combine these expectations.

Mock objects certainly help you make your tests run faster, but—more important—they help you test the really interesting aspects of your software, that is, how it behaves under extreme conditions. Whenever you have to integrate with external components (web services, databases, file systems, and so on), create mock objects for all of them, and test as many corner cases as you can think of. It's so easy with *RSpec*.

---

3. See http://rspec.rubyforge.org/rspec/1.1.11/classes/Spec/Mocks.html for a complete overview.

Also See

- See Recipe 49, *Improve Your Testing with RSpec*, on page 325 to learn the basics of *RSpec*.

Prototype Services with Sinatra

Your company uses a service-oriented architecture; in other words, each new application consists of distributed REST components. All components are developed independently and are tied together in an integration test. Usually, that happens rather late in the process, and to start integration tests earlier, it's often useful to build a prototype of a service. In this recipe, you'll learn how to create a mock-up of a REST service within minutes.

• Install the *Sinatra*[4] and *haml*[5] gems:

```
$ gem install sinatra
$ gem install haml
```

Although creating web services with Rails is a breeze compared to most other approaches, it still requires some ceremony. The biggest problem when building small applications or prototypes is that the code is spread across many files. For these purposes, better tools exist, and *Sinatra* is one of them, because it is a domain-specific language for creating web applications.

We'll use *Sinatra* to build a prototype of a catalog service, namely, a service managing a list of products. (Ramaze[6] is another lightweight web application framework that is certainly worth a look.) All its resources are encoded as XML documents, and it should support the endpoints described in Figure 11.1, on the following page.

---

4. http://rubyforge.org/projects/sinatra/
5. http://haml.hamptoncatlin.com/
6. http://ramaze.net/home/

HTTP Verb	URI	Action
GET	/products	Returns a list of all products
GET	/products/:id	Returns the product identified by :id
POST	/products	Creates a new product
DELETE	/products/:id	Deletes the product identified by :id

Figure 11.1: THE ACTIONS WE'D LIKE TO SIMULATE

Even if we are building a prototype only, it still will be backed by a database. To make things as easy as possible, we use SQLite,[7] and we create only a single table for our catalog's products:

```
testing/sinatra/catalog.rb
Line 1  require 'sinatra'
     -  require 'activerecord'
     -
     -  configure do
     5    ActiveRecord::Base.establish_connection(
     -      :adapter  => 'sqlite3',
     -      :database => './catalog.db',
     -      :timeout  => 5000
     -    )
    10
     -    class CreateProducts < ActiveRecord::Migration
     -      def self.up
     -        create_table :products, :force => true do |t|
     -          t.string  :name
    15          t.decimal :price, :precision => 10, :scale => 2
     -        end
     -      end
     -    end
     -    CreateProducts.up
    20
     -    class Product < ActiveRecord::Base
     -      validates_uniqueness_of :name
     -    end
     -    Product.create(:name => 'Beer', :price => 6.99)
    25  end
```

That's pretty straightforward ActiveRecord code, but you might wonder what the configure() call in line 4 does. Like Rails, *Sinatra* supports different environments (development, test, and production). In development mode, *Sinatra* reloads the whole program after every request,

---

7. http://www.sqlite.org/

which is nice, because it speeds up the development cycle; however, it can also be a problem. If you initialize a database at the beginning of your program, for example, it would be re-created after every request, which probably is not what you want. All code that is encapsulated in a configure() block is executed only once.

Now the database is ready, and we can implement the first REST endpoint. The following code makes sure that the whole catalog can be requested as an XML document at /products:

`testing/sinatra/catalog.rb`

```
Line 1  get '/products' do
          header 'Content-Type' => 'text/xml; charset=utf-8'
          products = Product.find(:all)
          builder do |xml|
     5      xml.instruct!
            xml.products do
              products.each do |product|
                xml.product :name => product.name, :price => product.price
              end
    10      end
          end
        end
```

Sinatra's get() method expects a route and a code block. Whenever a GET request is sent to the route, the code block will be executed, and its result is delivered to the client. You can modify other attributes of the response, too, so in line 2, we set the Content-Type header with the header() method. Then we read all products that are currently in the database and convert them into an XML document using Builder (to learn more about Builder, see Recipe 26, *Build Plain-Vanilla XML Documents*, on page 167). Let's start the catalog service:

```
mschmidt> ruby catalog.rb -e development
==  CreateProducts: migrating =====================================
-- create_table(:products, {:force=>true})
   -> 0.3044s
==  CreateProducts: migrated (0.3047s) ===========================

== Sinatra has taken the stage on port 4567 for development
```

Sinatra supports only a few command-line arguments, and we have used -e to run in the development environment (which is the default anyway). After the database has been initialized, Sinatra listens on its default port 4567 (you can set the port with the -p option).

It's time to initiate a first request:

```
mschmidt> curl -i http://localhost:4567/products
HTTP/1.1 200 OK
Content-Type: text/xml; charset=utf-8
Content-Length: 105

<?xml version="1.0" encoding="UTF-8"?>
<products>
  <product price="6.99" name="Beer"/>
</products>
```

First shot, first hit! We've successfully requested the first resource from our new service prototype. And it was not even a real fake: everything was read from a database and has been properly serialized with Builder into an XML document. Let's write the code for requesting a single product now:

testing/sinatra/catalog.rb

```
Line 1   helpers do
     -     def product_to_xml(xml, product)
     -       xml.product :name => product.name, :price => product.price
     -     end
     5   end
     -
     -   get '/products/:id' do
     -     header 'Content-Type' => 'text/xml; charset=utf-8'
     -     unless product = Product.find_by_id(params[:id])
    10       response.status = 404
     -     else
     -       builder do |xml|
     -         xml.instruct!
     -         product_to_xml(xml, product)
    15       end
     -     end
     -   end
```

At first we use another useful *Sinatra* feature: helpers. We know that we have to serialize a Product object into an XML document again, so we have written a small helper method named product_to_xml() that does it for us. Once defined, a helper method can be used everywhere in a program.

The business logic is implemented again in a code block that is passed to the get() method. This time we need a parameter from the request URL that is the ID of the product to be returned. In the first argument to get(), we can find a placeholder named :id. *Sinatra* extracts such placeholders and puts them into the params hash automatically, so we can access it in line 9. Then we try to find the referenced product in the database. We use find_by_id() and not find(), because it returns nil instead of raising an exception if no product can be found. If we cannot find it, we set the response's status to 404 (Not Found) and return an empty body. Otherwise, we turn the product into an XML document with our new product_to_xml() helper in line 14. See it in action:

```
mschmidt> curl http://localhost:4567/products/1
<?xml version="1.0" encoding="UTF-8"?>
<product price="6.99" name="Beer"/>
```

Looking up products in the catalog works like a charm, so it's time for the next level, that is, adding products:

testing/sinatra/catalog.rb

```
Line 1   require 'rexml/document'

         post '/products' do
           xml = request.env['rack.input'].read
    5      doc = REXML::Document.new(xml)
           product = Product.create(
             :name => doc.elements['/product/@name'].value,
             :price => doc.elements['/product/@price'].value.to_f
           )
   10      header 'Location' => "/products/#{product.id}"
           response.status = 201
         end
```

To make our service RESTful, we have to use the post() method this time. It works exactly like get() but gets invoked whenever *Sinatra* receives a POST request. In line 4, we read the payload that has been sent with the request (an XML document containing a product). At the moment we have to use this awkward syntax to get the request body, but it works without problems (*rack* is a library that is used by *Sinatra*). The rest of the code is easy: we turn the XML document that has been transmitted in the request into a Product object using REXML and store it in the database. In line 10, we set the Location header, and finally we set the response's status code to 201 (Created).

Now we can take this document:

testing/sinatra/product.xml

```
<product name='Fresh Donuts' price='0.99'/>
```

and add it to the catalog:

```
mschmidt> curl -i -H 'content-type:text/xml' -d @product.xml \
> http://localhost:4567/products
HTTP/1.1 201 Created
Location: /products/2
```

curl sends application/www-form-urlencoded by default in the content-type header, so we set it explicitly to text/xml. Otherwise, the posted data would be misinterpreted by *Sinatra*, and we could not read it. As expected, the status code is 201 (Created), and the Location header contains a link to the newly created product resource.

The opposite direction—that is, getting rid of a product—can be implemented as follows:

testing/sinatra/catalog.rb

```
delete '/products/:id' do
  if Product.exists?(params[:id])
    Product.delete(params[:id])
  else
    response.status = 404
  end
end
```

If a product can be found, it will be deleted. If not, 404 is returned. Here's what happens if you try to delete a nonexistent product:

```
mschmidt> curl -i -X DELETE http://localhost:4567/products/42
HTTP/1.1 404 Not Found
```

We're done with all the endpoints we needed, and we've covered a lot of *Sinatra*'s features (we didn't cover PUT requests, but I'm fairly sure you can guess how they are implemented). But I've saved some of *Sinatra*'s coolest features for the end of the recipe. For example, *Sinatra* automatically serves static files in the public directory. Put an informative README file into the public directory, and your clients can get it as follows:

```
mschmidt> curl http://localhost:4567/README
This is a prototype of the catalog application.
It is only meant for integration purposes.
```

It gets even cooler: *Sinatra* supports templates written in Embedded Ruby (ERb), XHTML Abstraction Markup Language (HAML), and Syntactically Awesome Style Sheets (SASS). It even has support for partials.

We'll use HAML and SASS to create an HTML view of our catalog. Here's the code that's needed:

testing/sinatra/catalog.rb

```
get '/screen.css' do
  header 'Content-Type' => 'text/css; charset=utf-8'
  sass :screen
end
```

```
get '/catalog' do
  @products = Product.find(:all)
  haml :catalog
end
```

When the URL /screen.css is requested, *Sinatra* reads the file screen.css from the views directory (all templates are stored in the views directory) and converts it into a Cascading Style Sheets (CSS) file with the sass() method. Similar things happen for /catalog: views/catalog.haml is read and is transformed into an HTML document. catalog.haml looks like this:

testing/sinatra/views/catalog.haml

```
%html
  %head
    %title Our Fancy Catalog
    %link{:rel => 'stylesheet', :href => '/screen.css', |
      :type => 'text/css', :media => 'screen'}          |
  %body
    %h2 Our Catalog:
    #content
      %ol
        = list_of(@products) do |p|
          = "#{p.name} ($#{p.price})"
```

Before the HAML crash course starts, point your browser to http://localhost:4567/catalog, and you'll see something like Figure 11.2, on the following page.

HAML is a markup language that frees HTML documents from a lot of redundant clutter. In the beginning it reads a bit strange, but when you get used to it, it's an invaluable time-saver. In HAML documents indentation matters, so you do not have to close elements. Regular HTML elements start with a percentage sign, and attributes are defined within curly braces and Ruby's hash syntax.

We've split the %link element across two lines, so we had to end those lines with a pipe symbol (|). #content is an abbreviation for the following:

```
<div id='content'>
```

and to generate a class= attribute instead of id=, we had to write .content.

You can embed arbitrary Ruby code into HAML documents. If the code is introduced by a hyphen (-), it gets executed only, but if it's introduced by an equal sign (=), its result is embedded into the document. The list_of() helper creates *<li>* elements for all elements in an array, and we use it to generate a list of all products.

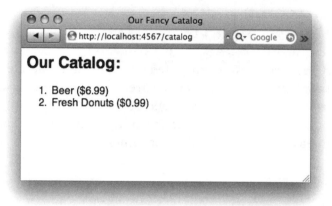

Figure 11.2: HTML VIEW OF CATALOG

SASS documents are structured in a similar way. Here's ours:

testing/sinatra/views/screen.sass

```
body
  font-family: sans-serif

content
  padding: 1em
```

After it has been interpreted by the sass() method, it will look like this:

```
body {
  font-family: sans-serif; }

content {
  padding: 1em; }
```

That's it! In 90 lines of code we have built a REST service that accesses a database. It not only implements all the endpoints we needed, but it also comes with nice add-ons such as an HTML view of the catalog.

In principle, you could use *Sinatra* to build small web services or applications, but it's best suited for prototyping interfaces and services. Instead of scribbling your ideas on a piece of paper, type them into your editor next time. The sooner you start to integrate all parts of a new distributed application, the better it will work.

Also See

- To learn how to build complete web services based on REST and SOAP, see Chapter 6, *Perform Basic Networking Tasks with Ease*, on page 175.

## Chapter 12

Get Documentation
Nearly for Free

Developing enterprise applications is expensive, and therefore many of them get comparatively old (do you remember how popular COBOL programmers were during the Y2K crisis?). Often they are maintained by generations of developers, and making this possible requires good documentation.

The most important parts of a software project's documentation are the so-called API docs generated from a program's source code and diagrams describing the structure of the database on which the application works. They are also the most unstable parts, and usually they change very often. Because of this, all modern languages have mechanisms for creating such documentation automatically, and Ruby is no exception. In Recipe 53, *Generate Documentation Automatically*, on page 357, you'll learn how to generate most of your project's documentation from comments in your source code and from your database.

Abstraction is a nice thing when it comes to databases, but sometimes you are interested in concrete information. If you are working with ActiveRecord, for example, you often need to know the structure of the table underlying your model. Usually, you have to look it up in the according migration or—even worse—in the database. In Recipe 54, *Annotate Your Models Automatically*, on page 365, you'll learn how to add table definitions automatically to your models.

An important feature of most enterprise applications is reporting, because many enterprise applications have no user interface and communicate with the outside world via reports. In Recipe 55, *Create Great Reports*, on page 369, you'll learn how to create reports in various output formats. No matter whether you need CSV, HTML, or PDF files and no matter how complicated your database is, Ruby helps you find a solution quickly.

Generate Documentation Automatically

You have finished your new Rails application, so now you want to deploy it to the production environment. But before that, the QA department wants to have database diagrams showing the relationships between your application's models, and it wants API documentation explaining all the classes and their methods.

In this recipe, you'll learn how to generate documentation automatically from the comments in your application code and from your database schema.

Ingredients

- Install *Railroad*,[1] a tool for generating database diagrams.

    ```
    $ gem install railroad
    ```

- Install the *Graphviz*[2] tool suite for visualizing graphs. It's free and open source.

Solution

Let's say your application's database contains the typical COLA tables: customers, orders, line items, and accounts. They have been created with the following ActiveRecord migrations:

```
create_table :customers do |t|
  t.string :forename, :surname
  t.timestamps
end

create_table :accounts do |t|
  t.belongs_to :customer
  t.string     :pay_type
  t.timestamps
end
```

---

1. http://railroad.rubyforge.org/
2. http://www.graphviz.org/

```ruby
create_table :orders do |t|
  t.belongs_to :customer
  t.string     :comment
  t.timestamps
end

create_table :line_items do |t|
  t.belongs_to :order
  t.string     :name
  t.integer    :quantity
  t.decimal    :price_per_unit
  t.timestamps
end
```

Although these migrations describe the attributes of all models, they do not explain their relationships (the only exception is the belongs_to() method, which creates a foreign key column). All relationships have to be declared in the model classes:

```ruby
class Customer < ActiveRecord::Base
  has_one  :account
  has_many :orders
end

class Account < ActiveRecord::Base
  belongs_to :customer
end

class Order < ActiveRecord::Base
  belongs_to :customer
  has_many :line_items
end

class LineItem < ActiveRecord::Base
  belongs_to :order
end
```

For software developers, these declarations read like a specification and would usually be sufficient. But QA departments often insist on database diagrams, and for more complex databases, that really makes sense.

Many tools are available for generating diagrams from databases automatically, but most of them do not produce decent results for Rails databases. Usually, such tools read all the information they need from the database's data dictionary. For example, they expect you to define relationships between tables with foreign key constraints. In Rails applications, you do this in your model classes, which aren't taken into account by regular tools. *Railroad* is different, because it has been explicitly designed for visualizing Rails databases.

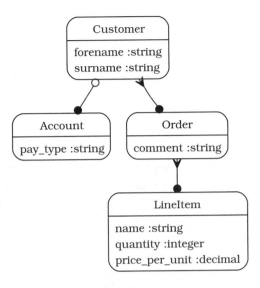

Figure 12.1: Database diagram

```
mschmidt> railroad -M --hide-magic -o models.dot
mschmidt> dot -Tpng models.dot > models.png
```

The railroad command scans the application's models and produces a .dot file. This file contains a textual representation of a graph describing the database tables and their relationships. It can be turned into images of various formats by the dot command that is part of the *Graphviz* tool suite. In the previous example, the .dot file is turned into the PNG image shown in Figure 12.1. See the *Joe Asks...* on the following page for details about DOT.

Railroad's output can be controlled by many command-line switches. We have used -M for generating a diagram of our models (-C would generate a class diagram of the controllers), and --hide-magic hides Rails' magic attributes like created_at. -o determines the name of the output file to be produced, and there are many more switches that are described in *Railroad*'s excellent documentation.

Because *Railroad* emits *DOT* files, you can export your diagrams automatically into every graphic format you need. It's especially useful to export them as Scalable Vector Graphic (SVG) files that can be imported by drawing tools such as Microsoft Visio, for instance.

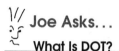 **Joe Asks...**

What Is DOT?

DOT is a text format for describing graphs consisting of nodes and edges. The following code specifies a simplified version of the relationship between the Customer and the Account model as it is shown in Figure 12.1, on the previous page:

`documentation/models.dot`

```
digraph models_diagram {
  graph[overlap=false, splines=true]
  "Account" [shape=Mrecord, label="Account"]
  "Customer" [shape=Mrecord, label="Customer"]
  "Customer" -> "Account" [
    arrowtail=odot, arrowhead=dot, dir=both
  ]
}
```

Even without explaining every detail, you should be able to understand most of the code: digraph defines a new directed graph, and with the graph declaration we set some global properties of the graph to be drawn (with DOT you do not only define nodes and edges but also their appearance). We do not want nodes to overlap, and it's OK if edges aren't drawn as straight lines but as splines if necessary.

Then we define two nodes named "Customer" and "Account" that both have a label and use the predefined *Mrecord* shape (a rectangle with rounded corners). Finally, we define an edge connecting these two notes, and we specify how the connection should look.

Creating .dot files is easy, and you should keep that in mind whenever you have to visualize a graph structure. Several tools are available for turning .dot files into various graphic formats such as PNG or Scalable Vector Graphics (SVG). One of the most popular tools is the *Graphviz* package from AT&T Research Labs.

Now that we have nice diagrams for our database, let's see whether we can create nice API documentation, too. Here we have an extended and fully documented version of the Order class:

documentation/sampleshop/app/models/order.rb

```
Line 1   # This class encapsulates all attributes of an order. In addition, it
   -     # provides some methods for calculating various figures.
   -     class Order < ActiveRecord::Base
   -       belongs_to :customer
   5       has_many :line_items
   -
   -       # Calculates the total amount of an order.
   -       def total_amount()
   -         self.line_items.inject(0) { |total, li| total += li.total_price }
   10      end
   -
   -       # Calculates the payment amount of an order.
   -       #
   -       # discount::
   15      #   Discount (percentage) that will be granted to the customer.
   -       # This method still has some *problems*:
   -       # * It does not check if discount is negative.
   -       # * It does not check if discount is greater than 100.
   -       def payment_amount(discount = 0)
   20        total_amount() * (1 - discount / 100)
   -       end
   -     end
```

All comments look pretty normal, but they contain some special features that will become obvious when we turn the inline documentation into pretty HTML pages:

```
mschmidt> rake doc:app
```

This command generates documentation for all classes belonging to your application in the doc/app directory. The HTML page documenting the Order class can be found in doc/app/classes/Order.html, and it is shown in Figure 12.2, on the following page.

As you can see, most of the comment text has been copied verbatim to the generated HTML documents, but some parts have been interpreted as a special kind of markup: RDoc. RDoc is the standard tool for embedding documentation into Ruby source code, and in contrast to similar tools such as Javadoc, it's refreshingly simple. Usually, it's sufficient to do nothing but write comments, and there are only a few special rules.

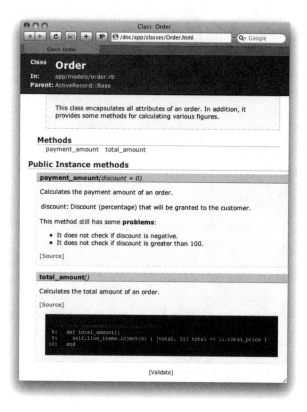

Figure 12.2: RDOC OUTPUT SAMPLE

In line 14, for example, we have appended two colons to the name of the discount argument to produce a labeled list (containing only a single item). This is a typical style for documenting method arguments, because there is no such thing as *@param* in Javadoc. The Rails project uses a different style and would have written the same comment as follows:

```
* +discount+ - Discount (percentage) that will be granted to the
  customer.
```

This produces a bulleted list and sets the word *discount* with a typewriter font. To emphasize a word, you can also make it bold by enclosing it in * characters, as we did in line 16, or you can use underscores for italics.

Every Ruby installation comes with the rdoc command-line tool, and running ri RDoc outputs excellent documentation. Whenever you are commenting code, make sure you're using RDoc style, because it's easy and pays off quickly.

Although RDoc and *Railroad* are completely independent, they create surprisingly good results when used together—not only for your QA department but also for you and your fellow developers.

Also See

You might also take a look at Recipe 54, *Annotate Your Models Automatically*, on page 365 to learn how to create documentation for your database.

Annotate Your Models Automatically

When working with ActiveRecord, you rarely think about database specifics. ActiveRecord simplifies your model classes, and migrations make it easy to create their definitions in the database. But during development you forget the table structure when editing models or writing fixtures, and you often find yourself switching between files just to look up a certain attribute.

In this recipe, you'll learn how to circumvent this by using annotate, a tool for annotating Rails models automatically.

Ingredients

- Install the *annotate-models* gem:[3]

  ```
  $ gem install annotate-models
  ```

Solution

For demonstration purposes, we create a simple customer model:

```
mschmidt> ruby script/generate model Customer forename:string \
> surname:string
```

This results in the following migration:

`documentation/annotate/annotate_sample/db/migrate/001_create_customers.rb`

```
create_table :customers do |t|
  t.string :forename
  t.string :surname
  t.timestamps
end
```

The migration describes the customers table's structure in a database-independent manner; that is, you cannot see the exact definition of a column (what's the maximum length of the forename column, for instance?), and you cannot see all the columns that are created in

---

3. http://annotate-models.rubyforge.org/

the database. For example, the previous migration creates an *integer* column named id and two *datetime* columns named created_at and updated_at. All these details are hidden in the model where you cannot see any of a customer's attributes, because Rails generates only two lines of code:

```
class Customer < ActiveRecord::Base
end
```

Classes derived from ActiveRecord::Base do not need more information, because ActiveRecord dynamically reads all attribute definitions from the database whenever it's necessary. Usually that's a good thing, because it eliminates redundancy. But during development you often have to switch from your model code to the appropriate migration file to look up the definition of a certain attribute.

With annotate, these times are over. annotate is a Ruby script that examines all your models and inserts a comment containing detailed schema information into the according source files:

```
mschmidt> annotate
Annotated Customer
mschmidt> cat app/models/customer.rb
# == Schema Information
# Schema version: 1
#
# Table name: customers
#
#  id         :integer          not null, primary key
#  forename   :string(255)
#  surname    :string(255)
#  created_at :datetime
#  updated_at :datetime
#

class Customer < ActiveRecord::Base
end
```

For our Customer model, annotate has inserted the table name and the definition (including column types and constraints) of all five columns.

By default annotate puts the annotation in front of the model class. Using the -p (position) switch, you can put it after the class:

```
mschmidt> annotate -p after
Annotated Customer
mschmidt> cat app/models/customer.rb
class Customer < ActiveRecord::Base
end
```

```
# == Schema Information
# Schema version: 1
#
# Table name: customers
#
#  id         :integer          not null, primary key
#  forename   :string(255)
#  surname    :string(255)
#  created_at :datetime
#  updated_at :datetime
#
```

As you can see, annotate is clever enough to remove the existing annotation and to replace it with a new one. In addition, it does not touch
your own comments:

```
mschmidt> cat app/models/customer.rb
# This is our customer model class.
class Customer < ActiveRecord::Base
end
mschmidt> annotate
Annotated Customer
mschmidt> cat app/models/customer.rb
# == Schema Information
# Schema version: 1
#
# Table name: customers
#
#  id         :integer          not null, primary key
#  forename   :string(255)
#  surname    :string(255)
#  created_at :datetime
#  updated_at :datetime
#

# This is our customer model class.
class Customer < ActiveRecord::Base
end
```

By the way, all this magic happens in your fixtures files as well:

```
mschmidt> cat test/fixtures/customers.yml
# == Schema Information
# Schema version: 1
#
# Table name: customers
#
#  id         :integer          not null, primary key
#  forename   :string(255)
#  surname    :string(255)
#  created_at :datetime
#  updated_at :datetime
#
```

```
# Read about fixtures at http://ar.rubyonrails.org/classes/Fixtures.html

one:
  forename: MyString
  surname: MyString

two:
  forename: MyString
  surname: MyString
```

If you want to get rid of all annotations, use the -d (delete) switch:

```
mschmidt> annotate -d
Removed annotation from: Customer
mschmidt> cat app/models/customer.rb
# This is our customer model class.
class Customer < ActiveRecord::Base
end
```

annotate works fine with legacy tables, too; if you've set the table name in your model explicitly with set_table_name(), it still produces correct results. It does not work, though, with multiple database connections as we have described them in Recipe 15, *Access Databases from Different Vendors Simultaneously*, on page 95.

To get the most out of it, it's best to make annotate part of your build process. For example, you could write a rake task that executes annotate every time rake db:migrate gets called. Even better, you can modify the db:migrate task directly:

documentation/annotate/annotate_sample/Rakefile

```
namespace :db do
  task :migrate do
    sh 'annotate'
  end
end
```

This works because Rake by default does not overwrite the db:migrate task but adds the new functionality to it. From now on, annotate is run automatically after new migrations have been applied to the database.

Create Great Reports

Many enterprise applications are implemented as background services and do not have a graphical user interface. They often write only to log files and databases and can communicate with the outside world only via reports. Sometimes these reports are as simple as the outcome of a SQL query, but they can also be complex spreadsheets, HTML pages, or PDF documents containing lots of tables and graphs.

Reporting features are often forgotten when planning new applications, and they usually get implemented hastily at the end of a project, because many programmers do not like to deal with these aspects of an application.

But if you have the right tools, reports actually can be fun, and in this recipe you'll learn how to create nice-looking reports in various output formats with ease.

- The reports in this recipe will be created using the *ruport* gem:[4]

  ```
  $ gem install ruport
  ```

- If you want to use *ruport* with *ruby-dbi* or with ActiveRecord in your Rails application, you have to install two additional gems:

  ```
  $ gem install ruport-util
  $ gem install acts_as_reportable
  ```

The most important thing when creating a report is its *basis*—the data to create a report for—because usually a report is only a highly condensed version of this database. A report can be as simple as a single number like the number of open orders, for example, but it can also be a PDF document comprising several hundred pages.

---

4. http://rubyreports.org/

To make things more tangible in this recipe, we'll assume that we're working for a company selling cell phones and have to create reports describing the cell phone models currently stored in the company's shop database. To achieve this, we'll use the *Ruport* framework, a powerful library for creating first-class reports with Ruby.

Although it's not limited to relational database systems, the main classes of the *Ruport* framework represent relational database concepts such as tables and groupings. *Ruport* adds some convenience methods for filtering and sorting data and a lot of functionality for creating various output formats.

We'll start with a simple Ruport::Data::Table object representing a cell phone with a manufacturer, a model, a certain weight, and a flag indicating whether it has a GPS receiver. To make things more interesting, we immediately create two cell phone data sets:

documentation/ruport/ruport_sample.rb

```ruby
require 'ruport'
phones = Table(%w(manufacturer model weight gps))
phones << {
  'manufacturer' => 'Nokia', 'model' => 'N95',
  'weight' => '120', 'gps' => true
}
phones << {
  'manufacturer' => 'Apple', 'model' => 'iPhone',
  'weight' => '135', 'gps' => false
}
puts phones
puts 'Column names: ' + phones.column_names.join(', ')
```

The previous program produces a simple report resembling the format MySQL uses to display query results:

```
+----------------------------------------+
| manufacturer | model  | weight |  gps  |
+----------------------------------------+
| Nokia        | N95    | 120    | true  |
| Apple        | iPhone | 135    | false |
+----------------------------------------+
Column names: manufacturer, model, weight, gps
```

As you can see, a Table object's to_s() method produces a nicely formatted text report, and column_names() returns an Array containing its column names.

The following program slightly modifies the report:

documentation/ruport/ruport_sample.rb

```
phones = phones.sub_table(%w(manufacturer model weight))
phones.rename_columns(
    'manufacturer' => 'Manufacturer',
    'model'        => 'Model',
    'weight'       => 'Weight (gram)'
)
puts phones
puts 'Column names: ' + phones.column_names.join(', ')
```

It produces the following result:

```
+-------------------------------------+
| Manufacturer | Model  | Weight (gram) |
+-------------------------------------+
| Nokia        | N95    | 120           |
| Apple        | iPhone | 135           |
+-------------------------------------+
Column names: Manufacturer, Model, Weight (gram)
```

With the sub_table() method, we have reduced the column set we're reporting on, and with rename_columns() we have made the column headings a bit more attractive. Now we'll swap the manufacturer and model columns and add another phone data set:

documentation/ruport/ruport_sample.rb

```
phones.swap_column('Model', 'Manufacturer')
phones << {
    'Manufacturer' => 'Apple', 'Model' => 'iPhone 3G',
    'Weight (gram)' => '133', 'gps' => true
}
puts phones
```

The program prints the following:

```
+-----------------------------------------+
|   Model   | Manufacturer | Weight (gram) |
+-----------------------------------------+
| N95       | Nokia        | 120           |
| iPhone    | Apple        | 135           |
| iPhone 3G | Apple        | 133           |
+-----------------------------------------+
```

Please note that we have to use the current column names to add a new phone and that the gps attribute will be stored but not printed.

OK, our text report is as nice as a text report can be, but it certainly will not win a beauty contest, and it has some disadvantages, too. For example, it cannot be imported by a spreadsheet application.

A CSV file could be imported, so let's create one:

`documentation/ruport/ruport_sample.rb`

```
puts phones.to_csv
```

Here's the program's output:

```
Model,Manufacturer,Weight (gram)
N95,Nokia,120
iPhone,Apple,135
iPhone 3G,Apple,133
```

It starts to pay off that the data we're working on is represented by Table objects, because they come with some useful standard formatters, and new formatters can be added if needed. HTML is supported by default, too, and a single statement such as the following:

`documentation/ruport/ruport_sample.rb`

```
puts phones.sort_rows_by(%w(Manufacturer Model)).to_html
```

produces the following *<table>* element:

```
<table>
  <tr>
    <th>Model</th>
    <th>Manufacturer</th>
    <th>Weight (gram)</th>
  </tr>
  <tr>
    <td>N95</td>
    <td>Nokia</td>
    <td>120</td>
  </tr>
  <tr>
    <td>iPhone</td>
    <td>Apple</td>
    <td>135</td>
  </tr>
  <tr>
    <td>iPhone 3G</td>
    <td>Apple</td>
    <td>133</td>
  </tr>
</table>
```

Before the HTML report has been created, the table data has been sorted by the manufacturer attribute first and then by the model attribute. This has been achieved by using the sort_rows_by() method that expects an array of column names to sort the table data by.

Grouping is as easy as sorting with *Ruport*, and it's such an important task that it's represented by its own class named Grouping. It is used in the following program to group our cell phone data by the manufacturer attribute:

documentation/ruport/ruport_sample.rb

```
grouping = Grouping(phones, :by => 'Manufacturer')
puts grouping
```

The program outputs the following:

```
Nokia:

+----------------------+
| Model | Weight (gram) |
+----------------------+
| N95   | 120           |
+----------------------+

Apple:

+--------------------------+
|   Model   | Weight (gram) |
+--------------------------+
| iPhone    | 135           |
| iPhone 3G | 133           |
+--------------------------+
```

That's all nice, and *Ruport* has tons of more useful methods for filtering, grouping, and sorting data (take a look at *The Ruport Book* [BMtRc08] for a detailed reference). But reporting is more fun when data comes from a real database, so now we'll combine *Ruport* and ActiveRecord.

We'll do it the right way; that is, we'll use two separate tables for representing cell phones and their manufacturers. First we'll create and initialize the manufacturers table with the following migration:

documentation/ruport/phones/db/migrate/20080704153504_create_manufacturers.rb

```
create_table :manufacturers do |t|
  t.string :name
  t.timestamps
end

# Load sample data:
Manufacturer.create(:name => 'Nokia')
Manufacturer.create(:name => 'Apple')
```

And we have a table for cell phones, too:

documentation/ruport/phones/db/migrate/20080704153604_create_cell_phones.rb

```
create_table :cell_phones do |t|
  t.belongs_to :manufacturer
  t.string     :model
  t.integer    :weight
  t.boolean    :gps
  t.timestamps
end

# Load sample data:
[
  ['Nokia', 'N95',      120, true],
  ['Apple', 'iPhone',   135, false],
  ['Apple', 'iPhone 3G', 133, true],
].each do |p|
  CellPhone.create(
    :manufacturer_id => Manufacturer.find_by_name(p[0]).id,
    :model => p[1], :weight => p[2], :gps => p[3]
  )
end
```

That's similar to the initialization we did manually when creating our Table object, but now we are working with a database using model classes to represent the database tables:

documentation/ruport/phones/app/models/manufacturer.rb

```
require 'ruport/acts_as_reportable'

class Manufacturer < ActiveRecord::Base
  has_many :cell_phones
  acts_as_reportable
end
```

documentation/ruport/phones/app/models/cell_phone.rb

```
class CellPhone < ActiveRecord::Base
  belongs_to :manufacturer
  acts_as_reportable
end
```

The only special thing in these classes is the acts_as_reportable() declaration. It makes sure that we can use all the *Ruport* methods we have used directly before in both the Manufacturer and CellPhone classes.

Now we'll create a ReportController class for generating reports as CSV files, HTML tables, and PDF documents. But before that, we have to add something to the mime_types.rb file.

documentation/ruport/phones/config/initializers/mime_types.rb

```ruby
Mime::Type.register 'application/pdf', :pdf
```

And we have to make sure that the following statement appears in routes.rb:

documentation/ruport/phones/config/routes.rb

```ruby
map.connect ':controller/:action.:format'
```

Everything is prepared, so we can create a ReportController with an action for creating a report that shows all cell phones in the database grouped by manufacturer:

documentation/ruport/phones/app/controllers/report_controller.rb

```ruby
Line 1  class ReportController < ApplicationController
          def all_phones
            report = CellPhone.report_table(
              :all,
     5         :only => %w(model weight),
              :include => {
                :manufacturer => { :only => %w(name) }
              },
              :transforms => lambda do |row|
    10          row['weight'] = '%.2f' % (row['weight'] * 0.035274)
              end,
              :order => 'model'
            )
            report.rename_columns(
    15        'model'             => 'Model',
              'manufacturer.name' => 'Manufacturer',
              'weight'            => 'Weight (oz)'
            )
            report = Grouping(report, :by => 'Manufacturer')
    20      respond_to do |format|
              format.csv  {
                send_data report.to_csv,
                          :type => 'text/csv',
                          :filename => 'all_phones.csv'
    25        }
              format.pdf  {
                send_data report.to_pdf,
                          :type => 'application/pdf',
                          :disposition => 'inline',
    30                    :filename => 'all_phones.pdf'
              }
              format.html { @report_table = report.to_html }
            end
          end
    35  end
```

That's a fairly big amount of code, but it contains only four statements that we'll dissect now. The first ranges from lines 3 to 13 and calls the report_table() method that has been added to the CellPhone model by the acts_as_reportable() declaration. Basically, report_table() creates a Table object, as we did manually in the former examples. Here's an explanation of all the arguments we have passed:

- *all* specifies that we'd like to read all cell phones from the database. You can use all the specifiers that ActiveRecord's find() method supports, including first and last, for example.

- With the *:only* option we define the columns in which we are interested.

- Every CellPhone object is associated with a Manufacturer object, and the *:include* option allows us to define which manufacturer attribute we'd like to see in the report.

- The *:transforms* option is a powerful one and accepts an array of Proc objects (or a single one as in our case). Every object is passed the current row of data, so the data to be reported can be transformed up front. We use this mechanism to convert a cell phone's weight from grams to ounces before displaying it.

- *:order* specifies which attribute should be used for ordering the data.

To set default values, many of the options passed to report_table() can be passed to acts_as_reportable(), too.

In line 14, we rename some columns, and in line 19 we group the cell phones by their manufacturers. These statements look exactly like the ones we have used before, because report is an ordinary Table instance that has been initialized from a database.

report contains all the data we need in the right format, so the only task left is rendering its content. As promised, we will support three different formats, so we use respond_to() to distinguish them. This way you can determine a report's output format from an extension added to the URL. For the PDF report, point your browser to /report/all_phones.pdf; for an HTML version, point it to /report/all_phones.html, and so on.

For rendering CSV and PDF, we don't have to do anything special. We call send_data(), passing it the report in the right format, the content's disposition (inline embeds the result in the browser window; otherwise the content would be stored in a local file), and a filename for the data

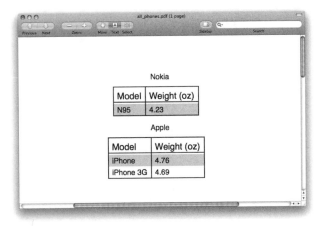

Figure 12.3: PHONE REPORT AS A PDF DOCUMENT

in case the user wants to store it locally. In Figure 12.3, you can see the PDF version.

For the HTML view, add the following file:

documentation/ruport/phones/app/views/report/all_phones.html.erb

```
<div class="report">
  <%= @report_table %>
</div>
```

This template embeds the HTML table produced by *Ruport*'s to_html() method in a *<div>* element with the class report. This way you could add some CSS styles to turn the report into something beautiful.

We have barely scratched the surface of *Ruport*'s capabilities, and you should use this recipe's code as a starting point for experiments. There are many more ways to transform and filter data; *Ruport* also addresses important topics such as eager loading of dependent data and so on. In addition, it gives you nearly endless possibilities to format your reports or to create graphs.

Bibliography

[BK05]   Mark M. Burnett and Dave Kleiman. *Perfect Passwords.*
            Syngress Media, Rockland, MA, 2005.

[BMtRc08] Gregory Brown, Michael Milner, and the Ruport commu-
            nity. *The Ruport Book: Your guide to mastering Ruby Reports.*
            Rinara Press LLC, 2008.

[CE08]   Jeff Cohen and Brian Eng. *Rails for .NET Developers.* The
            Pragmatic Programmers, LLC, Raleigh, NC, and Dallas, TX,
            2008.

[For03]   Neal Ford. *Art of Java Web Development: Struts, Tapestry,
            Commons, Velocity, JUnit, Axis, Cocoon, InternetBeans, Web-
            Work.* Manning Publications Co., Greenwich, CT, 2003.

[Fow03]   Martin Fowler. *Patterns of Enterprise Application Architec-
            ture.* Addison Wesley Longman, Reading, MA, 2003.

[HT00]   Andrew Hunt and David Thomas. *The Pragmatic Program-
            mer: From Journeyman to Master.* Addison-Wesley, Reading,
            MA, 2000.

[RR07]   Leonard Richardson and Sam Ruby. *RESTful Web Services.*
            O'Reilly & Associates, Inc, Sebastopol, CA, 2007.

[TFH08]   David Thomas, Chad Fowler, and Andrew Hunt. *Program-
            ming Ruby: The Pragmatic Programmers' Guide.* The Prag-
            matic Programmers, LLC, Raleigh, NC, and Dallas, TX, third
            edition, 2008.

Index

All About Ruby

If you're programming in Ruby, you need the PickAxe Book: the definitive reference to the Ruby Programming language, now available in a new version for Ruby 1.9. Fix a traditional weak spot in testing, and see how to automatically test graphical user interfaces using Ruby.

Programming Ruby 1.9 (The Pickaxe for 1.9)

The Pickaxe book, named for the tool on the cover, is the definitive reference to this highly-regarded language.

- Up-to-date and expanded for Ruby version 1.9
- Complete documentation of all the built-in classes, modules, and methods • Complete descriptions of all standard libraries • Learn more about Ruby's web tools, unit testing, and programming philosophy

Programming Ruby 1.9: The Pragmatic Programmer's Guide for Ruby 1.9
Dave Thomas with Chad Fowler and Andy Hunt
(900 pages) ISBN: 978-1-9343560-8-1. $49.95
http://pragprog.com/titles/ruby3

Scripted GUI Testing with Ruby

If you need to automatically test a user interface, this book is for you. Whether it's Windows, a Java platform (including Mac, Linux, and others) or a web app, you'll see how to test it reliably and repeatably.

This book is for people who want to get their hands dirty on examples from the real world—and who know that testing can be a joy when the tools don't get in the way. It starts with the mechanics of simulating button pushes and keystrokes, and builds up to writing clear code, organizing tests, and beyond.

Scripted GUI Testing with Ruby
Ian Dees
(192 pages) ISBN: 978-1-9343561-8-0. $34.95
http://pragprog.com/titles/idgtr

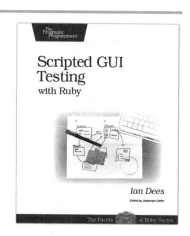